The Political Economy of Egyptian Media

The Political Economy of Egyptian Media

Business and Military Elite Power and Communication after 2011

Maher Hamoud

I.B.TAURIS

LONDON · NEW YORK · OXFORD · NEW DELHI · SYDNEY

I.B. TAURIS
Bloomsbury Publishing Plc
50 Bedford Square, London, WC1B 3DP, UK
1385 Broadway, New York, NY 10018, USA
29 Earlsfort Terrace, Dublin 2, Ireland

BLOOMSBURY, I.B. TAURIS and the I.B. Tauris logo are trademarks of
Bloomsbury Publishing Plc

First published in Great Britain 2023
This paperback edition published 2025

Series design by Catherine Wood & Adriana Brioso

Cover image: Shennawy

A catalogue record for this book is available from the British Library.

A catalog record for this book is available from the Library of Congress.

ISBN: HB: 978-0-7556-4307-3
        PB: 978-0-7556-4311-0
        ePDF: 978-0-7556-4308-0
        eBook: 978-0-7556-4309-7

Typeset by RefineCatch Limited, Bungay, Suffolk

To find out more about our authors and books visit www.bloomsbury.com
and sign up for our newsletters.

To my mother, Soraya Al Hadek, her endless love and a long life full of new adventures still to come.

To the spirit of my father, Salama Hamoud, and his life of resilience, pride, and hard work until almost the last hour.

To my siblings, Mohamed, Emad and Dina, and the bright futures that await their children, who can always count on my support to reach the highest levels of education.

To Professor Adel Beshei, former chair of the Economics Department at The American University in Cairo, for his mentorship and the support he provided me in my early academic career, and the love that he and his wife, Dr Magda Barsoum, continue to send my way despite the geographical distance between us.

Contents

Acknowledgements

This research was begun at the Department of Conflict and Development Studies, Ghent University. Its journey continued and it settled at the Department of East Asian and Arabic Studies, the University of Leuven, where it became a book. In this context, I would like to thank the chair of the department, Professor Umar Ryad, for welcoming me into their academic family, and my colleague Dr Osama Diab for his invaluable feedback on parts of the first draft of this book. This book could not have materialized without the invaluable input of Mr Belal Fadl, Mr Hisham Kassem, Dr Hossam El-Hamalawy and the rest of the fifteen media experts interviewed in this book, to whom I am indebted for the knowledge they shared with me. I would like to thank the editors of this book series, Professor Dina Matar and Professor Zahera Harb, for giving me the opportunity to be part of this series and for their invaluable input. Many thanks as well go to the peer-reviewers for their invaluable comments on the first draft of the book. I would also like to thank Professor Charles Tripp for honouring this book by writing its foreword and linking my work to the larger theoretical picture. Many thanks are also due to the great cartoonist Shennawy, who did not hesitate in agreeing to illustrate the image on the cover of this book. I owe huge gratitude to my dear friend and early reader of my work Dr Peter Verkinderen, whose feedback on my early work was very important and helpful. And of course, it goes without saying that this book would not have seen the light in such a good shape without the editorial team that worked behind it: Merv Honeywood, Sophie Campbell, Judy Tither, Rory Gormley, Faiza Zakaria, Yasmin Garcha, and others working behind the scenes. I recognize all the great contributions of these wonderful minds to this book, while solely holding complete responsibility for any shortcomings in this work. Lastly, I would also like to thank Dr Kholoud Saber Barakat for being the reliable friend she is, and every other friend, who I do not mention by name here but who stood by my side in difficult times, whether back home in Egypt, in Belgium, or in other parts of the world. To each and every one of them, I owe this book and more.

Foreword

Charles Tripp

'The army and the people are one hand' was the slogan that gave heart to many at the outset of the Egyptian revolution in 2011 since it seemed to imply that the army was siding with the popular uprising against the sclerotic and corrupt regime of President Mubarak. Others mistrusted it from the start, seeing it not as evidence of military support for the uprising but as a sign of the determination of the armed forces never to lose control of events, inserting itself into the narrative of the Egyptian popular revolution and using violence to suppress alternative accounts. As the following years were to show, this was closer to reality.

Indeed, the early commissioning by the armed forces of billboards foregrounding this slogan beneath an image of an Egyptian soldier awkwardly holding what seemed to be a struggling child indicated both the military's attachment to this image, but also its ambivalence. Less ambiguous was the response of one of Egypt's emerging street artists, 'Sad Panda', who responded by painting a large mural on Mohamed Mahmoud Street depicting an Egyptian soldier throwing a child onto a bonfire. In doing so, he found himself in danger of being mobbed, not by the security forces but by enraged passers-by, offended by this denigration of an institution that had enjoyed so long a history of image creation as 'heroes of the nation'.

These themes resonate in Maher Hamoud's detailed and forensic dissection of the role of the military in the gradual take-over of the media landscape in Egypt in the years since 2013. As an experienced journalist himself he had the good fortune to be able to practice his profession in Egypt during the brief window of 2011-2013 when print media were freer to report and to express themselves than at any time in Egypt's modern history since 1952. He was able therefore to witness at first hand the developments that he analyses so ably here. Chief amongst these has been the gradual takeover by the Egyptian military, under the direction of President Abdel Fattah al-Sisi, of much of the country's mass media and its main advertising agencies. This has led many talented and creative Egyptians, such as the author himself, to leave the country, finding that the atmosphere of uncritical adulation of the president and the violence done to those who would voice critical opinions make it dangerous and pointless to remain.

As countless historical and comparative examples demonstrate, efforts to control the image of power is part of the fabric of the political itself even if its trajectory is not always predictable. Any cursory view through the ages bears witness to the attention and artistry involved across the world in shoring up authority, whether divine or profane, through image cultivation. It was that supreme political realist Niccolò Machiavelli who was among the first to analyse the part this plays in the constitution of political power when he examined the conditions in which it was important for the Prince not only to be all-seeing, but also to control the ways in which he would be seen. The visual and the spectacular become part of the performance of power both in the sense of its theatrical display, and in the sense of performatively bringing about changing relations – fear, command, obedience but also devotion and affection – through the way that the powerful are made to appear to others.

In the modern world, of course, the arena extends far beyond the visual arts and involves all the ways in which power comes to be known to the public, reinforcing their self-empowerment as citizens or fixing their subordinate subject status, depending on the nature of the political regime. This will shape the ways in which otherwise similar forms of mass communication will work in different systems, although the logic of authoritarian power is common to both. More open systems, with a plural politics, and a recognition of the rights of diversity and of counter-publics, can provide a more robust activist and legal framework to keep in check the natural tendency to unaccountability and to monopoly that characterize both state and capital. Vigilance, however, is always necessary, as is the enforcement of rights.

In authoritarian systems, such as that of contemporary Egypt, these checks and their enforcement face in the other direction: they are aimed at those who would contest the government's monopoly of state and capital. Al-Sisi and his allies entrench themselves through their monopoly not only of the mechanisms of power but also of the narratives by which their hold on power is made to seem both natural and virtuous. In this way, they seek to produce the subjects who will fit into their own highly restrictive view of political order. Their intention is to cement a hegemony that normalizes inequalities of power and opportunity, through the manipulation of a politics of appearance in which all forms of communication are pressed into service. And if the narrative fails to persuade there is always a violent alternative ready to hand.

This is the strength, but also paradoxically the weakness of a regime like al-Sisi's that is based on the military as an institution. It is a strength since the ground will long have been prepared by the myths of nationalist and anti-colonial struggle for the projection of an image of the armed forces that identifies them with the nation, carefully disguising their class character, their hierarchies, their arbitrary use of force and their incompetence. With the state's resources at their disposal and free of any judicial oversight it also allows, indeed compels, the military to take control of all forms of mass media, enabling them to propagate the versions they want to create of themselves and of the country that they rule.

However, it is also a potential weakness in some ways. The relentless projection of narratives, images and performances, however positive and uplifting in intent, can be subject to dramaturgical decay. Even amongst those willing to support the current regime uncritically, constant repetition can lead to boredom, cynicism and a growing tendency to satirize the very images that are intended to inspire. The uniform control of all forms of mass media not only degrades journalism as a profession but also creates a growing sense of disbelief or lack of interest in the printed or visual output. In both areas, it is fertile terrain for mockery, an art long practiced with skill and acumen by the Egyptians, whether by word of mouth, disguised electronic communication or through the internet connections that authorities are unable to block.

In addition, hegemony is never as complete as its champions might wish. This is well borne out in the current situation of the media in Egypt. Controlling the mass media, the publishing houses, the TV companies and the advertising agencies that are part of the same ecosystem has created enormous opportunities for financial profit, free of any independent audit while the image, the message and the narrative work to the advantage of the president and his cohort. But they also create internal competition and rivalries amongst those who seek to extend and cement that control. In this sense, the logic of capital competition tends to displace that of collegial solidarity of the kind that might be expected to be integral to the ethos of a military institution.

Finally, there is a systemic weakness in this situation. The deceptive ease of control by the military of the media landscape in Egypt after the violence of 2013 and the following years, the material rewards that it has produced for them, even the all-consuming rivalries between the neo-Mamelukes who operate the system create a greater risk. Of all countries, Egypt and its military establishment should remember the disasters of the 1960s when the military had become so deeply involved in games of patronage, political competition and image projection that it was deflected from its primary professional tasks, whether in Yemen or in the Sinai. No amount of image projection or media manipulation could then disguise the military defeats that so changed Egypt's standing in the world.

Introduction

The following quote is not taken from a thriller novel but is from an editorial by Magdy al-Gallad, one of Egypt's most influential journalists. Al-Gallad, who took positions as the editor-in-chief of some of Egypt's top privately-owned newspapers such as *al-Masry al-Youm*, once wrote:

> The ambitious and polite man walks his political path carrying on his shoulders savage creatures that survive on his blood, differing in size from worms to rhinoceroses and aggressive monsters. Most of these [animals] don't like Gamal Mubarak as much as they desire to maximise their political and financial gains from his own living flesh. The man pays this price without knowing. And the price creates a greater distance between him and the average citizen.[1]

As a politically well-connected editor, Al-Gallad wrote his famous editorial titled 'Life on the Shoulders of Gamal Mubarak', in July 2009, almost two years before the 2011 uprising. Ironically, when reading Denis McQuail's discussion of the development of the newspaper industry in the seventeenth century, there are similarities between the world described by McQuail and al-Gallad's work today. Newspapers at that time were an extension into the public domain of an activity that had long been going on for governmental, diplomatic or commercial as well as for private purposes. The early newspaper was marked by its regular appearance, commercial basis and public character. Thus, it was used for information, as a record, for advertising, diversion and gossip.[2] *Al-Masry al-Youm* and *al-Watan* newspapers might appear from a distance to be as modern as other well-established international newspapers. However, a closer look from the perspective of someone inside the news industry, or a just critical reader, might give one a strong sense of seventeenth century journalism as McQuail describes it, disguised in twenty-first century clothing – the same century that witnessed the 2011 uprising that brought down Mohamed Hosni Mubarak, former Egyptian military leader and fourth president of the Arab Republic of Egypt since 1981. For a few years until Mubarak's ouster under the pressure of mass protests across the country and particularly in the iconic Tahrir Square, his son, Gamal, was being prepared and introduced by both state-run and private media as the country's next president.

The mission failed, as we have seen in 2011, but al-Gallad was ready again to serve as a propagandist for hire with similar content to that he had produced in Mubarak's time. Al-Gallad wrote later, 'Personally, I adore staring intensely at al-Sisi's eyes when he speaks about the future. His looks seem like confidently and strongly jumping forward. And since the beginning of his presidency, he has persistently created a spirit of hope.'[3] This is a quote from an editorial by al-Gallad, published at Masrawy on 20 January 2018 with the title: 'A Journey in the Mind of al-Sisi', shortly before al-Sisi ran for his second term in presidency, which he won by 97 per cent of the votes. Almost all other candidates were put in prison.

Al-Gallad is in fact not as shallowly hypocritical or simplistic as his writing might imply. Among the expert journalists interviewed for this book, Belal Fadl and Hossam el-Hamalawy[4] – both opposition journalists who have seriously suffered and are now living in exile – express opposing opinions regarding the period when they worked with al-Gallad while he was editor of *al-Masry al-Youm*. Belal opined that al-Gallad 'is the best editor-in-chief I have ever worked with',[5] while Hossam expressed in offensive terms that imply he was the worst.[6] The phenomenal and controversial al-Gallad as well as other media people and media investors will be considered in detail in this book while discussing Egypt's media market both before the uprising and after the military coup.

Concerning this uprising, it is observable that media accounts have elevated the Tahrir Square episode to the status of a 'pure event', echoing a Biblical clash between Good and Evil, where Tahrir became the place where *al-Shab* (the people) fought a victorious battle against *al-Nidham* (the regime).[7] The fall of Mubarak on 11 February 2011 was not in fact the fall of his regime's elites, contrary to how this was portrayed in the local and international media at the time. The military and business elites had been in control of the state's institutions for decades until that day and they were coordinating with each other to protect the political and economic gains they had made since Egypt's independence from colonialist Britain in 1952. Over the years, until the fall of Mubarak, they had changed face and control mechanisms several times. Among the most important tools in the elites' hands were the state-run and the privately-owned media.

Egypt is not the only country in the world where elites control and influence how media content is produced. However, Egypt is relatively different in the influence that this content has beyond its national borders, throughout the Arab region, given the country's political importance, as will be discussed in later chapters. Simply by the use of Arabic as a common language in these countries, gave the country's media industry additional importance and influence, at least until the rise of Al Jazeera, not to mention the political and economic influence of the United States on Egypt from the 1978 Camp David Accords and, in parallel, the shift to a free-market economy, from 1974.

One of the major outcomes of the 2011 uprising, which in 2012 brought to power a civilian and a somehow democratically elected president from the Muslim Brotherhood, Mohamed Morsi, seemed unacceptable to the historically politically engaged Egyptian army. A military coup in 2013 was the response.[8] This was also supported by the masses, who headed to the streets in unprecedented numbers across the country. News agendas controlled by the military and business elites,[9] alongside fatal political mistakes by the Muslim Brotherhood, were the main reasons for such mass support for this coup. It is in this context that this book *critically* discusses the political economy behind the controlled media market in Egypt's contemporary history. Observing how the Egyptian masses revolted against Mubarak in 2011 and then two-and-a-half years later as greater numbers headed to the streets to support a military coup highlights how crucial the media's role was in this. Or, as this book asks: How did al-Sisi succeed in restructuring the media market of Mubarak's business elite in favour of the military? Answering this question will require tracing back selectively political and economic events that occurred decades earlier. Nevertheless, before delving into the core content of this book, it is important to understand today's Egypt through a brief introduction to its economic model of capitalism and to the business empire of its military.

The critical political economist Jonathan Hardy wrote, thought-provokingly, 'If there have been times when the political and economic aspects of communication could be neglected by scholars then it is surely not ours'.[10] This book will question and analyse the role of Egypt's business elites, whether civilian or military, in controlling the country's media market. The discussions and findings of this book will provide us with explanations for an important aspect of the dynamics of power relations between the political (military and civilian) and business elites in Egypt, who are heterogenous and interrelated. Understanding these dynamics will help us understand why, for example, a newspaper like *al-Masry al-Youm* was founded in 2004, and why there was a need for a new paper, *al-Watan*, to be founded in 2012. It will also explain why, following the 2013 coup, the military gradually took over the media scene. The afore-mentioned two newspapers had successfully developed and dominated the press market by the time a military coup was on the horizon in 2013, especially *al-Watan*. It is also almost equally important to understand the role of some of the individuals belonging to these elites in a country where many of its businesspeople belonged, under Mubarak, to the same ruling party, the Nation Democratic Party (NDP), and of no less importance, we should understand the role of the media personnel at their service, such as Magdy al-Gallad quoted at the beginning of this introduction, as the actual producers of media content. Interestingly, some international sources, whether academic or journalistic, label Egypt's private newspapers as 'independent'.[11] This book refers to these news outlets as clearly 'private' but not independent, since they are influenced by many political and economic factors, especially following the coup. Such a clarification allows for a fresh critique of their newspapers' content and aids a better understanding of the political affiliations of their owners as members of the business elite.

To better inform the analysis of the background of Egypt's business and military elites and their interests in influencing the media, this book takes a Critical Political Economy (CPE) approach. CPE, as its name implies, critically studies the political economy of power relations and the socioeconomics that shape the communication of information from the mass media to its public.[12] In this sense, the main question of this book will be answered by analysing the relevant literature covering Egypt's business elite and its private media market critically, along with a series of interviews with media experts. This book will in turn answer a set of related sub-questions in each of the following chapters. Through this, a general picture of the post-Mubarak media market will be gradually drawn while explaining how the country's business elite has controlled the private media in their favour and in favour of the military, pushing certain political agendas, and how they continue, willingly or unwillingly, to maintain this control to the present day. To provide and analyse these details, the book will also discuss their initial position before the 2011 revolution as a power group interested in protecting their privileges in a free-market economy. The topic of Egypt's political economy of communication has been partially and insufficiently covered in some literature, but never in one comprehensive book.

> Social production takes place in the economy, politics and culture. Humans produce use-values, collective decisions and meanings. The economy and work are not limited to the production of physical goods. Also, culture and politics are on the one hand part of the economy: humans produce and communicate meanings and collective decisions in social processes. But culture and politics are not identical with the economy. They are simultaneously part and no-part of the economy. Once produced, rules and meanings take effect all over society.[13]

Christian Fuchs, in stating the above, introduces us to arguments about the commodification of culture and politics, which cannot be separated from economic influences. This opens the door to a multi-layered discussion on the relation between the economy, politics and society and how rules are communicated or, as will be argued later, enforced over a society as messages through the media. CPE is introduced in this chapter and will inform most of the discussions throughout this book of political economy with the purpose of understanding the power position of Egypt's business and military elites. The use of CPE in this book starts with a theoretical discussion of the position of the elites in general in relation to the concepts of hegemony and social relations. Then the principles of these discussions will be applied to the Egyptian case in the following chapters, topic by topic, where the literature will be discussed and combined with interviews conducted during this research.

CPE is rooted in diverse traditions, strands and clusters (across time, subject area and regions) that have developed over decades and continue to do so today. Despite the fact that CPE can be traced back to earlier points in the twentieth century, namely the Frankfurt School, the 1960s and 1970s were particularly important for CPE, which was largely influenced by Western Marxism, the rise of dissident social movements, and anti-imperialist sentiments worldwide at that time.[14] After a period of relative decline of Marxist thought in the 1980s, communications scholarship in the 1990s developed to more affirmative accounts due to the growth of digital media and analysing the rise of neoliberalism, which gave an edge to CPE analysis of the media industries.[15] Proponents of the democratization theory and free market economy recognize the mass media as a potential and influential actor of democratization because, unlike earlier instances of democratization, the current 'global wave of democracy' is taking place in a media-saturated environment.[16] This argument is supported by a well-established 'conventional' political economy tradition, which argues that the free market guarantees independence, diversity and the accountability of commercial media. In this view, the free market ensures that the free media are independent of governments, and hence it produces a diverse media system since all are free to publish. It also ensures the media are representative of society, since media enterprises must respond to their audiences. However, what actually happens is that media investors make arrangements with governments, because they share agendas and benefit mutually from cooperation.[17] Hardy's strongly critical view of the neoliberal media is interestingly also supported by free-market media economist Gillian Doyle, who says that since the early days of printing, the ability to communicate with mass audiences has been subject to many forms of intervention by state authorities, and that media industries are affected not only by 'normal' economic and industrial policy concerns, such as growth and efficiency, but also by a range of special considerations that reflect the socio-political and cultural importance of mass communication.[18] In the end, the assumption of democratization, in the sense that the more private media we have, the more likely democracy and free media will prevail, seems very challenging in terms of its materialization on the ground, if this is indeed even possible. In the case of Egypt, we can see that despite the country's fairly large private or commercial media market, the 2013 military coup occurred and was largely supported by most state institutions and the masses that consumed the same private media.[19] Having said this, it does not necessarily mean that CPE is only limited to Marxist or Marxian thought, as it shares some of the liberal pluralist thoughts about media in terms of serving citizens. The difference is that it critically challenges the role of capitalist corporate media in serving these citizens, as they claim.[20]

CPE is essential for understanding Egypt's media market in the context of the hegemony of power and money (political and economic) relations. Due to this focus, this critical approach stands out in the very diverse domain of political economy of communication. Two of the major scholars to whom this book pays particular attention throughout its critical approach to communication are Jonathan Hardy, referred to earlier, and Vincent Mosco, who had a developed approach to understanding commodification and how it relates to social change and power relations. Edward Herman and Noam Chomsky with their 'propaganda model' are also important to this book as they helped to empirically understand the practice of control over the media from a critical political economy perspective as well. Although the propaganda model of Herman and Chomsky is US-focused, it is insightful in analysing hegemony in the American media, which provides some lessons to reflect on when considering the Egyptian media. The following paragraphs involve a theoretical discussion on CPE and how it relates to Egypt's political economy and its media market.

In an initial answer to the question of what political economy is, Mosco argues that it is a broad-based and variegated approach to social analysis. He highlights two general characteristics, which have been used in communications research. One concentrates on social relations, particularly in power relations, governing production, distribution and the exchange of resources; the other concentrates on the broader problems of control and survival of the elites.[21] Mosco's understanding of political economy in relation to media research and power relations is key to understanding the Egyptian media market, and understanding this market entails addressing the political economy of the country and the power of its business elite, which goes hand in hand with a critical discussion of their historical and contemporary backgrounds. This book pays attention to the cultural production of the private media, which in turn is a part of the broader political economy.[22] The specific interconnections of the political and the economic are understood as structures that shape practices and strongly influence national media systems. Here it is important, in the Egyptian context, to ask ourselves who has the means and the power to produce media content, and who has access to them? To what extent do specific political and economic structures form media institutions and thus regulate flows of information? Conversely, how does media shape the economic and political practices that eventually create structures?[23] Fuchs argues that there are major principles that should be considered when studying political economy: the historical development of the economy; whether power and wealth are related and how these in turn are connected to cultural and social life; and basic moral questions of justice, equity and the public good.[24] Therefore, it is crucial for this book to study the history of Egypt's business elite in periods of political, economic and social transformation, i.e. Nasser's statist developmental project, Sadat's *Infitah*, Mubarak's hyper-neoliberalization, aided by his son Gamal, and al-Sisi's advancements in militarizing Egypt's neoliberal economy. In many cases we can diagnose an increased intertwining of political elites and business elites in Arab countries. Increasingly, media institutions seem to have become part of this trend, providing instruments of control and regime legitimization. As we will see in the Egyptian case, Mubarak's last governments included several ministers in key sectors such as construction or transport, who were at the same time owners of major firms contracting with the very same ministries. As we will see in Chapter Two, many members of this business elite resurfaced after Mubarak's fall, and enlarged their investment portfolios through adding TV channels and newspapers, in what can be seen as clearly politically charged activity in support of the military.

Mosco is critical of conventional economics where economists agree on a set of narrow rules about research and discourse. However, this set of rules succeeds because it serves power by providing information, advice and policies to strengthen capitalism. Between sources in the government institutions and sources in the business sector, a business news story produced by a journalist is mostly (intentionally and unintentionally) a reconfirmation of unchallenged 'conventional' economic narratives imposed by the former two. Important as it is to view the so-called 'normal economics' as a system of rhetoric, it is at least as important to see it as a system of power. To understand this system and to propose ways to change it we need political economy.[25] This is what makes CPE scholars stand out in their analytical approaches to the economic, the political and the social. By so doing, CPE is best placed to understand the role of the uprising in 2011 in changing and re-positioning power structures in Egypt, and the military coup in 2013. By studying both we can learn a lot about power and media control for the sake of political and economic influence in that period of a little longer than a decade. Here the instrumental character of the media becomes obvious. It becomes apparent not only when one investigates the relationships between the owners of the media and the ruling elite, but also when one considers how the content produced is most often loyal to the regime.[26] This in turn reinforces the need to take a critical approach, which occupies a significant space in the history of the political economy of communication from a multidisciplinary perspective,[27] in order to understand the case of Egypt and talk about future change that might, or might not, come about.

The development of CPE started by defining communication as a social process of exchange, where its outcome is the mark of a social relationship. In keeping with the broad approach to the field, the definition includes both the transmission of information and the social constitution of meaning. Mosco's and Hardy's critical approaches are important to this book due to their understanding and inclusion of recent technological advancements in communications, which include mediated communication with its many forms, from traditional newspapers to social media. Mosco's adapted approach to studying communications grew from concerns about the shortcomings of mainstream research, and with the policies that protected large media businesses from the development of a more democratic media system. Pertinent to the Egyptian context, he pays attention to the 'less developed world', where concrete political struggles over the shape of the post-colonial world played a large part in the growth of a political economy approach. Mosco also argues that the *commodification* of media content, audience and labour is the entry point at which to begin to theorize the political economy of communication. He defines commodification as the process of transforming goods and services, including communication, all of which are valued for their use, into commodities which are valued for what they will bring to the marketplace.[28] This brings us back to the importance of communication to the economy; not only to communicate economic messages relating to the marketplace, but also in conveying political messages to the general public, as a form of directly and indirectly influencing and controlling a society. Jürgen Habermas argues earlier along the same lines that Mosco and Hardy take later, that a critical approach would question the media as an attack of money and power, and in turn, as a structure that the elites use to dominate a society,[29] from which the importance of examining this structure that the elites use in the Egyptian case (briefly in this book with regard to the eras of Nasser and Sadat, and in more detail Mubarak and al-Sisi) comes, where a significant concentration of wealth lies in the hands of the elites.

Critical approaches also tend to be followed more during times of crises in the capitalist system, such as the 1968 protests and the world's financial meltdown in 2008. It should therefore come as no surprise that a CPE approach will be used in a book that investigates the political economy of Egypt around the 2011 uprising and the developments that has followed. We can see that one of the major structural patterns that relate to the Egyptian media system, which will be discussed in detail in Chapter Two, is that the extreme inequality of wealth distribution in Egyptian society was not affected or changed by the 2011 uprising, but was probably increased, as power and wealth remained in the hands of the country's elites despite the brief period of threat they experienced between the uprising and the coup. Comparatively speaking, it is also true that even 'established' democracies like the United States show a significant concentration of wealth among the elites. Most major US media are linked through ownership structures and boards of trustees connected to big businesses, which pose a serious challenge to media freedom. However, when comparing Egypt with the United States, one must note that not all capital in the US is 'loyalist' in the sense that it can be identified with one particular political player. The US media capital is somewhat more competitive, and political parties, social institutions and civil society at large are less vulnerable than they are in Egypt.[30] The 'propaganda model' of Edward Herman and Noam Chomsky is a critical approach towards understanding the American news industry and how it is controlled by the elites and their economic interests, and provides many lessons to be learnt from when analysing the Egyptian news industry. Ultimately, we cannot deny American political and economic influences on Egypt dating from the signing of the Camp David Accords in 1978.

Herman and Chomsky see the mass media as a system that serves to communicate messages and symbols to the general public. It is the function of the mass media to amuse, entertain, inform and inculcate individuals with the values, beliefs and codes of behaviour that integrate them into the institutional structures of the larger society. In a world of concentrated wealth and major conflicts of class interests, fulfilling this role requires systematic propaganda.[31] Both Herman and Chomsky focus mostly on the politics of American media, which is largely privately owned. In our case, the Egyptian private media, established shortly before the 2000s (private media during monarchical Egypt was nationalized following the 1952 military coup), were intended to produce more entertaining political and apolitical content to draw the public's attention back to local media after Al Jazeera and other international media outlets had pulled it away. At the point when new media strategies were introduced to regain the attention of the masses, the business elite of the time provided a service to the political and military elites by stepping into the private media market.

In countries where the levers of power are in the hands of a state bureaucracy, monopolistic control over the media, often supplemented by official censorship, makes it clear that the media serve the goals of a dominant elite. Herman and Chomsky argue that criticism of the elites in the American media is of a very limited nature and does not question the entire system, thus effectively strengthening it rather than criticizing it. Moreover, they point to the importance of a huge inequality in access to news sources in the American system, which in turn decides who has influence and who does not.[32] Their propaganda model promotes the view that elite domination of the media can lead to marginalizing dissenting voices. Similar to the way the American media may depict 'enemy states' in a certain way – compared to the way they depict 'friendly states' – the Egyptian media depicted the Muslim Brotherhood and revolutionary voices or whoever supported or sympathized with them as enemies of Egypt, and whoever took the elites' position as a friend. In such an environment, the private media are being used, both willingly and unwillingly, to produce content that meets the political and business elites' interests, or at least to limit the 'harmfulness' of critical content in order to maintain the elites' power and protect their position. The 'consent' notion of Herman and Chomsky goes hand in hand with Mosco's and Hardy's understanding of hegemony, which draws its strength from achieving the consent of those it would control. Mosco argues that this hegemony requires the exercise of power to maintain consent under changing conditions.[33] On the foundation of this understanding, this book's framework introduces a critique of the private media under changing conditions: primarily under Mubarak, who was toppled by a popular uprising, and under al-Sisi, who seized power by a popularly supported military coup.

In line with this framework, this book in adopting a CPE theoretical approach applies a methodology of qualitative analysis of semi-structured elite interviews and embeds them in discussions of the literature and observations of the field. The application of this tailored methodology starts with a critical analysis of Egypt's business elites and their political interests in addition to the media landscape that they dominate to their benefit and to the benefit of the military elite. A critical qualitative analysis approach using the literature covering Egypt's political economy in general and the media market in particular from the 1950s until the present day will be applied throughout the chapters. This book will pay particular attention to themes of hegemony imposed by the ruling elites, and political, economic and social changes that might accompany the process of political enforcement, where relevant. This will include, for example, the process of change under Nasser and the Free Officers Movement following the 1952 military coup and building a post-independence state, Sadat's *Infitah* and his approach which reinforced his position internally to later gain support from the West, Mubarak's relatively similar approach to that of Sadat, and al-Sisi's excessive militarization of the economy and media. These politics of hegemony and their relation to the media will be discussed critically, while an extra focus of analysis will be given to the period from 2011 to the present. In many sources, mostly non-academic, the two major political upheavals frequently mentioned in this book about Mubarak's fall in 2011 and the military coup in 2013 are commonly known as the 'January Revolution' and 'June Revolution' respectively. However, throughout this book the first is called an 'uprising' and the second 'military coup', since the first attempt at a revolution failed and the second, in an operation led by a field marshal, deposed a democratically elected president who was subsequently put in prison, and was later arguably killed through medical negligence. With relatively similar logic the 1952 events are called a 'military coup' in this book.

The responses of fifteen Egyptian expert media personnel interviewed for this study are embedded in arguments as qualitative analyses throughout the coming chapters. These expert/elite interviews play an important role from two perspectives. The first is that of adding depth to the arguments made throughout the course of this book. The second relates to the importance of each respondent and the special access they have to information and experiences, influence and insights that can be shared here, which is different from other forms of interviews that might require a larger number of respondents, depending on the topic and its scale. The sources interviewed here were all influential media professionals who have contributed significant portions of the daily news production in or about Egypt before and after the 2011 uprising, whether as actual producers of content or through managing (mostly news) media businesses. Their strategic positions give them an awareness of the almost inaccessible and strategic side of the news industry not available to other junior or medium level media personnel. All experts here are anonymized with gender-neutral pseudonyms as first names, except for the iconic publisher Hisham Kassem (founder of *al-Masry al-Youm* and other media outlets), popular journalist, author and TV presenter Belal Fadl, and pioneering blogger and socialist journalist Hossam el-Hamalawy, who all insisted on being quoted with their real names. The anonymization of the other twelve experts is very important for their own security, although the majority live abroad now. To distinguish the voices of the experts from that of the literature, the first are referred to by their first names (mostly pseudonyms) and their responses and views are expressed in the past tense, while voices of the literature are referred to with full names in their first mentions and then only family names in subsequent mentions, while their voices are expressed in the present tense.

Based on the theoretical and methodological frameworks set out above, the following chapters will discuss five topics in response to this book's major question: How did al-Sisi succeed in restructuring the media market of Mubarak's business elite in favour of the military? In answering this question, Chapter Two draws a profile of the contemporary Egyptian economy and media market from the time of the 1952 military coup with a focus on the decade before the 2011 uprising until the present. This chapter pays particular attention to the role played by the business elite before the uprising and how this role changed afterwards in terms of military ownership in the media market. It additionally analyses the profiles of two media investors, Salah Diab and Mohamed al-Amin, including the differences in their positions following the 2013 coup, as well as two influential media personnel, Magdy al-Gallad and Yasser Rizk, as facilitators of the roles and balances of interests of the business and military elites in the media. Chapter Three discusses the under-studied advertising sector in Egypt. Ideally, advertising revenues would be the incentive for investing in the media in a free market economy, but in the case of Egypt, as discussed in the chapter, media investments are not primarily profit-seeking. Chapter Four provides a review of social media in Egypt from the uprising until today, considering that social media is famously thought to have played a major role in the uprising. The chapter starts by considering the existence of the internet as a 'political space' before the uprising, the role of social media during the uprising and the coup that followed, the military use of social media in recent years, and the increasing use of the internet and social media surveillance technology against critical voices.

The first four chapters having provided the foundational discussions and analyses of the Egyptian media market, Chapter Five provides a review of media coverage of selected topics and periods around and after 2011. It starts with the coverage of the 2011 uprising itself, the 2013 coup and the period in between, and the changes observed following the coup. This chapter also discusses the introduction of the pro-military Tamarod Campaign, and the promotion of al-Sisi as 'saviour' of the country. Chapter Six discusses the deterioration of freedom of expression, allowed only where expressed against the Muslim Brotherhood, in addition to organized and random violence against journalists and the demonization of local and foreign critical news outlets. The chapter ends by looking at peculiar, poorly planned and sudden investments by the military in the regionally popular Egyptian soap opera market. The book concludes with Chapter Seven, which provides a summary of discussions and considers the findings of all previous chapters.

A Critical Overview of Egypt's Media Market

After the assassination of Sadat in 1981, his successor, Hosni Mubarak, leaned on the rentier economic structure for a transformist politics toward the political opposition. Political prisoners were released, civil rights such as freedom of press and of association were restored – to a degree – and in 1984 parliamentary elections were held. Relations with the Arabic nations, which had soured over the separate peace with Israel, were improved. The political 'détente' was not a process of 'democratisation from above', but a tactical retreat of the dictatorship, leaving limited spaces open in civil and political society for contentious politics that remained subordinated to regime interests [...] The rules of the new democratic game were set by the government and the NDP. Elections were manipulated and voters were systematically bought or intimidated.[1]

The above quote from Brecht De Smet, who works on revolutionary politics, political economy of capitalism and neoliberalism in Egypt, draws a three-dimensional picture that echoes the focus of this book more generally – and this chapter in particular – which is political authoritarianism, the associated neoliberal economic model and the controlled media. Taking a diverse approach to studying Egyptian media goes in line with Dina Matar's notion of studying the 'here' and 'now' by considering the contexts of the 'genealogies' of the particular histories of nation-states, religions, capitalist class formations, national, regional and international politics as well as cultural and discursive formations.[2] This is a notion that is shared with Mohamed Zyani, who says that studying Arab media necessitates an understanding of dynamics that cuts across vital activities that include the social, cultural, political, economic and religious, as a 'part of an evolutionary historical process'.[3] Contexts in which, when put together, make the Egyptian media appear eclectic and paradoxical in nature, as Sahar Khamis describes when drawing a picture that combines sets of binary opposites between authoritarianism versus resistance, public ownership versus privatization, official versus popular spheres, and secularization versus (re)Islamization.[4] This brings our focus back to the work of Vincent Mosco, discussed in Chapter One, which considers the need for a critical discourse when dealing with conventional economics – which is mostly the case when dealing with the political economy of Egyptian media, as a cross-cutting topic that includes the political, the economic and the social all-in-one media market. As Mosco argues, conventional economics fails to succeed only because economists agree on a set of narrow rules about research and discourse. Mainstream economics also succeeds because it serves power by providing information, advice and policies to strengthen capitalism. As important as it is to see economic orthodoxy as a system of rhetoric, it is also important to see it as a system of power. To understand that system and to propose ways to change it, especially having observed how Egypt's elites managed to outfox the 2011 uprising leading to a widely supported military coup two-and-a-half years later, we need critical political economy to be able to understand and inform the public about power games and social control. The game played by the Egyptian elites to maintain their powers will be critically discussed here. This chapter will introduce the interconnectedness between the business elite, the military elite and the media, and also introduce the role of media personnel and the politics behind their jobs.

Egypt's neoliberal capitalism and the business elite

To better understand how Egypt's business elite control the media, we have to go back through history to understand their nature, how they came about, how they evolved, and what their interests are. Samir Amin says that Egypt has never witnessed any genuine democracy in its modern history, as repression was the norm, while the elites and the imperialist powers have always 'feared communism' and its influence on Egypt.[5] Bearing in mind the notion that Egypt has constantly been authoritarian, this section will start with a brief historical overview from the start of Nasser's rule, as the beginning of the Egyptian Republic and move swiftly to the later stages in the country's political history with a political economy lens. We thus start with the foundation of the state of Israel in 1948 and the debate about this major event, which signaled the collapse of the monarchy, the central political pillar of imperialism and the reactionary domination of the country's political elite.[6] The Cairo Fire in January 1952,[7] in which many of Egypt's colonially symbolic buildings were burned down in mysterious circumstances, unresolved to this day, was one of the major signs of the end of British colonialism and the rule of Mohamed Ali's dynasty in Egypt. The change in the world order following the end of the Second World War, the *Nakba* in 1948,[8] the rise of nationalism, and other factors including the significant corruption and brutality of the local monarch-supported elites and aristocracy, were all important in leading to the huge change in Egypt that started on 23 July 1952. On that day, a group of young military men, the Free Officers, led by Mohamed Naguib and Gamal Abdel Nasser, carried out a military coup against King Farouk I. This group of young officers initiated a series of fundamental political, economic and social changes that played an important role in shaping today's Egypt. Social justice, the abolition of feudalism, the establishment of a strong national army, and full independence and sovereignty for Egypt were all pillars of the Free Officers' plan for the future of the country,[9] while building a post-independence economy, a main goal for the movement.

The Free Officers realized the need to build new political structures for the new Egypt they aspired to. The country was the stage for class struggles against the elites, especially the feudalists, where violence against farmers and small landowners was common. Nasser and his officers decided, with the support of large segments of the society, to push the monarchy – and the British-supported elites – out of the picture, especially since the majority of these were considered as allying with the counter-revolutionary camp. From the start, the Free Officers were briefly hoping for Western (but non-British) support, as they made some concessions. However, they realized they could expect nothing from the US.[10] There was also other mounting international pressure on the new Egypt, which was giving signals of moving towards socialism – later understood to be a 'statist development model' – to align with the 'Western camp', given the strategic importance of the Suez Canal for international economy.

Within six weeks the movement passed a land reform law that significantly changed the whole rural social landscape by limiting land ownership, which in turn caused hundreds of the pre-coup elite to lose large amounts of their wealth. The application of this law mandated to a newly formed body called the Higher Committee for the Liquidation of Feudalism. Farmland ownership was reduced to a maximum of 200 *Feddans* (a unit of land measurement used in Egypt and several other countries in the region that equates to about 0.41 hectares) for individuals and 300 for families. By 1969, around 12 per cent of Egypt's cultivated land was in the hands of previously landless or near-landless farmers.[11] The industrialists and big business owners also had their share of nationalization, as by 1960 the state was responsible for 74 per cent of the country's GDP.[12] The public sector grew dramatically because of an expanding welfare state and the need to fill the gaps left by Egyptian capitalists' unwillingness to invest in the economy.[13] These actions, alongside the 1956 nationalization of the Suez Canal and the Suez Crisis,[14] which was brought on by an abrupt US withdrawal of support for the High Dam in Aswan in the south of Egypt, are now seen as a turning point in Egypt's politics.

However, Nasser and his fellow officers did not seize power with the aim of only carrying out land reform or building a postcolonial state around the Aswan project. Concerned principally with the incompetence and corruption of the army's high command, and fearing arrest due to the opposition they had created within the army following the *Nakba*, they had taken control.[15] Similar to other newly independent states in the world at that time, 'the post-war order institutionalized a populist authoritarian bargain, in which workers and peasants accepted the authoritarianism of Nasser's one-party state [The Arab Socialist Union Party] in return for job guarantees, employment protection, health care, pensions and tenure security', writes Angela Joya.[16] It seems that, particularly following the nationalization of the Suez Canal, the newly reborn state became confrontational, nationally, regionally and internationally, in order to survive the internal and external pressures on it. Allies were therefore needed to support this fragile independence project. They were drawn internally, through a loyal elite created almost from scratch and which mostly consisted of military men and state bureaucrats. Meanwhile, externally, Nasser and the Free Officers leaned towards the Soviet Union and more generally the Eastern bloc. In turn, and as a start of collaboration, the Soviets arranged to provide Egypt with Czech weapons in response to the nationalization of the Suez Canal.[17]

Ambition and fear were both important elements in shaping what followed the Free Officers' military coup, leading to the birth of their post-independence state. Nasser and his colleagues, with the support of the Egyptian masses and solidarity in some parts of the Arab region, had the big ambition of building a strong pan-Arab nationalist state. They hoped to position Egypt and the region on solid ground in the new world order following the post-Second World War realignment of power, which was shifting the compass towards the United States. However, fear was naturally present in their political and economic strategy planning, as they seemed aware that their ambition would be opposed by the former elites, which were well connected to the West with its old colonialist powers as well as the rising American ones. That new post-war bipolar world provided the Free Officers with a great chance to press on with their plans, since both the Soviet Union and the United States were competing for alliances in the Middle East, a fact well realized by the young officers and which they took advantage of by claiming to hold a balance between the two powers. By doing so, they managed to create for themselves a space to reinforce the country's national sovereignty.[18] Amin argues that the emergence and evolution of 'Nasserism' had shifted from 'the strategic to the immediate', imposing an internal question for the local political players of whether to be a critical support or in opposition to the new regime.[19] This could be seen with more clarity in the early 1960s through the formation of a new elite that Nasser could trust and depend on in building his statist development model, which almost completely replaced the previous monarch-supported capitalist model. Indeed, a new elite that consisted of state bureaucrats, military men and a few rural and urban political leaders was on the rise. This was established with control over all labour movements, which were overarched by the single entity of the Egyptian Trade Union Federation (ETUF), founded in 1957. Charles Tripp highlights the relationship between Nasser's state and the workers in Nasser's own words: 'The workers don't demand. We give'. In this sense, the only permitted stage for union activity became deeply implicated in the operations of the one-party state, with labour leaders rarely standing up to the government and almost always siding with the authorities.[20] In parallel, a media propaganda machine owned and controlled by the new state was established to guarantee popular support for the Free Officers' ambitions. This will be discussed in more detail later in this chapter. However, the defeat of the

Egyptian Army in 1967 and the occupation of Sinai and other Arab territories by Israel[21] was a major set-back for Nasser's state. This defeat was followed by significant political and economic pressures, which marked the beginning of the end of the only decade of relative success in attempting to transform Egypt through a statist development project. The economic crisis and the defeat by Israel both clearly undermined the material and ideological base of the so-called 'Nasserist project'. While in a parallel view, it also showed the contrast between the support of the United States for the state capitalism of countries like South Korea and Taiwan in comparison with violent opposition to state capitalism in Nasser's Egypt.[22]

Nasser's untimely death in 1970 coincided with the beginning of a dramatic shift in the global economy as the United States unilaterally dismantled the post-war arrangements established under the Bretton Woods Agreements. President Muhammad Anwar el-Sadat (1970–81) re-oriented Egypt away from the Soviet Union, abandoned Nasser's commitment to the non-aligned movement, and allied Egypt closely with the United States and oil monarchies in the Persian Gulf.[23] To attract foreign capital, the ruling elites led by Sadat forcefully reconfigured the dominant class alliances and accumulation strategy along neoliberal lines.[24] The pace of this setback accelerated when the Free Officers divided into two factions: one pro-Soviet, led by Ali Sabri,[25] and another that later was to become pro-American, led by Sadat. The bureaucratic pro-Soviet Nasserist left was then weak and uncomfortable with mobilizing the masses.[26] Hence, Sadat, with the support of Islamists – mostly the Muslim Brotherhood – succeeded in winning the political battle against the Nasserists and enforced new measures to gradually reshape Egypt's political and economic model towards a free-market economy in what became known later as *Infitah* or Open-Door Policy,[27] starting around 1974. The Higher Committee for the Liquidation of Feudalism was disbanded right after Nasser's death. Landowners and some earlier feudalists were able to reclaim some of their farmland, and rents were raised for the first time since 1952.[28] When Sadat took the path of making peace with Israel and de-militarizing the state, he decided to provide the military with the opportunity to develop its own business capacity and interests as a means of 'coup-proofing' his rule.[29] In 1978, the Camp David Peace Accord[30] was signed between Egypt and Israel, which in turn took Sadat's policies to a higher level of economic liberalization, with the support of the

United States where the peace treaty was signed. In this context, Adam Hanieh considers the agriculture sector as the initial focal point of Sadat's neoliberal project, which Mubarak continued. They liberalized the sector by letting the prices of agricultural inputs and output to rise to the level of international markets, leaving private companies as the only players that could benefit.[31] Timothy Mitchell describes a snapshot of the dramatic change during this period:

> Transferring farmland out of village control into large commercial hands coincided with the interests of American agribusiness corporations, including Coca-Cola and Pepsico, for whom Camp David confirmed the ending of the Egyptian boycott of American soft drink companies and the opening up of an important new market. Both companies embarked on investment projects in Egypt in the late 1970s, including a twenty-thousand-acre citrus-growing project to produce soft-drink concentrates negotiated jointly by Taha Zaki (an advisor to the Egyptian government on 'food security') and a director of Pepsico – the White House advisor Robert Strauss.[32]

This close economic and political cooperation between Egypt and the United States continues on the basis of these ties in one way or another to this day, depending on the historical phase. They might strengthen or weaken depending on the changes that occur under successive American administrations, but they still exist and shape a large part of Egypt's so-called free-market policies. It is important to shed light on the fact that the changes in economic and political policies since Sadat have been supported by, among others, three Washington-based institutions; the International Monetary Fund (IMF), the World Bank (WB), and the United States Agency for International Development (USAID). These institutions presented a hegemonic approach that Sadat allowed to penetrate Egypt's economic policy making following the death of Nasser, and which continued to grow in terms of involvement and enforcing change ever further towards a free-market economy under the watch of President Muhammad Hosni Mubarak (1981–2011), who slowly followed in Sadat's footsteps after his assassination in 1981.

During that period, a form of 'rentier capitalism' was in service for the benefit of both state bureaucrats and the private sector. Rents were accumulating and distributed centrally through the state based on connections, while private capital entered the rent distribution process through subcontracting and the informal market.[33] Under Mubarak, as a continuation of Sadat's policies, the second phase of forming a politically loyal elite commenced, to further replace Nasser's military and bureaucratic elites. This more or less constitutes the origins of today's business elite. The process of creating this elite was predicated on a lack of confidence, on the part of Sadat, in Nasser's loyalists, which was shared by his successor. Mubarak followed Sadat's path and reinforced the emerging business elite. Some were from the former monarch-loyal elite who had had their wealth nationalized under Nasser, such as the Mansour family, while some were state bureaucrats who were turning into businessmen using their connections with the state, and still others were just born of the re-launched free-market economy. These changes additionally acted as preconditions for the 'internationalization of Gulf capital into the Egyptian agribusiness', where Gulf capital deepened the process of Egypt's economic liberalization.[34] Egypt has since become the Gulf's largest food supplier, and buyer, in the Arab World, and at the same time a centre for Gulf capital accumulation.[35]

The central problem of political and economic reform from the period of *Infitah* until today lies in the ways it has been conceptualized and implemented through a free-market ideology that transfers power from the state to new 'hybrid' governmental arrangements where the 'state' and the 'market' seem to become a symbiotic pair.[36] One supports the other, and vice-versa, which plays a pivotal role in creating political, economic and social consent, or at least attempts to. We can briefly remark that Sadat's *Infitah* policy almost led to an erosion of Nasser's bureaucratic class and to the rise of a new upper class concentrating its investments in the service, trade and finance sectors rather than manufacturing, as had been the case in the 1950s and 1960s. However, in Mubarak's time, this new upper class became massively richer after joining the Sadat-founded National Democratic Party (NDP),[37] which later became the regime's strongest ally. Joya explains that the period of the NDP's political precedence and the economic rise of those associated with it can be considered against the background of a set of internationally imposed changes, which she describes as follows:

> The Third World debt crisis of the mid-1980s increased the pressure on Egypt to dismantle the statist development model it had inherited from the Nasser era. By the end of the decade, Mubarak was cashing in his geostrategic

rents to reduce some of its external debt as it entered negotiations with the World Bank and the International Monetary Fund. The result was Economic Reform and Structural Adjustment Programme, a comprehensive structural adjustment program conforming to the broad agenda of the so-called Washington Consensus.[38]

In line with Joya's external factors, we can ascribe faces to the dramatic economic changes in the late Sadat and early Mubarak eras, as Timothy Mitchell provides us with three representative examples from among many families who were supported by Sadat's and Mubarak's regimes to become well established in the new business elite in exchange for political support for the state. The Mansour family were cotton traders prior to 1952 and then found their way back into the business world in the mid-1970s as major private investors. They managed to gain exceptional access to international – mainly American – brands, and became local agents for Western companies. Among a diverse pool of brands, the Mansours were sole agents for Chevrolet, General Motors, Caterpillar, Marlboro and McDonald's. Besides the fast-food sector, they generally dominated Egypt's automotive market at that time, and still maintain a leading position in the same market today. A second example, very different to the pre-1952 returning elite of the Mansours, is the Bahgat Group led by Ahmed Bahgat, who has no aristocratic history and who did not previously number among the elite. The Bahgat Group became the biggest producer of television sets in the Middle East with a dominant position in the Egyptian market. Bahgat was always publicly seen to be Mubarak's friend, which gave him access to financing opportunities in other non-electronic sectors such as irrigation systems, tourism, real estate, retail trade, and later as the founder and owner of Dream TV Network. The third example, the rise of whom also post-dates 1952, is the Sawiris family (who also had a business presence before the 1952 military coup, although this does not seem to be so significant in comparison with other families like the Mansours). Onsi Sawiris, the father, was working as a contractor in Libya before the *Infitah* and the new policy encouraged him to return to Egypt. The family's wealth initially grew rapidly, following their introduction to the market as local agents of Hewlett-Packard and AT&T, besides building US-funded communication networks for the Egyptian military.[39] Later, in the 1990s, the son Naguib revolutionized the family's business, reaching a much higher peak by investing in telecom services and construction through their holding company Orascom, with investments located in more than twenty countries in Europe, Africa and Asia. The son later became the founder and owner of ONTV Network and cofounder of the popular privately-owned newspaper *al-Masry al-Youm*, and most recently the founder and funder of the prestigious el-Gouna Film Festival.

What the above-mentioned investors have in common is that they were all well-established and enjoyed watching their investment portfolios massively and diversely grow during the last few years under Sadat and the whole period under Mubarak. During the period from the mid-1970s till the mid-2000s the common features of their cooperation with the state were almost the same: based on government contracts, projects promoted and supported by USAID, and special access to private bank credit – already owned or managed by relatives or members of the same business elite – again, born under Sadat and grown during Mubarak's first twenty-five years in office. These three examples of business elite represent the key diversity within their power group: Mansour as a returning aristocrat, Sawiris as a returning businessman, and Bahgat as a newly home-grown tycoon. Despite these differences in backgrounds and beginnings, they all enjoyed remarkably similar benefits, interests and privileged access to resources, as explained earlier. Two Bahgat and Sawiris had their own media companies, and the third, Mansour, tried to buy the giant al-Hayat TV Network in mid-2016, but the deal was not sealed. They all benefited from the state, and they all became interested in the private media market after having become well-established in other business sectors. As Tripp briefly indicates, 'in the decade or so that followed the introduction of the 1991 [privatization] law, the balance between state and private enterprise changed dramatically, such that by 2005 some seventy per cent of the Egyptian economy was privately owned'.[40] From 2003 to 2010, as the work of Ishac Diwan finds, the bulk of bank loans went to politically connected private companies.[41] The exchange of interests between business and political elites, whether military or civilian, is common in liberal economies. Joya, however, makes a distinction between liberalization and neoliberalization in her work on the Egyptian economy. For her, liberalization refers to the elimination of constraints on economic activity and can be understood as a process of negative reforms, in the sense of removing legislation and regulation. She distinguishes neoliberalization as a project that entails far more substantive reforms that target the nature of the state itself, and thus far more ambitious and radical than mere liberalization. In Egypt's case, these reforms entailed not only removing constraints on market activities, but also transforming the state with the goal of creating new markets and enhancing market discipline.[42] In this sense, the year 2004 represented an important shift within the Sadat-Mubarak era of politics and their neoliberal project. This was the year when Gamal Mubarak was introduced to Egypt's political sphere as the head of the Policies Committee at the NDP. In the same year, Egyptian-Canadian graduate of McGill University, Ahmed Nazif, was appointed as the country's prime minister, with two goals to achieve. The first, pushed by the international Washington-based institutions, was to accelerate the process of privatization of the public sector. For example, in the cement and steel production sectors, privatization worked to the benefit of the Sawiris family, Ahmed Ezz and others. The second was to provide the support required and a friendly legislative environment for Gamal to run for presidency at an appropriate time in the future – most likely after his had father stepped down for him to take his place, or perhaps through inheriting the presidential palace as political heir upon his father's death. Obviously, this big plan stumbled and then failed following the 2011 uprising.

Generally speaking, the politics from 1991 to 2011 can be viewed as a struggle within the NDP between neoliberal modernizers pushing forward with their structural reforms, and pragmatic conservatives, many of whom were linked to the military, cautioning restraint.[43] One can now judge that Gamal, a Western-minded and neoliberally educated young man with the burning ambition to inherit his father's throne, was too enthusiastic and insistent on reaching his goal. The change that he needed to pave his road to presidency was not happening quickly enough for the purpose of his plans. For this reason, he decided to introduce a new business elite to Egypt: a new power group that was younger than the existing one and closer to him personally, to act as stronger allies and respond more quickly to his ambitious plans. Gamal's new elite, or the hyper-neoliberal 'new guard', were not intended to conflict with the existing 'old guard', grown under Sadat and Mubarak and mostly connected with the military. It was instead an alternative solution that was intended to work in parallel, and no significant conflicts occurred between the two sub-groups, at least not publicly. Similar to what had previously been provided under Gamal's father and under Sadat, the new guard had privileged access to economic benefits and were allowed to grow quickly. The neoliberal modernizers of the NDP were clearly politically on the rise by the early 2000s.[44] The success of this rapidly enforced political and economic project resulted in Gamal attempting to unite forces in his favour: both the business and civilian political elites, together in one ruling elite. This worked well at the beginning, however it was one of the main factors that accelerated the fall of the Mubaraks, once economic and political corruption reached an unprecedented level as a result.

One example of many that relate to this attempted merger of the political and business elites into almost one body was highlighted in what is known as the Palm Hills court case. Looking through the details of political, legal and financial corruption in this case brings to light how the influence of the business elite promoted by Gamal Mubarak, the new guards, quickly spread economically and politically. Palm Hills was a company with a registered total capital of EGP 2 billion, 55 per cent of which was owned by al-Mansur and al-Maghraby companies. The two businessmen, Mohamed al-Mansour and Ahmed al-Maghraby, ran other diverse investments in different sectors in cooperation with the state. While running these businesses they were both appointed to Nazif's cabinet. Al-Mansour was the minister of transportation from 2005 to 2009, while al-Maghraby served from 2004 until 2009 as minister of tourism, and from 2009 until Mubarak's fall as minister of construction. The Palm Hills company, owned by Gamal's close friends and the new business elite, became richer and stronger, while the Mubaraks also benefitted financially.[45] Alaa Mubarak, Gamal's brother and a shareholder in Palm Hills, was profited from state assets such as public land allocated to the private sector in exchange for money channelled in and out of companies in which he held shares. Another example is the case of Moataz al-Alfi, the CEO of Americana, the Kuwaiti food giant, who was a close associate of Mubarak's family, particularly of Gamal, and a prominent member of the NDP. In the 2000s, when public sector companies were being privatized, al-Alfi made use of his connections with the Mubaraks to secure Americana the acquisition of large public assets with significantly less than half their market value, which was only revealed after Mubarak's fall.[46] Generally, land sales were a lucrative source of financial gain for corrupt officials, who worked as brokers of these deals.[47] This high level of manipulation was indeed reflected in a survey by the Pew

Research Center, which revealed that in 2010 (just before the 2011 uprising) corruption was the top concern of 46 per cent of Egyptians, and was ahead of their concerns about lack of democracy or poor economic conditions.[48] The strategy for Gamal Mubarak's new guards, according to which they should not clash with Mubarak senior's old guards, did not work perfectly in the end. It seems that the military did not fully approve of the 'presidential inheritance plan' in favour of the son, but also did not want to clash with the father, who they were loyal to as their military leader. Almost immediately after Mubarak's fall, this factional conflict clearly intensified, as the military went first after numerous prominent neoliberals who had been associated with Gamal Mubarak. However, later developments following the 2013 coup suggest a certain qualified rapprochement that took place between the military and the neoliberals, albeit under the hegemony of the former, which still retained a certain nationalist political orientation[49] in the eyes of the public. One indication that supports this argument is the decision by the Supreme Council of Armed Forces (SCAF), a body which took over following the fall of Mubarak, to state its support for the uprising and to meet some of the protesters' demands of placing many from the son's new guard under arrest in a media-sensational fashion. The old guard, however, were only arrested after the masses took to the streets again demanding the trials of Mubarak, his family and his corrupt old guard. The members of the old guard were arrested in a subtle way, without any contrived media shaming, in marked contrast to the treatment of the new guard. Another indication of favouritism and respect for the old guard by the military can be drawn from the post-coup period starting late 2013. There were many court acquittals for both groups of these business elites.

There is not yet sufficient in-depth literature published on the relations between al-Sisi and the business elite. Since the military coup of 2013 there have been indications that he follows Mubarak's approach. However, he tends to come across as more conflicted and ambiguous in his approach. Al-Sisi's promise to reward all Egyptians who had massively supported the coup against Morsi and the Muslim Brotherhood, was unrealistic. Al-Sisi flirted with the public wearing his military suit and speaking a language that appealed to nostalgic Nasserist ears among the poor. He also partially followed a Sadatist style in his use of Egyptian nationalist language. The term 'Egypt above all' could be heard and seen on banners all over the country at that time. Al-Sisi approached the existing business elite with promises of lucrative investments.[50] This is in addition to the further deepening of Gulf capital into several sectors of the Egyptian economy. As one example, by the end of 2016 close to half of the food and agricultural companies listed on the Egyptian Stock Exchange were either controlled or had significant ownership stakes held by Gulf capital.[51] However, and as Joya pointed out previously, the military continues to exercise a hegemony practised over the business elite based on a 'certain nationalist political orientation'. To understand this orientation, the business empire of the Egyptian army needs to be discussed, connecting its post-independence roots to today's post-coup militarized model of neoliberalization.

Structural phases of the military's business empire

The relationship between the Egyptian military and the country's business elite was not born, or reborn, during Sadat's era, as many mayt think. It had actually existed since the very beginning of the 1952 military coup. There are indeed points in history when this relationship was weak. However, the two remained connected. One example of this is Sayed Marey, a feudalist from the liberal and pre-independence al-Wafd Party, and the brain behind the Agricultural Reform Programme that managed the redistribution of farmland to landless farmers discussed previously. Later in the 1970s under Sadat, Marey became one of Egypt's biggest producers of fox fur. We should also not forget that most of the offspring of Egyptian presidents have been businesspersons with links to the military. Even today's several 'hipster' tourist camps in the highly militarized Sinai Peninsula are owned or run by descendants of superior intelligence officers.[52] To put it simply, the Egyptian military following their 1952 coup did not particularly have a socialist agenda, but they had an urgent need to rebuild a strong post-independence national economy. Such plans always face the need to invest in infrastructure, which the private sector usually is unlikely to be involved in, hence nationalization programmes were introduced. Joya argues that instead of representing a form of socialism, the military's role evolved as a pragmatic response to the contingencies of post-colonial development, particularly the lack of capital, where they gradually developed organizational capacity to accumulate assets and control strategic sectors of the economy.[53] The leading giant construction 'public sector' company, the Arab Contractors, was founded and managed for decades by the pre-independence business tycoon Osman Ahmed Osman (1917–99). He accumulated his initial wealth from construction projects in the Gulf countries and founded his company in Egypt in 1956. It was nationalized in 1961 without resistance, and he continued to manage and receive government construction contracts thereafter. His offspring continue to run the company today. Therefore, working with the hypothesis that the Egyptian military have always been involved to some degree in business, this section will shed some light on five structural phases of the military's business empire.

The first phase was from 1952 until Nasser's death in 1970. Following the deposal of King Farouk I (r. 1936–52) in 1953, Egypt was declared a republic. As early as 1954, the Ministry of Military Production was established, which marked the official beginning of the direct involvement of the army in business, even though this was then limited to military purposes. Nasser was a highly influential figure in the Free Officers Movement from its beginning, even under Mohamed Naguib's presidency from 1953. In 1956 he was elected as the president, marking a period of even more significant transformation, where the military became increasingly involved in the economic development of the post-independence economy.[54] This was also a period in which the military were called on to hold managerial roles in the state's bureaucracy.[55] However, the military's involvement in civilian production, which started in the late 1950s, was not a success story[56] until Sadat's presidency. The year 1961 witnessed a new wave of military involvement in the economy, as more private companies and assets were nationalized. In the same year, the defence minister Abdel Hakim Amer was appointed as the head of the Higher Council for Public Enterprises. He was later largely blamed for Egypt's dramatic defeat of 1967 by Israel, although – apart from of successes and failures in the military's involvements in the civilian economy – we can still say that Egypt's modern defence industry was built under Nasser in the 1950s and 1960s.[57]

The second phase took place during Sadat's reign from 1970 to 1981. As discussed earlier, the *Infitah* policies began in this period, particularly in 1974, and were later reinforced with the signing of Camp David Accords with Israel in 1978. Both led to a rise of neoliberal economic policies and 'openness' to the free market and the West, as the term *Infitah* implies. On the military side of associated economic events during this period, particularly in 1975, Sadat founded the Arab Organization for Industrialization (AOI), which was funded by Saudi Arabia, Qatar and the United Arab Emirates, as a means of drawing significant investment to Egypt.[58] The economic role of the military was then increasing as a form of compensation for the army's formal depoliticization.[59] One of the forms of this compensation was delegating the military to be a leading player in the reconstruction of post-war urban areas and rebuilding infrastructure in the Suez Canal governorates, which set them to claim economic civilian assets and activities in that part of country,[60] in addition to other business projects in the food and consumer goods sectors. However, these sectors were still mostly directed towards consumption by military personnel, as a form of 'self-sufficiency' under the post-war cuts to military budgets in line with the Camp David Accords.

The third phase of the military's business empire took place during Mubarak's three-decade-long rule, a significant upward shift in the sophistication of the military business empire. This section is not sufficient to cover all transformations relating to how the military carried out business in Egypt, but it will focus on the developments that are considered to be game-changers or significant shifts in power relations. Abd al-Halim Abu Ghazala was already appointed as the minister of defence and military production in March 1981, seven months before Sadat's assassination in October of that year. He continued his role under Mubarak, until 1989. This was a time of pressure from international financial institutions to reduce the defence budget, and this in turn encouraged the growth of a largely off-budget military economy.[61] Abu Ghazala was given the green light by Mubarak to unleash military involvement in the civilian economy, during a period that can be considered the real breakthrough of a parallel military business empire, and which explains its expansion during the following four decades. During the first year of his term in office Abu Ghazala established both the General Services Agency (GSA) and the Land Projects Agency (LPA). In 1984, the National Authority for Military Production (NAMP) was established, and in 1985, the Ministry of Defence began its ongoing business of constructing civilian bridges and roads using military conscripts as labour. Through these and other similar agencies, the military started investing in food production, housing and infrastructure projects, leasing state-owned facilities placed under their authority, and leveraging their control of military zones around the capital and other cities to acquire a financial return on approving the use of land for state-funded projects.[62] This economic expansion helped Mubarak keep the military well-compensated under the enforced 'demilitarization' of Camp David. However, it caused Mubarak a headache, as Abu Ghazala became internally popular among the military, due to the increase of wealth of officers and increased living standards among conscripts. He was also internationally popular in the West, particularly in the United States, due to his role in supporting the Iraqi army in their war against Iran and the Afghani Mujahidin in their war against the Soviets, supplying Egyptian-made arms and ammunition.[63] It is widely known that Mubarak did not like influential political figures to become too popular. In 1989, Abu Ghazala was fired from his position, a move which he did not resist as there had already been a media campaign aimed at tarnishing his reputation through portraying him as a flirtatious person.[64]

The dismissal of Abu Ghazala was intended to introduce a new simple trade-off between Mubarak and the military, according to which the latter could increase its economic engagement, in return for staying out of politics.[65] Sabry Abou Talib was assigned to Abu Ghazala's former position, but probably did not meet Mubarak's expectations as he was also a relatively popular figure, though less so than Abu Ghazala. By 1991, Mubarak seemed to have found his ideal candidate for the job: Mohamed Hussein Tantawi, who stayed in office until the end of Mubarak's reign. Ironically, Tantawi also headed the Supreme Council of the Armed Forces (SCAF) which led the country following Mubarak's fall in 2011. Under Tantawi, the military business empire quietly expanded, based on Abu Ghazala's economic models, with the addition of a couple more agencies. One of these was the Maritime Industries and Services Agency (MISA), which was put in control of the Egyptian Shipbuilding and Repair Company and Alexandria Shipyard. This growth occurred under Tantawi without his claiming any personal popularity, exactly as Mubarak wished, hence both the presidency and the military found themselves in political harmony – although there was some minor tension and a clash of interests, as explained in the previous section, that arrived with the introduction of Gamal Mubarak and his new business elite in 2004.

The fourth phase was as short as just three years, which represents the period from Mubarak's fall in 2011 to the beginning of al-Sisi's first presidential term in

2014. This includes the rule of the SCAF, headed by Tantawi, and the short-lived presidency of Morsi. The military business continued as usual, although at a lower level due to the political turmoil created by the aftermath of the uprising. In the end, it was obvious that the military were determined to 'restart the Egyptian economy not restructure it' and to return to more or less the lines it had followed since the 1990s.[66] There were, however, two major developments that may be important during this phase. The first is that during this period the military managed to present itself as 'the one organization with the greatest degree of national legitimacy', as Joya puts it, 'enabling it to either expropriate or co-opt the neoliberals [of Gamal Mubarak], and usurp power from the Muslim Brotherhood. By doing so, it was able to emerge as the dominant fraction of Egyptian capital – the only one that was capable of promoting a vision of national reconstruction'.[67] The second development, which is related to the issue of economic legitimacy, was a confrontation between the military and Morsi over development plans for the Suez Canal zone, which ended in favour of the military, following the July 2013 coup. This coup was initially supported by Saudi Arabia, the UAE and Kuwait, who together pledged a total amount of US$ 12 billion to the military regime in the wake of Morsi's ouster, which was followed by additional other forms of support including subsidised supplies of oil, loans, promises of massive investments, and the deposit of Gulf financial reserves in the Egyptian Central Bank.[68] In September of that year, the military did not wait but launched massive major public works and procurement contracts managed by the same military agencies discussed earlier. However, this time it was with overwhelming popular support, unlike previous decades where the military business was mostly discrete. Such support encouraged the military to seek even further legal legitimacy for their control over the economy by enforcing constitutional amendments in 2014, enshrining its budgetary and operational autonomy from any civilian authority – attaining complete power.[69]

The fifth and last phase starts with the election of al-Sisi and the beginning of his first term in 2014. Apart from his popularity as 'saviour' of the country from the Muslim Brotherhood – which will be discussed in Chapter Five – he was handed a country fully obedient to the army's control, both militarily and economically, with a civilian business elite which had realized that there was no option other than to work under the military's terms, whether willingly or unwillingly.[70] Like the previous long-serving presidents, al-Sisi launched his own mega-project, or in fact two of them. The first was the expansion of the Suez Canal in what was propagandized as 'the New Suez Canal', and the second was the 'new capital' project, which still does not have a name even today. As a further legal detail that would increase the level of cooperation and control over the civilian economy, in 2015 the Land Projects Agency was authorized by a presidential decree to form joint ventures with Egyptian and foreign companies, and was also permitted to use military land as equity in these investments. Before the 2013 coup, Egypt had already been the regional leader in the so-called Public-Private Partnership (PPP), which allowed the government to allocate business opportunities to the private sector. This strategy came to a halt by the time of the 2011 uprising, however, it regained prominence following the coup and has since broadened its scope to encompass a wider array of urban services.[71] In this final phase, we can see that al-Sisi depended on the already existing economic power of the military, in terms of both accumulated capital and reinforced legal structures that had been built up since 1952. This accumulation of power and capital has significantly helped him to unleash the powerful military dictatorship that Egypt has today.

Despite the strong grip of al-Sisi and his military over the Egyptian economy, his policies are not necessarily a great success. Elke Grawert and Zeinab Abul-Magd argue that al-Sisi's economic policies in Egypt are contradictory and have brought discontent among both the civilian business elite and the underprivileged classes that joined the 2011 uprising:

> On the one hand, he imposes a state and military upper hand in running the economy and extends government support to the middle and lower classes, a la Nasser's model. On the other hand, he pursues market reforms by eliminating subsidies and stimulating the investments of the business elite, following in Mubarak's footsteps. Wrapped in ultra-nationalistic discourse, al-Sisi aspires to revive Nasser's socialist state under military control, and yet he is in dire need of local and foreign capital that is only attracted to and thrives in a liberalized market. His confused economic policies have thus far not assuaged post-revolutionary discontent on the side of the very social groups that voted for him; on the contrary, unrest persists.[72]

The assumptions of Grawert and Abul-Magd, published in 2016, still hold their validity, however the impression that al-Sisi was trying to revive Nasser's 'socialist' state can now more clearly be understood as merely hyper-military-neoliberalization of the economy. Nevertheless, the position of the military within Egypt's politics has always been complex and still warrants further research, especially concerning the changes in power relations between the military and business elites in favour of the former, which have stepped into more and more business territories such as the media market, which will be discussed later in this chapter.

Hazem Kandil founds his analyses, like most political economists working on Egypt, on the introduction of *Infitah*. He argues that by adding the interior as a 'civilian' entity to the picture, the military's destiny under Sadat and Mubarak was temporarily tied to the security apparatus. He posits that the interior had a stronger position during the period following Camp David. At the beginning of the 2011 uprising, the masses chanted: 'The people and the military are one hand!' This was based on the common understanding among Egyptians that the military would not intervene in the uprising in favour of the security forces, which was not entirely true. However, those who chanted in praise of unity between the army and the people also began to chant furiously: 'The people demand the execution of the field marshal' – who was then the head of the SCAF, Mohamed Tantawi. Praise for the 'patriotism' and 'integrity' of the military turned into sour denunciation by activists against the corrupt and complacent officer corps. Even passive citizens who did not engage in the uprising have come to observe the military with suspicion. Generally speaking, the public image of the army during 2011–12 deteriorated from a partner in the revolution to the leader of the counter-revolution. At that point, the military seems to have decided to cross to the other side, into the usual territories of the security apparatus handling civilian security affairs, and to engage more in politics. According to Kandil, 'it appears that the army had surrendered to the power formula by Sadat and maintained by Mubarak, whereby the security apparatus dominates its political auxiliaries, enjoys status and wealth, and the military watches passively from a faraway corner'.[73]

I disagree, however, with some parts of Kandil's overall excellent evaluation of the military's position within the political sphere. His assumption that the army surrendered to Sadat's formula of leaving space for the security apparatus was not accurate, because in 2013 a military coup took place. It was difficult to draw a proper conclusion at that time, as it was still too early. I do agree, however, with the existence of what Kandil calls a 'formula' for how power is shared or 'enjoyed' between the military and the security apparatus. Indeed, there was what appeared to be a political retreat by the military from political life from Camp David until the fall of Mubarak (not economically though). There was an exchange of political power for economic power, as discussed earlier, especially under Mubarak and Tantawi's three decades of military leadership. In this exchange, both sides won and Egypt as a country does not appear too militarized in the eyes of the West. We should not underestimate that the administration of almost every seaport and airport in the country was awarded to retired generals. The same applied to hundreds of state and privately-owned companies. The army was given the chance to directly invest in a variety of business sectors, from the construction of bridges and real estate, to the production of pasta, and even providing entertainment in their resorts and hotels. Ultimately, the relationship between the military and the security apparatus as a relationship of struggle, was more of ongoing negotiations over territories, which has endured not only from the time of Camp David but since the foundation of Nasser's state, up until the 2013 coup. From that moment on, the military took over the political sphere, including that of the interior, alongside the economic sphere they already enjoyed, and almost ceased negotiating with other players as had been the case from the 1950s. However, since the factors behind the 2011 uprisings are still present, violent suppression by the military of all critical voices remains the direct response, while the reinvention of an augmented propaganda machine is its tool of reassuring its hegemony to the public.

A brief history of Egyptian media

Egypt is generally seen as the leading force that has shaped today's Arab media. This is rather an exaggeration, as other places in the Arab region have played a vital role in developing the Arab media landscape, both before and after independence from colonialist powers and the rise of pan-Arabism. Lebanon, Syria, Iraq and Morocco also have their own pioneering experiences, some of which have greatly influenced the direction that the Egyptian media have taken as it has developed. Although several newspapers first appeared in Egypt during the nineteenth century, Lebanon hosted the largest number of newspapers per capita[74] during that time. However, it is important to acknowledge that the Egyptian media became the most influential in the region particularly under Nasser, and then to lesser degrees under subsequent presidents, as will be explored in the rest of this section.

Today's pan-Arab or regional media have grown into large industries operating under either state control or self-censorship by those who own them and wish to preserve their advertising revenues or to remain on good terms with the authorities. Most Arab news broadcasters are controlled by totalitarian governments that exercise wide powers over media organizations. Although it is hard to perceive authoritarianism as a nurturing environment for commercially vibrant media systems, the Arab region represents a rather good example where the commercialization and liberalization of selected media industries have gone hand in hand with continued state intervention and increasing self-censorship.[75] The situation of today's Arab media with a heavy influence imposed by the authorities raises the question of when and how this tradition of censorship or control emerged and developed. To answer this question, which applies to Egypt as well as to almost every Arab country, we need to shed some light on the development of pan-Arab media in general before shifting the focus to Egypt, since Egypt has always been a major player in the region's politics.

Coming before Nasser's pan-Arabism, the concept of 'news' was in most cases introduced by the colonial authorities in the several Arab colonies and protectorates with the main aim of informing officials in their local administrations of laws and regulations. Later, Arab intellectuals used the press as a new channel for their intellectual debates and literary productions. This trend was particularly associated with the nineteenth century bourgeoisie of Syria, Lebanon, and Egypt. In the first half of the twentieth century, the press was used as a forum to discuss independence. This developing role of the press was significant in terms of mobilizing public opinion against the imperialist powers. Because of this role, newly independent governments realized that the press was a powerful weapon, which they sought to monopolize. National governments then used the media as a vehicle to promote their national policies and to mobilize pan-Arab public opinion. Nasser, for instance, used the Egyptian radio station Sawt Al-Arab (Voice of the Arabs) to mobilize public opinion both in Egypt and the wider Arab region. Cultural genres have also been used to mobilize the public.[76] Of course, other media such as cinema, theatre and books were also used to mobilize the public. However, these non-news media were not controlled by the state to the same extent that the news media were.

Before the 1952 military coup, widely known in the Arab region as the July or 1952 Revolution, the media landscape in Egypt was clearly diverse and decentralized, to say the least. This does not mean that it was significantly developed or reached distinguished professional standards, but it did represent the views and agendas of diverse political orientations from right to left, in the relative absence of state control. Towards the end of 1952, the Free Officers made sure that all media outlets, both print and radio, were in the hands of the state under one authority represented by Wizarat al-I'lam (the Ministry of Information). This move was intended to provide support for the newly born state. It was also meant to exercise control over how the state's sovereignty was perceived both locally and regionally. The pan-Arab Nasser was portrayed in the media as a president of Egypt and an inspiration or re-creator of the newly independent Arab nations.

Al-Ahram[77] was one example of a popular newspaper that turned 'revolutionary' overnight following its nationalization. It became a voice of state propaganda not only in Egypt but across the whole Arab region. It even expanded its reach to Arabs in the diaspora, mainly in Europe, with a large circulation base and a large network of offices in many world capitals. *Al-Gomhuria*[78] (*The Republic*) was another example of state media propaganda, but unlike the older *al-Ahram* it was established after the 1952 coup. It followed almost the same administrative pattern and editorial line as *al-Ahram* in being a tool in the hands of the state and controlling the people's access to news and information. However, *al-Gomhuria* was targeted towards the middle and lower classes, while *al-Ahram* was targeted towards the middle and upper classes. *Al-Akhbar*[79] and *al-Masaa*[80] were both further examples of state-run newspapers, the only permitted model between the 1950s and 1970s.

All radio stations played almost the same propaganda role, especially Sawt al-Arab,[81] which became a highly popular pan-Arab transnational media outlet. It was listened to from the Arab Gulf in the east to the Atlantic Ocean in the west. It had a slogan at that time: 'Umma waheda min al-moheet ila al-khaleej', which translates as 'One nation from the Ocean to the Gulf'. In this sense, Nasser used the radio as a primary means of strengthening his position in Egypt and in the Arab region at large.[82]

The al-Télévision al-Masry (Egyptian TV) project was initiated in 1956 but encountered delays in implementation because of the escalation of the Suez Crisis in the same year, and it only broadcast its first signal in 1960. It fitted the same state propaganda model as the newspapers and radio stations. In 1956 Nasser also founded the Middle East News Agency (MENA), which was intended to serve the whole region.[83] However, this sparked competition between Arab countries, as each rushed to establish their own national news agencies. Over the years, the press became more focused on foreign news, as local Arab news became uninteresting and shallow due to excessive control.

In 1971, following Sadat's political victory against the pro-Soviet faction of the Free Officers led by Ali Sabri in what he called *Thawrat al-Tashih* (The Corrective Revolution),[84] the media landscape changed slightly. A few private, mainly partisan, newspapers were allowed to operate. However, they were all essentially under the control and the censorship of the state. *Al-Wafd, al-Lewaa al-Islamy, al-Ahaly* and *al-Shaab* were all newspapers given very limited space to operate and circulate. In fact, they all played an important role in providing Sadat's *Infitah* state a different face – one that seemed less authoritarian than the state of his predecessor, Nasser. Hisham Kassem when interviewed opined that if Sadat hadn't been assassinated in 1981, the media could have become free by the 1990s.[85] In any case, generally speaking, the media landscape remained largely unchanged under Mubarak until the mid-1990s. All these presidents, directly and indirectly, supervised the appointment of new editors-in-chief. This consequently forced journalists into a vicious circle of self-censorship to ensure that their work would be published.[86] This circle, however, was very briefly broken following the 1967 defeat, as the Egyptian government tolerated criticism as a way of absorbing public resentment.[87] Later, the media development in Egypt during the late Sadat era and then Mubarak's, moved from being partisan to being the mouthpiece of one party – the NDP – and then the privately-owned media emerged.

The introduction of satellite technologies to many Egyptian and Arab homes – Arabsat in 1976, and Nilesat in 1996 – played a very important role in changing the media landscape in Egypt and the Arab region. This trend particularly intensified following the establishment of the Doha-based Al Jazeera TV network in 1997. Soon after the 11 September attacks of 2001, the region became the centre of international media attention. Al Jazeera grew rapidly and gained in popularity when it was founded, however in the aftermath of the attacks the channel provided alternative war coverage, beginning with Afghanistan and then Iraq. This was almost the first time that war has been seen through the lens of Arab media.[88] This new development in news production drew attention even further away from traditional Arab media, which either copied Western news producers, or broadcast governmental statements on the wars, or both. The Arab populations suddenly had overwhelming access to totally different editorial agendas and unprecedented narratives of news and documentary films that contradicted those that existed since 1952.

The two satellite projects, Arabsat and Nilesat, were not intended to play a mind-opening role, but what happened, against the Arab rulers' will, was the use of these facilities by Al Jazeera for producing and spreading Qatar's own regional political agenda. The initial reaction of the Egyptian government to Al Jazeera's narrative of news and historical documentaries was arrogant and short-sighted. The Egyptian media thought it was sufficient to accuse the Qataris of lying, assuming that their audience would believe what the state and its controlled media (both state-run and private) would say. However, this Egyptian discourse of defamation of Al Jazeera failed, and the network gained in popularity.

Even before the American invasions of Afghanistan and Iraq, in 2001 and 2003 respectively, the Egyptian authorities realized the danger of the rapidly growing influence of external news narratives and media content and the loss of trust of Egyptians in their own national media outlets. They attempted to counter this by introducing and allowing new home-grown forms of critical news narratives that might be able to win back the trust of people in local media outlets and reduce their dependence on external sources. They allowed already existing partisan newspapers from Sadat's era such as *al-Sha'b*[89] (which translates as 'The People' and belongs to the Labour Party) and new ones such as *al-Dostor*[90] (The Constitution) to operate semi-freely. The latter became very popular, reaching a circulation of 150,000, according to Belal Fadl, who teamed up with its provocative chief editor and founder Ibrahim Issa to achieve the success of their newly born newspaper.[91] However, this success never reached the level of being able to compete with Al Jazeera the giant, for example. Their success briefly became out of control later and the government did not tolerate the criticism of these newspapers: *al-Sha'b* was permanently shut down in 2000 and *al-Dostor* was forced to soften its news narrative following frequent security and judicial harassment and a shutdown lasting from 1998 until 2005.

Another tactic to attract audiences to a state-supportive media outlet was the launch in 2001 of the Dream TV Network,[92] owned by Mubarak's friend and business tycoon Ahmed Bahgat, mentioned earlier in this chapter as a member of the business elite and one of the old guard. The network succeeded in attracting significant viewership, but more as an entertainment network rather than the provider of political content. Such channels were a necessary safety valve to ease public pressure and suppression, and as a way to absorb the inherent tensions[93] which were increasing in Egypt as well as among audiences in the Arab region. The success of Dream TV and similar media was a result of the highly unattractive content screened on state TV channels, which became material for humour against the state rather than creating the impression of being a trustworthy media outlet in the eyes of the average Egyptian. Reda, one of the interviewees for this study, said: 'The private media is a little bit more free. It has a wider space and [a greater variety of] subjects to focus on more than the state-owned ones. Another difference is that private media tends to have a better pool of talented people.'[94] Another respondent, Wesam, more straightforwardly commented: 'Both [state-run and private media] are unprofessional. The state media serves the authorities and the private one is directed [according to] the owners' visions and personal interests.'[95] However, this was not enough as the authorities realized that what the audience needed was serious programming, not only entertainment.[96] This realization came too late, as attention to proper news content was already increasingly diverted towards Doha and its then growing giant Al Jazeera, the channel that had put Qatar on the political map and gave it greater regional influence.[97] Later, this phenomenon proved to be of even greater influence during the Arab Uprisings, when Al Jazeera's coverage of the events was in favour of the Muslim Brotherhood in Egypt and opposition groups in other Arab countries,[98] which will be discussed in later chapters. To sum up from a CPE perspective, from the early 2000s onwards it was obvious to the political elites that the state-run media had lost their influence on the public and had become an economic burden on the state. For example, the state-run TV and radio broadcasts were suffering a continuous increase in deficits from US\$ 200 million in the year

2000 up to US$ 327 million in 2017, all next to an accumulation of debt compounded interest, together adding up to US$ 2.5 billion.[99] This is particularly challenging for any government to manage, hence its reliance on the private media, also somehow controlled, which has become its strategy to counter Al Jazeera and other external narratives.

The year 2004 marked a significant change in the position of Egypt's political elite towards the freedom of the media. They started to follow a more intelligent approach of attempting to bring audiences back to local sources of news by introducing higher quality and more professional news content. This was the year that Gamal, Mubarak's son, was introduced to the political scene and also when the newspaper *al-Masry al-Youm* was launched. The paper was co-founded by Naguib Sawiris, the richest member of Egypt's business elite and among the world's richest individuals, as a minority shareholder. The newspaper was administratively chaired by its other co-founder, Salah Diab, who was the majority shareholder. However, the mind behind this 'new' model of journalism was the pioneering publisher Hisham Kassem, who was approached by Diab initially to establish an 'opposition' newspaper, which Hisham rejected and he turned the project into a giant mainstream newspaper.[100] Diab and another media investor, Mohamed al-Amin, are discussed later in this chapter. *Al-Masry al-Youm* was privileged from its beginning with high profile access to news sources and connections with the political and business elites. This access gave the newspaper unprecedented critical news narratives that brought credibility to the local news production scene for the first time since 1952. Ihsan, another respondent in this study, said:

> The state's press lacks credibility and neutrality in the public sphere due to its support for all the state's policies. The same applies to the partisan press, which always align with their parties. As for the private newspapers, they try in one way or another to benefit from such tendencies [in order] to attract readers searching for information that carries truth. However, complete truth does not exist, in my opinion, due to the presence of complex interests between private newspapers' owners, the government and businessmen.[101]

Al-Masry al-Youm produced truly critical news stories that could have been seen as damaging to the state and its political elite, especially under Hisham's leadership from December 2003 to November 2006. However, later under subsequent editorial leaderships this became part of a game, with the double goal of attracting a news audience to locally produced content and giving Mubarak's political and business elites a democratic face. This new face was necessary to address mounting criticism both locally and internationally regarding Mubarak's authoritarian rule. This was the case across the Arab region, as pressures from the World Bank and the IMF were already pushing for deregulation of the media sector.[102] Regarding this change in the private media, Nour, an interviewee for this study, said: 'I think that most of them orient their editorial policies according to their owner's interests, which in many cases are linked as well to the different security bodies, or [else] they are afraid of those bodies, which can put several pressures on those businessmen'.[103] This change caused the so-called deregulation of media to be more cosmetic than real. Eventually, this 'tripartite ownership' of Egyptian media, whether state-run, partisan or private, brought about significant contrasts in the political economy of the sector and its journalistic practices.[104]

In 2012, one year after Mubarak's fall, it seemed that the military and the business elites decided to repeat the model they were familiar with through launching the new *al-Watan* newspaper, owned by another business tycoon, Mohamed al-Amin. This newspaper plays almost the same role as *al-Masry al-Youm* did previously. Both newspapers have very similar agendas in relation to the business and political elites, but they differ slightly in editorial lines. They both maintain a solid position in the press market today as the two top newspapers both in terms of circulation and setting the national news agenda, not only for the rest of the press, but also as a source for broadcasters. Alaa, an interviewee for this study, commented 'The state-run media is the voice of the government. The private media is the voice of those with power. And between them there are [just] small margins [to] express the street's opinion to secure attention to the media'.[105] The sort of critical news that attracts readers' attention remains in the margin. Even this limited margin was made to shrink following the 2013 coup, as will be discussed in later chapters. It is worth mentioning that the Egyptian constitutions, including the constitutions of 2014 following the 2013 coup, have guaranteed the freedom of expression, as discussed in the following section. However, the reality on the ground has always been a different matter, especially in recent years. The government has often relied on laws that impede freedom of expression, including the Emergency Law and articles from the penal code, and has used these to censor content and intimidate journalists, bloggers and broadcasters. Over the years this has caused many of those working in the media to censor themselves and has led to the acknowledgement of 'red lines' that demark areas deemed too sensitive to tackle.[106] This 'legal' control is one of the tools used by the business and military elites, which they continued to use to control the media market for their interests.

The business elite's interest in media control[107]

Understanding the issue of economic injustice and the role of Egypt's business elite as an ally of the political elite for the sake of protecting the interests of both groups is important in understanding what was happening in Egypt at the time of the historic 2013 military coup. One of the most valuable hegemonic tools at the hands of the Egyptian elites was the private media they owned, and control over them ensured that the old regime could survive even after the fall of Mubarak in 2011. Egypt's business elite and their relation to the state are intimately connected with the process of accumulating capital under a free market economy. Certain political decisions are always needed to help and reinforce the process of accumulation of capital. David Harvey argues that the private sector always seeks to maximize its benefits/profits. This can conflict with the political elite or the two forces may simply reinforce each other. However, the process of cooperation between political and business elites is complex, as it is hard to manage either sphere of life – except indirectly.[108] In Egypt's case, reinforcement is common, as the rest of this section discusses in detail. We can see that the relationship between the business and political elites in the country is in a similar position to Harvey's understanding. Both entities – with their controlled state and private media – support an aggregate, the free market economy. Clearly, the institutional arrangements embedded within the state have an influential role to play in setting the stage for capital accumulation.

We can see the dynamics in Mubarak's politics between the political and business elites as a sort of continuation of Sadat's *Infitah*. From Mubarak's time we may single out, as one example from many, the steel tycoon Ahmed Ezz, who managed to accumulate colossal wealth in a relatively short period of time. Ezz was allowed to dominate the Egyptian steel market, while at the same time playing a significant political role in the NDP by holding the position of Secretary General of Organization. This one tycoon, with his wealth, power and several arms in the business sector and political domain, was a leading player in the process of political enforcement in a top-down manner, as was apparent in both the parliamentary elections of 2005 and 2010. Fraud occurred in both elections, but this was evidently more in favour of the NDP during the latter election.

The relationship between capital and political power would appear to be a set of mutual interests, where the accumulation of control over the political sphere is an important goal. Today's Egypt has a top-down enforced neoliberal model, as many evident realities highlight. This model and the injustices it brought about were a reason for the people to rise against the ruling elites in 2011. However, the uprising was not simply born at that moment in history, nor did it end with the fall of Mubarak.[109] It was a chapter in a recent history of free market dynamics, both local and global, that led to the contemporary Egypt becoming an 'emerging market' in the international political economic system. The rise of political activism and public discontent can be traced to at least ten years before the masses poured out onto the squares demanding the fall of Mubarak and his regime. However, while only Mubarak was removed, his regime and legacy remained. The current political instability in Egypt is more likely to continue for the foreseeable future, since the reasons for the uprising are still present, as Maha Abdelrahman argues:

> After the initial euphoria and laudatory comments, the supposedly victorious masses were soon relegated to the back seat while the focus returned to traditional political actors: the military, the [Muslim] Brotherhood [ousted by the 2013 military coup] and regional powers. The millions and their continuing struggle receive cursory attention and only in so far as they are seen to have been subdued and defeated by counter-revolutionary forces [...] Increasing poverty, high unemployment rates and a youth bulge combined with the absence of political freedom under an authoritarian regime are by now the stable ingredients of the mainstream narrative of the causes of the Egyptian uprising.[110]

The crucial role and power of the private media in Egyptian political life should be evaluated in light of the context summarized above. As the private media is still powerful and is controlled by the same elites (although more by the military, as will be discussed later), the masses will keep receiving the same cursory attention. The media play an important role in conveying political and economic discourses to the public. Egypt's private media and those who own it are in no different position, as they frame their messages to the masses, attempting to shape their political compass, as happens with any form of media. Journalists have been found to use a multitude of methods to frame the news, including commonly used themes such as emphasizing conflict, the emotional aspect of a story, and/or grim economic consequences. Such 'frames' can promote a particular definition of a problem, causal interpretation, or moral evaluation[111] and thus influence debates and structure political outcomes. Media production is always influenced by frames which in general match with the interests of private media owners, both politically and economically.[112] Regardless of the proven influence of news coverage on the public, we still have to deal case by case, learning about how this influence prevails within certain news agendas. We also learn from each case how politicians, including members of the business elite in the Egyptian case, formulate their responses to both the news agendas they control and the public they target.[113] We should also pay attention to the fact that different news agendas have different influences on citizens and politics.[114] However, in the case of the Egyptian media market, although citizens have access to several news outlets, agendas are mostly similar in their political and economic interests.

The concentration of media ownership is a significant variable of great importance in terms of the power it brings to the owner. This is particularly the case if media power can be used to project political influence, such as an investor would aspire to gain. In their book *Arab Media Moguls*, published in 2015, Naomi Sakr et al. see the Middle East as fertile ground for media moguldom, where a general business tycoon – coming from the business elite with all associations with the political one – invests in the private media. This phenomenon is particularly applicable to the Egyptian case. As has happened in many countries in the region, Egyptian media tycoons have emerged together with the opportunities afforded by steps towards the liberalization and privatization of the media sector, which are not separate from the liberalization and privatization of the economy in general, and with the rise of an expanding media market. These media tycoons rose under the watchful eyes of political authoritarianism, and they made sure not to challenge the rulers directly.

These autocratic rulers envisaged media regulation and censorship, not to prevent a concentration of media but to curb political opposition and to foster a submissive public. The authoritarian power holders of Egypt could live with the rise of media tycoons, and the media tycoons could live with them.[115] However, particularly in the Egyptian case, the media tycoons did not rise entirely organically in response to liberalization; rather they were indirectly, or sometimes even directly, pushed into playing that role and fostering a submissive mass for their counterparts in power, the political elite. Ihsan, an interviewee for this study, confirmed the presence of such a relationship between the business and the political elites, saying: 'Yes, I believe that this relation exists, however in different variations. The business community desires to support its own activities through influencing the economic press'.[116] The profitability of media investments, especially in Egypt, where business tycoons like Salah Diab and Mohamed al-Amin are strong examples, is not a priority in comparison with other non-media investments (these two cases are to be discussed in detail later in this chapter). There are indeed increasing trends towards media concentration and no effective controls against this. The concentration of ownership has spurred a downswing in pluralism in the Egyptian media. For example, the prominent journalist Ibrahim Eissa, who founded *al-Dostor* newspaper, mentioned in the previous section, and al-Tahrir TV right after the fall of Mubarak, later sold the channel to Suleiman Amer, a businessman closely connected to the remnants of Mubarak's elite.[117]

Skovgaard-Petersen defines a media tycoon as a person who owns and operates major media companies, who takes entrepreneurial risks, and who conducts these media businesses in a personal or eccentric style.[118] However, in the case of Egypt the risks are not necessarily high, at least not during Mubarak's era, since the gains in other non-media investments increase due to connections to the inner circle of political power. Reda, another interviewee for this study, took a similar view, saying: 'A quick look at the media scene in Egypt will tell you that all private media is owned by big business names. They all have huge investments in areas other than the media, and all have a foot in the media scene by holding one or more media outlets, and they defiantly control that space'.[119] This explains how an Egyptian media tycoon would win favour with the political elite, and hence have more access to economic power. We can see this clearly in the cases of Diab and his investment in *al-Masry al-Youm*, and al-Amin in *al-Watan* and several TV networks. Hanan Badr more or less confirms this argument, in which the business elite use the media to 'protect' their other businesses, even when making losses, which they compensate through the latter.[120]

Profit-seeking cannot be an overriding expectation because distortions in the advertising market and restrictions on editorial content do undermine the commercial potential of media operations. Controlling a network of media is a good way to demonstrate loyalty and thus curry favour with the rulers of a country,[121] which is the main goal of the investment. In Mubarak's era, all the major media tycoons tended to be close to the regime. However, being close does not mean that they approved of the regime, nor that they actively sought its patronage. Rather, it was often an inevitable consequence of the economic importance and interests of the business groups that they were heading.[122] And thus developed the role of newspapers such as *al-Masry al-Youm* and *al-Watan* and their owners. Nour elaborated this further, saying: 'Many businessmen, whether [they] founded their media outlets before or after 2011, used them to achieve certain goals, or to deliver certain messages to the recipients. This is very clear when comparing the way famous broadcasters and writers change their tone according to the outlet they're working for. In addition, some businessmen use those outlets to send direct messages, either through being hosted on one of the TV programmes, interviewed in their newspapers, or even writing opinion articles under pseudonyms.'[123]

As in many countries, wealth and power have been concentrated with the upper class of society, which in turn requires organized propaganda to normalize injustice and integrate citizens into a public moral conduct that accepts the 'norms' enforced by elites.[124] In today's Egypt, the private media market has grown strong enough to be even more influential than the state-run media; however, the two types of media outlets almost never contradict each other in terms of the political discourses conveyed to the public. Alaa commented: 'All private newspapers and TV channels owned by businessmen have limitations for [freedom of] expression regarding public opinion in order [to avoid] a clash between the owner and the government that might harm his [non-media] businesses.'[125] Hisham said that businessmen thought having media investments would mean having more power, keeping an eye on the Berlusconi model or that of the Russian oligarchs.[126] Another goal for them, as Tayseer said, is buying loyalties and authors to defend them against other media outlets, as well as the regime's loyalty through producing favourable news coverage. Hisham, however, said he believed that *al-Masry al-Youm* was a 'mistake', referring to the period that he was in charge (December 2003 to November 2006). He said that the government believed it would be just another small opposition newspaper, which were usually without influence, according to Hisham. However, it was soon a 'shock' to the government when *al-Masry al-Youm* quickly became a 'paper of record' that people actually started to believe in, and which quickly grew. Hisham added that once he left in 2006, 'they' started getting rid of staff members that were thought to be personally connected to him.[127]

If we consider *al-Masry al-Youm* and *al-Watan*, the two most-circulated private newspapers in Egypt (no reliable sources are available for accurate data on the exact numbers), we can see that these dominate access to information and high-profile official sources. We can also observe the interrelationships between newspapers' editors, investors, and the government. For example, *al-Masry al-Youm* was founded by Salah Diab, who was already the founder and main shareholder of Bico, which dominates agricultural trade in Egypt. He has also had strong relations with Israeli companies since the Camp David Accords of 1978. *Al-Watan* was founded and chaired by Mohamed al-Amin, who was a top Mubarak supporter and a business tycoon with a diverse portfolio. Al-Amin interestingly hired Magdy al-Gallad as *al-Watan's* editor-in-chief. Al-Gallad, known for being politically highly connected, was a former editor-in-chief of *al-Masry al-Youm*, as we mentioned earlier is owned by Diab. This indicates that the Egyptian media market is dominated by the business elite, which largely owns its news outlets and controls them. This domination happens either through such elite taking on direct management roles, or by delegating highly connected media personnel to serve their investors' interests. These vary between directly economic interests for corporations owned by the same investors, interests of other business groups, and interests of the political elite with its two factions: the civilian and the military. However, this exchange of mutual interests does not happen in a vacuum, as there are laws and regulations that facilitate the existence and growth of this practice.

Tailoring press legislation

Despite several notable changes in Egypt's media legislation from the military coup of 1952 until the present, the theme of control has always been evident, with the purpose of protecting those in power, whether civilian or military. Nasser placed the press industry under the state's complete control. His presidency marked the beginning of the detachment of the Egyptian press from its main function, namely that of informing readers, to unconditionally supporting the state. None of the governments since Nasser have ever undermined this role. Further, they have all directly and indirectly controlled or influenced the choices of the editors-in-chief appointed.[128] Journalists in Egypt were, and still are, under the influence of both government censorship and self-censorship due to the fear that their work will not be published, or worse, that they could be persecuted. Nasser said on one occasion that there were 'no restrictive laws on the press' and that journalists themselves chose to ignore certain issues due to self-censorship.[129]

As mentioned earlier in this chapter, the state's grip on press freedom slightly softened following the 1967 defeat of Egypt by Israel, with the purpose of absorbing some of the public's anger. However, laws that allowed the government to control the press were never revoked, so the government could always enact them again whenever the need to exercise strict control arose, depending on the political situation the country might be going through. Law 156 of 1960 turned journalists into public servants, while the preceding Law 162 of 1958 had already given the president the right to declare a state of emergency and thus censor publications and hinder the freedom of expression if it was deemed to conflict with national interests. The law of 1958 is still in effect, with a few amendments made in 1980 and 1981. Although private media ownership was (re)enforced by law in 1980, the government at the time, under Sadat's rule, simultaneously enforced Law 148 (also known as the Law of Shame), which prohibited the publishing or broadcasting of pictures or texts that may offend 'the dignity of the state'.[130]

The press market was slightly less controlled under Mubarak, especially from the mid-1990s until his ouster in 2011. However, the laws have been essentially the same since the time of Sadat, and in turn not very different to Nasser's era. During the first two decades of Mubarak's presidency, the media faced substantial legal and regulatory challenges that limited their independence and hindered their ability to criticize and hold the government accountable.[131] The situation following the fall of Mubarak led to relative freedom that allowed uncensored journalism and the establishment of new newspapers – which was more due to political chaos in the aftermath of 2011 than an actual permanent freedom for the media. Nour shed a brief light on that period, saying: 'Directly after Mubarak's fall, there was a good margin of freedom. However, newspapers and TV channels did not make use of it and engaged in self-censorship. Then gradually things returned to how they were, maybe even worse'.[132] Additionally, the Egyptian Journalists Syndicate was long dominated by the Mubarak regime. During the years until the 2013 coup, the syndicate witnessed a power struggle between pro- and anti-Muslim Brotherhood forces. As a result, it has never been able to fully free itself from state interference. Although at several points in history the syndicate protected journalists, it can also be said to have tolerated corruption within its ranks.[133]

By 2013, the press industry in Egypt had a force of 6,378 journalists registered at the syndicate.[134] In this regard, Alaa said that following the fall of Mubarak, many were allowed to work in the media. According to Alaa this was shown by the big numbers of those who joined the journalists syndicate during the three-year period from 2011, when more than 2,000 journalists registered. The same number joined the syndicate over a period of six years during Mubarak's time. Alaa further remarked that, 'However, now things are going into the direction of suffocating the media'.[135] The number of journalists operating in that period was probably much higher than reported as many journalists are unregistered. By 2013, there were fifty-six state-run newspapers and sixty-five partisan ones affiliated with political groups.[136] The Muslim Brotherhood's newspaper *al-Horreya wal-Adala* was the first to be shut down following the 2013 coup. There are no reliable numbers available for the privately-owned newspapers, however there are many that have been licensed following the fall of Mubarak, probably in the hundreds, based on the observation of their online presence.

Toby Mendel has examined the details of journalism laws relating to issuing new private newspapers in Egypt and he has analysed the controversy and control that continues to be practised by the authorities. Anyone intending to establish a newspaper must obtain a license from the Supreme Press Council (the SPC – although it later changed its name, as will be explained). The application for a license must include various types of information, including the title, the language, periodicity, business sector, budget breakdown, sources of funding, editorial structure, nationality and place of residence of the proprietor, the name of the editor-in-chief, and the address of the printing house. The law also says that anyone who is prohibited from exercising political rights may not own or publish a newspaper. The SPC is required to decide on a submitted application for a newspaper license within forty days. If an application is refused, the council is supposed to provide specific reasons for the refusal to the applicant who may then appeal to the Court of Administrative Adjudication within thirty days. However, the law does not indicate what might justify a refusal to issue a license. The law also states that obtaining a license to publish a newspaper is a 'special privilege', a label that explains why such strict conditions for the establishment of private newspapers exist. Such newspapers must take the form of co-operatives, owned exclusively by Egyptians, with no one owning more than ten per cent of the overall capital. It is unclear whether these rules are enforced in practice, as at least some major newspapers appear to be owned, or at least controlled, by individual businessmen.[137] It is also observable that ownership may be manipulated through dividing a newspaper's shares among fake partners, mainly relatives and/or friends of the private newspaper's major investor. There is no information available showing whether the SPC has ever tried to investigate such practices.

The requirement to apply for security permission from the interior ministry to obtain a license is essential. There exists in Egypt a strong culture of asking for security permission for any press activity, from establishing a newspaper to holding a camera in the street. For example, a new newspaper that has not been granted security permission will definitely find nowhere to print. A positive aspect of the temporary change between 2011 and 2013 was that the SPC's procedures became speedier following Mubarak's fall. However, being quick or not does not mean a lot to journalists such as Ihsan, who strongly believed that 'There are no differences. The deep state is in control, and hence policies are the same'.[138] Wesam took an even more pessimistic position, saying that '[the media situation] is going from bad to worse'.[139] More or less since the early 2000s, the Egyptian state has been engaged in applying legal authoritarianism that conveys the impression of maintaining the rule of law, while the goal was in fact restricting freedoms and controlling the political economy of state-capitalism, where the media remain in the hands of their loyalists among the business elite.[140]

As a setback following the marginal positive developments that the media market witnessed during the two years following Mubarak's fall, the 2013 coup took it even further backwards than the position before 2011. A new unified media law that was intended to replace all the ambiguous legislation of the past was issued. The current constitution (voted for and passed by a referendum in January 2014) mandates the formation of three media regulators. Article 211 stipulates the formation of the Supreme Media Regulatory Council (SMRC), which replaced the SPC and is responsible for regulating the affairs of audio and visual media, print and digital press and other forms of media. Article 212 outlines the formation of the National Press Authority (NPA), which manages and develops state-owned press institutions. Finally, Article 213 orders the formation of the National Media Authority (NMA), which manages and develops state-owned visual, audio and digital media outlets, a model that Rasha Allam labels 'a prime example of the failure' that represent 'a real challenge to meet the requirements of the new law in terms of providing public service content'.[141] In accordance with the law, the SMRC's board is composed of thirteen members, three of whom are appointed by the president, including the council's head. In response to these changes, the Journalists Syndicate issued a statement reiterating its call for a unified media law that would adhere to the constitution, notably Article 71, which prohibits all punitive measures curtailing freedom of the press. The syndicate's position contrasts with many pro-state journalists and the government itself, which see regulation as a necessary means to combat what it considers the dissemination of false news, a claim that is often deployed to challenge positions other than the government's own.[142] However, the position of the syndicate later changed to conform with that of the presidency. Reda observed: 'Unfortunately, it seems that they [...] bend the laws to the benefit of the regime as usual'.[143] Needless to say, small independent broadcasts disappeared,[144] as well as other forms of traditional or digital media. However, the laws were not only bent – as Reda was rightfully pessimistic about – but even tighter control is now exercised through the military stepping into media ownership. Mandating media control to media investors following the 2013 coup was no longer enough. However, before elaborating on this recent shift in mandated control towards the military, the relationship between civilian media investors and content producers since 2004 needs to be discussed first.

Teaming between investors and media personnel[145]

Based on previous discussion in this chapter and to understand the interest of Egypt's business elite in controlling the private media further, this book considers the business affairs of two major profiles in the sector. Understanding their backgrounds and going through their stories one by one can provide us with an extra dimension in the context of the picture sketched earlier, in order to explain this strong interest in the media which reinforces the business elite's economic and political powers. These two investors are chosen because they own Egypt's top two newspapers. The first is Salah Diab, the agri-business tycoon and the co-founder and CEO of *al-Masry al-Youm*. The second investor is Mohamed al-Amin, a diverse-portfolio investor and sole founder of *al-Watan* and several other media outlets.

Salaheddin Ahmed Tawfiq Diab, known simply as Salah Diab, does not have a diverse media portfolio like al-Amin's, who will be discussed later. Hisham said that his experience of working with him for about three years was that Diab was a focused person and a good listener.[146] However, Diab's non-media investments are much more diverse. His father, Tawfiq Diab, was a critical journalist in the first half of the twentieth century, opposing the British occupation. Diab has a political background, given his relation to the liberal *al-Wafd* and probably had a 'supressed desire to have a political role'.[147] It is not documented anywhere that the son, Salah, ever practiced journalism before deciding to step into the sector as an investor towards the end of 2003 and launching *al-Masry al-Youm*. However, according to Tamam, another interviewee for this study, his choice of Hisham Kassem as a media pioneer to work with on founding the newspaper says a lot about Diab's sophisticated personality. Indeed, this alliance created high quality media that did not exist before.[148] Diab is known to have several connections with Israeli companies. His power lies in the portfolio of his family, which controlled about 70 per cent of the major American brands operating in Egypt until at least a few years ago. According to the American Chamber of Commerce, the family represented forty-three American companies in the country. One of these companies is the American oilfield services giant Haliburton,[149] which is known for several overseas corruption scandals, especially in Iraq following the US invasion in 2003.

To give Diab some credit, *al-Masry al-Youm* under Hisham once published an article against Diab himself, which he was 'very shocked about', however did nothing about, which was unimaginable with other media investors of the time.[150] However, regardless of this level of media maturity, there was always a question then about his relationship with the authorities, which is normal in the Egyptian case to be able have access to the media market.[151] Diab was once briefly detained in a corruption case following the ouster of Mubarak and later released on bail. The case was about a deal between him and Mubarak's oil minister Sameh Fahmy, wherein the latter sold Diab a piece of land with potential oil investments for less than the market price. The case did not garner much attention for the authorities at the time, which was a chaotic period between the fall of Mubarak and al-Sisi's coup.

Mohamed al-Amin, our second case in this article, came to the public sphere right after the fall of Mubarak, as he was not previously significantly known to the public. Tayseer, another interviewee for this study, commented that al-Amin was just someone who was requested to play a 'particular role' as a representative of the military's interests and had no media vision, and Tayseer thus never watched any of al-Amin's media production with any respect.[152] Al-Amin's wealth was estimated at about US$ 3 billion.[153] However, his rising diverse investment portfolio, from real-estate to media, especially after 2011, is considered to be extremely opaque when it comes to documentation or public records. In a period of about two years, al-Amin managed to establish, buy or inject capital into what is estimated to be fourteen media outlets. No clear documentation can be found, however. What is confirmed among his media portfolio, whether full or partial investments around that period and before the military stepped into the media sector, are the TV networks of CBC, al-Nahar, Modern, Panorama and Moga. He also bought the Cairo-based Arab News Agency from its Kuwaiti owners, and the local newspaper of *al-Fagr*. However, most importantly for this book's focus, he founded *al-Watan* and chaired its board. The newspaper quickly became known as Egypt's richest newspaper with the highest salaries ever paid to journalists. It is widely known in the journalists' community that al-Amin has heavy Kuwaiti financial support. This rumour is supported by the successful acquisition of the Arab News Agency, formerly owned by the Kuwaiti billionaire Mohamed al-Kharafi. Another indication of Kuwaiti involvement in al-Amin's sudden media investments following the uprising, were his frequent one- or two-day trips from Cairo to Kuwait at the time he was acquiring all these media companies.[154] It is worth mentioning that alongside Saudi Arabia and the United Arab Emirates, Kuwait was a strong supporter of Mubarak and the 2013 military coup.

While investigating al-Amin's life and his origins, the information available seemed conflicting and vague. What seems to have been confirmed about him in media circles is that he worked as a construction site manager in Kuwait in his early career. He later became the manager of a Kuwaiti construction company, and then returned to Egypt to start his own business. He started with an agriculture company licensed by then agriculture minister Youssef Wali, a controversial character known for corruption and being a loyal Mubarak ally who served as a minister for more than twenty years. Al-Amin heavily invested in the Amer Group, owned by his friend Mansour Amer, who was briefly detained for several corruption cases in 2011. Regarding al-Amin's wealth and its undeclared sources, a lawyer called Tarek Mahmoud officially used 'the right of reporting against citizens with suspicious wealth'. However, following a brief investigation, the case was closed by the order of the pro-Military prosecutor Abdel Meguid Mahmoud,[155] who was hired by Mubarak and survived the uprising until October 2012.

Despite the similarities in suspicious connections, allegations of corruption, and proximity to Mubarak's regime and then the military, there are some differences among the two tycoons concerning their backgrounds and media practices. When the interviewees were asked to draw comparisons between the two, Reda commented that 'some [investors] are more professional than others [in] dealing with the media they own. As an example, Diab was raised [in his family] close to the media, so he understands most of the process very well. Al-Amin jumped [into the media] from elsewhere with the aim of playing a big role in no time, which raises many questions'.[156] Wesam was very direct in commenting that 'Salah Diab possesses enough experience to own a media institution and use it as a magic wand. Mohamed al-Amin is a façade, [he is] executing what he has been ordered to do'.[157] Nour viewed Diab as a tycoon who 'started his media activities before the revolution, which played a political role in many cases. After the revolution the political role of his media tools became more noticeable in serving his economic interests, but we cannot ignore his relation to the security services.'[158] As for Mohamed al-Amin, Nour said: 'Nobody knew of him before the uprising as he entered the media suddenly with a huge amount of money invested in *al-Watan* newspaper and CBC. What we know is that he represents the counter-revolution'.[159] In headline style, Alaa labelled the two media investors as follows: 'Diab, a media investor at the service of businessmen and their interests. Al-Amin, a façade for a capitalist bloc within the government, for business interests'.[160]

Looking at these two businessmen from another perspective, it is useful to learn about the management capacity of members of the business elite who stepped into the media sector from different business backgrounds. We should assume that they would need someone to help them execute their media agendas professionally. Key to this is the role of editor-in-chief, TV channel director or even prominent TV host, as the media tycoon's assistant or executive. This brings us back to the distinction drawn by Sakr et al. in their book *Arab Media Moguls,* discussed earlier in this chapter. The media tycoon (or mogul as Sakr terms it) may be supported by several 'executives' who normally manage divisions or companies within the tycoon's larger interests (which Sakr labels as barons). The executive can be a chief executive who may also take entrepreneurial risks, but they are not the ultimate owner or controller of the overall enterprise.[161] Within this division and collaboration notions of tycoons and executives (or moguls and barons), this section looks at Magdy al-Gallad, former editor-in-chief of *al-Watan,* and before that *al-Masry al-Youm,* as one of those executives. He did not work for just one media tycoon, as his services were much in demand in the sector. Business tycoons seemed to compete to hire him, as happened between Diab and al-Amin, when he moved from *al-Masry al-Youm* to *al-Watan.* The list of this type of executive is an extensive one in Egypt, but al-Gallad is notable. Yasser Rizk is another example that will also be described here, even though he is not as famous as other executives such as TV presenters Ahmed Moussa or Lamees el-Hadidi, who are also highly influential in the view of the interviewees in this book. However, Rizk's case and its interconnectedness with those of Diab, al-Gallad, *al-Masry al-Youm* (as a private newspaper), and *Akhbar al-Youm* (as a state newspaper) can say more about the role of these executives than other more famous cases. Therefore, this section focuses on Diab and al-Amin from the perspective of investors and al-Gallad and Rizk from the perspective of executives.

Several years before the rise of al-Gallad, Mohamed Hassanein Heikal, who served under Nasser as the editor-in-chief of Egypt's leading state newspaper *Al-Ahram*, wrote the story of his exclusive dinner invitation by the late Yemeni President Ali Abdullah Saleh during one of his visits to Egypt in the 1980s. Heikal explained that Saleh was telling him about a discussion that took place between himself and Mubarak earlier during the same visit, regarding an issue Saleh had with the Egyptian press:

> The Yemeni president had expressed [to Mubarak] how annoyed he was because of an article written by a journalist (whose name he mentioned). Mubarak's response was unexpected by the Yemini president. Mubarak asked him without an introduction 'Has not Yemen become an oil-producing state?' Ali Abdallah Saleh was surprised by how [Mubarak's response] seemed far from what he was talking about, however Mubarak re-connected what he interrupted and continued: 'Man, shake your pocket, give him a bite and he will stop attacking you'.[162]

Mubarak's response to Saleh's complaint about the annoying journalist tells us a lot about how Mubarak was dealing with the media and what type of journalism he was encouraging. He chose to corrupt critical voices rather than using his predecessors' heavy-handed punishment, mostly in the form of imprisonment. Corruption was already common practice in the state-run media when the green light was given for the private media market to form itself through the business elite, and hence these practices were transferred. Based on observations and interviews, *al-Masry al-Youm* and *al-Watan* are part of this normalized financially corrupt media atmosphere that has existed since Mubarak's early years in office. It is important to note that Magdy al-Gallad was known to receive the highest monthly salary (EGP 200,000) ever paid to an editor-in-chief in the history of Egyptian journalism when he was hired for *al-Watan*.[163]

As mentioned earlier, *al-Masry al-Youm* was founded in 2004 (December 2003 was when Hisham commenced his employment there). Many editors had run the newspaper since its foundation, but none had the power that al-Gallad (later discussed as *al-Watan*'s editor as well) maintained, nor spent as many years in his position (2005–2012). The period when Hisham was the newspaper's publisher, hired by Diab to design the project, was exceptionally professional, however this did not last after his departure towards the end of 2006. Al-Gallad started his career as an investigative journalist at the state-run *Al-Ahram* newspaper before he moved to *al-Masry al-Youm*. Regarding al-Gallad, Tamam commented: 'It was the first time to see an editor-in-chief without grey hair'.[164] He was listed among the top 100 influential Arabs in 2009 by Arabian Business, and he hosted at least three television shows.[165] Hisham remembers that everything at the paper was based on improvisation and without proper planning. The newspaper did not develop as it should have done and it turned its focus on 'satisfying' the shareholders and coordination with the security.[166] It is clear that al-Gallad made *al-Masry al-Youm* bigger than it was before him, but less independent.[167]

Al-Gallad effectively created a network of loyal editors and journalists over the years. These people have not necessarily been loyal to their newspapers or their profession, but mainly to him as a person. As such, their loyalty was rewarded by being appointed to higher positions in his newspaper, and in other cases by finding them freelance opportunities in television channels as programme editors or as hosts using his personal connections.[168] Al-Gallad was famous for having close connections with Mubarak and his family, especially with Gamal, who was being prepared to inherit power from his father. This plan, however, was interrupted by the 2011 uprising. Here we should remember the rather bizarre passage from the article that he wrote in 2009 with the title 'Life on the Shoulders of Gamal Mubarak', quoted at the beginning of this book.[169] It was heard in press circles that al-Gallad warned his reporters against siding with the 2011 uprising in its first days. '[He] stood in the newsroom in the first days of the revolution and said: "Whoever wants to go to Tahrir Square to participate in the protests and the revolution should not say that he belongs to *al-Masry al-Youm*. Otherwise, he will be sent to the Investigations Department."'[170] This position towards the 2011 uprising is in line with al-Gallad's close relations with Mubarak's family, which clearly appears in the article mentioned earlier about Gamal. However, following the fall of Mubarak, he always introduced himself as a supporter of the uprising. He also continued to claim the same support even after his move to *al-Watan*, although it is owned by al-Amin, who is one of the most openly anti-revolutionary members of the business elite

During the 2013 military coup, Yasser Rizk was *al-Masry al-Youm*'s editor-in-chief. He is known in press circles for having a very good relationship with al-Gallad, his former superior before al-Gallad moved to then the newly founded *al-Watan* in 2012. Al-Gallad clearly left one of his loyal men behind at *al-Masry al-Youm* before moving to *al-Watan*, although Rizk was not as powerful or well-connected as al-Gallad. He was quickly appointed as *al-Masry al-Youm*'s editor once al-Gallad was chosen by al-Amin to lead the foundation of *al-Watan*. Rizk graduated from the same faculty of communication as al-Gallad did in 1986. He worked as a journalist for the state-run newspaper *Akhbar al-Youm* from when he was still a student at Cairo University. He later became a military editor at the same newspaper, and then a reporter at the presidential palace until 2005. In the same year, he was appointed as the editor-in-chief of the state-run weekly magazine *al-Itha'a wal-Tilvizyun*. One week before the 2011 uprising, he was appointed as the editor-in-chief of *Akbar al-Youm* but was quickly dismissed from the position following Mubarak's fall. Later in August 2012, he joined *al-Masry al-Youm* as its editor-in-chief, after al-Gallad moved to *al-Watan*.

Rizk ran *al-Masry al-Youm* exactly as al-Gallad did before him. The same policies and same editorial line continued. Al-Gallad was known to be behind what is called the 'Ahramization' of *al-Masry al-Youm*, i.e. running it as a state newspaper, which Rizk did not change.[171] Rizk's journalistic career has grown mostly under the state-run press. He worked for *Akhbar al-Youm* before *al-Masry al-Youm*. In late 2013, he returned to *Akhbar al-Youm* as he was selected as its chairman following the coup. This was a supposedly dignifying return ordered by the military that seemed like compensation for his humiliating dismissal in 2011. Rizk wrote an opinion article for *al-Masry al-Youm* on its tenth anniversary in 2014. The article was published with the title 'Yasser Rizk on *al-Masry al-Youm*: Days that Have History':

> I remember each of those days with fondness and nostalgia, when I turn the pages of *al-Masry al-Youm*'s volumes from 2012 and 2013, reading through

the stories and the wide coverage of the year of rage under the Muslim Brotherhood's rule, going through the headlines: 'Down with the Guide's rule', 'The Forgers', 'Illegitimate', 'Morsi speaks about another country', 'The country is on top of a pit', 'Too late', and finally '30 June Revolution' and 'Morsi deposed by the people's order'. I testify that the founder of *al-Masry al-Youm* Salah Diab never complained to me because of a headline, a news story or an opinion article [...] And what is most dear to me of all those memories at *al-Masry al-Youm* is its exclusive first interview with then Colonel General Abdel Fattah al-Sisi; an interview that had a huge political and media role locally and internationally and which hit the Muslim Brotherhood and their tails with a plague of rabies, whose barking echo is still heard.[172]

The article above, in his own words, reveals Rizk's political and editorial biases as an editor-in-chief working in the service of a media investor – Diab in this case – who in turn works in the service of the military elite. The article almost too directly tells us about *al-Masry al-Youm*'s position towards politics in general and the 2013 coup in particular. Rizk considered his relationship with al-Sisi to be as iconic as that of Heikal with Nasser, while he was merely a 'representative of the Ministry of Defence to the media'.[173] He has been always supportive of subsequent governments following Mubarak using an anti-Islamist approach, a role that fitted well during the 2013 coup.[174] Kai Hafez argues that before the coup, Egypt was a rather immature and radically polarized but vivid public sphere. After the coup, however, the country witnessed an authoritarian roll-back like that of Nasserist times. He adds that one can and must be critical of the Muslim Brotherhood, but Morsi was legitimately elected, and the military has not aimed to stabilize democracy but to seek absolute control over Egyptian politics and the economy.[175] In this context, changes in media ownership in favour of the military, to be discussed in the next section, had their influence on both media investors and the media personnel in their service.

We can consider Salah Diab and Magdy al-Gallad as military loyalists, Mubarak style, where the pro-regime propaganda allows a small margin of criticism that makes it look convincing. On the other hand, we can consider Mohamed al-Amin and Yasser Rizk as military loyalists, al-Sisi style, where the only allowed media content is pure pro-military propaganda and the slightest form of (even fake) criticism is punishable. Diab had his political views, clearly pro-military, but these were not very identical to those of the military. For example, he was slightly critical of the military operations in the Sinai Peninsula and the so-called war on terror there which has caused significant casualties among civilians and increased local unrest. He was punished following a wave of defamation in other state and private media, arrested several times, and the old court cases of corruption against him, closed since Mubarak's era, were re-opened. Al-Amin was punished for something no one knew about through a defamation campaign that targeted his private life. Al-Amin's reasons for punishment remains a mystery to this day, especially as he was much closer and more obedient to the military than Diab. It appears that al-Amin had made some 'mistake in his private' life and the result was a 'violent and public' punishment, a message that says 'everyone is replaceable'.[176] Whether he was expelled from the media market based on accusations of economic or personal corruption, it is clear that now that the military no longer appoints business tycoons to run their political propaganda and has already taken running the machine directly into its own hands.

From the side of the executives, al-Gallad, as a pro-military and open propagandist for al-Sisi, attempted to use his previous small margin of criticism in an editorial article two years after the coup. It was titled 'I'm a Cockroach and You are Too'. In this article he referred to the insignificance of the life of Egyptian citizen and criticized the state for a lack of transparency concerning several security incidents.[177] Al-Amin forced him to resign from *al-Watan*. Now he hosts a programme on CBC, previously owned by al-Amin and currently by the military, which is a significant step down for someone of his profile. Furthermore, the programme is very clearly pro-military fitting with full propaganda and no margin for criticism. Media voices have no other option now than 'complete' submission to the military, who wish to be supported in the style they want, not in any other way.[178] The punishment was however not as severe as that of Diab, for al-Gallad remains an influential pro-military media figure. The article was probably a mistake, which taught him a lesson. Al-Amin as a media investor has had his share of media companies seized by the military As for Rizk, the fierce pro-military propagandist who has most frequently interviewed al-Sisi, he continued to be one of al-Sisi's favourite media personnel. Rizk remained in his position atop the giant state-run newspaper *Akhbar al-Youm* until September 2020, when he fell ill and died in January 2022.

Shifting media ownership: from the business elite to the military

During the first year of al-Sisi's presidency he made it clear how he sees the role of the media in relation to his model of authoritarian governance. At the inauguration of a Suez Canal development project, he addressed the audience concerning a variety of issues, among which was his concern about the media. Al-Sisi said, 'The late leader Gamal Abdel Nasser was lucky, because he was speaking while the media was on his side'.[179] Several changes in the media market took place in Egypt after this telling speech, both legally, as explained earlier, and structurally, in terms of investments, as this section will discuss. Al-Sisi simply, as a classical dictator would, wanted the media to take only one side: his own. The set of new laws that were intended to centrally control media content and silence critical voices, additionally helped the military to gain even more control over the already existing private media owned by their allies in the business elite. However, new media ownership was also introduced to the market, whether by re-arranging existing investments from Mubarak's time or by creating new investments directly 'owned' by the military themselves. This is a new and unprecedented phenomenon in Egypt, as even during Nasser's era, which was also more or less a military dictatorship, the media was 'owned' by the state, not the military.

To understand this shift in media control through ownership it is helpful to focus on the leading model of the Egyptian Media Group (EMG), which is a company ambiguously owned by the military.[180] The company's profile on Reporters Without Borders (RSF) website provides some solid information about the mysteriously established company and this is confirmed by other sources including Mada Masr,[181] the Association for Freedom of Thought and Expression (AFTE),[182] and respondents interviewed for this book. They all agree that the EMG is owned by Eagle Capital for Financial Investments (ECFI), which is owned by the General Intelligence.[183] EMG was founded in 2013 by the young businessman Ahmed Abu Hashima, who is known to be close to both the security apparatus and the military. The EMG became the biggest media conglomerate in Egypt between 2016 and 2018. It now owns two large TV networks, five print outlets and their digital versions, a video platform, and another seven companies in the advertising and marketing sector,[184] or at least this is all we are aware of.

Regarding the television sector, in May 2016 EMG acquired the ON TV network by purchasing 100 per cent of the shares of Hawa Limited, owned by businessman Naguib Sawiris.[185] In July 2018, the group acquired al-Hayat TV network, which was previously owned by the Falcon Group, which in turn is owned by Egypt's leading private bank the Commercial International Bank (CIB). In September 2018, it acquired 51 per cent of the shares of the Future Media Holding Group (FMHG), owner of the CBC TV network, in turn is owned by al-Amin. Regarding the print media, in 2016 alone it acquired *al-Youm al-Sabea* newspaper, its website, and a number of its affiliated websites such as Video 7, Photo7, Infrad, Parliament, and The Cairo Post.[186] In July 2016, the group seized the Dot Masr website. In November 2016, Abu Hashima bought the weekly newspaper *Sawt al-Ummah* from its owner Ahmed Fahmy for EGP 12 million, after which EMG acquired the weekly newspaper *Ain Al-Mashahir*, which is also owned by Ahmed Fahmy.[187] As for drama production, in June 2016, EMG acquired 50 per cent of the Egyptian Cinema Company (ECC), owned by businessman Kamel Abu Ali. In November 2016, it acquired 50 per cent of Synergy Media,[188] which is owned by Tamer Morsi, a pro-military enthusiast and dark horse businessman, who quickly became the major representative of the military's media investments. He will be discussed again in Chapters Three and Six under the topics of advertising and drama production respectively. In the field of marketing and advertising, in June 2016 and in addition to owning Synergy Agency, EMG acquired Point of Differentiation (POD), an agency specializing in advertising, marketing, graphic design, internet services and public relations.[189]

The ECFI, which now owns EMG, is headed by former Investment Minister Dalia Khorshid, wife of Tarek Amer, the Governor of the Central Bank of Egypt (CBE). The ECFI is a private equity fund owned by General Intelligence, as mentioned earlier, and was founded to manage the apparatus' partial and full equity in several private sector projects and companies, not only in the media.[190] Unsurprisingly, Abu Hashima's stake in EMG never exceeded a few stocks, and his role as chairperson of the board of directors at the time the company was started up was confined to representing the group and signing the company's deals.[191] According to an official document obtained by Mada Masr on condition of anonymity, EMG was registered on 2 June 2013, almost a month before the military coup, under commercial registration number 66705 at the General

Authority For Investment (GAFI). The acquisition was sealed through the Zulficar law firm, which represented ECFI.[192] EMG's most important deal was signed on 20 January 2019 with the National Media Authority (NMA). Both entities signed several protocols to launch new TV channels and develop content on the state-owned TV channels. According to the deal, advertising rights were to be upgraded and developed. This extended the control of the EMG to the state-owned media sector, reinforcing the influence of the military-controlled General Intelligence over the entire media landscape in Egypt,[193] both state-run and private. More on Egypt's distorted advertising market will be discussed in Chapter Three, and more on how the above media market reshuffle has influenced drama production will be discussed in Chapter Six.

As mentioned earlier, al-Sisi, envious of Nasser, wanted the media to be on his side. Whether the business elite liked it or not, it appears that they had no choice in this. We must always remember the threat that the 2011 uprising brought to all elites. The business elite, as discussed earlier, enjoyed privilege and access to opportunities of capital accumulation in a balance of power and exchange of benefits with the military elite under Mubarak. The uprising was an existential moment for them, which threatened their very existence as a corrupt power group. Therefore, they fiercely supported the 2013 military coup through the media.[194] This support seemed willingly unconditional in the beginning, given the revolutionary threats around them. Hossam believes that following the coup, many of them did not like how the military were engaged in the process of monopolizing all sectors: 'The business elite had no other choice. There was a revolution that made them sleepless for almost three years.'[195] This is why a slogan such as '*Ofrom ya Sisi*' ('Grind them, oh Sisi') appeared in Egypt around the time of the coup. They did not even mind al-Sisi's own 'blindness' to harming them on the way while 'grinding' the uprising.[196] However, this enthusiasm ended for many of them after about two years, but they cannot do any anything about it.[197]

Nour's opinion is that the military have been in control of everything since the coup, while the business elite have become nothing but a tool in their hands. 'You're either with or against us,'[198] said Nour, referring to how the military sees members of the business elite. Aseel, an interviewee for this book, however argued that some media investors gradually voluntarily withdrew from the market, as it has become clear that their media investments would cause them problems and would not provide them any political power as had been the case previously.[199] Those who stayed in business hoped that they would be rewarded for their service in getting rid of the Muslim Brotherhood, however, the reality showed that the military gradually took over their investments.[200] Tayseer said that the regime works according to what al-Sisi believes are 'lessons from Mubarak's fall', where the 'slightly open door' should be shut. This was indirectly encouraged by the presence of Donald Trump at the top of the American administration, in a way that could not have as easily happened during the time of Barack Obama.[201] Let us not forget that Trump famously called al-Sisi 'my favourite dictator'.

There is a striking difference to the relationship between media investors as a business elite and the military elite under Mubarak, in comparison to that under al-Sisi. 'In the past, during the Mubarak days, lovers [of Mubarak] were placed in one basket, but now there are several baskets with several degrees.'[202] This explains, to some extent, the differences in the very small margin of criticism that was acceptable under Mubarak from one media outlet to another. Back then, all media investors were allies of the military, and this small margin of 'freedom' was tolerated. Now, under al-Sisi, they are also allies but there are degrees of how much a media (or non-media) investor is expected to support the military in permanent propaganda. If it is not enough, one might be punished. Such propaganda, whether under Mubarak or al-Sisi, needed coordination between the media investors and the executives who produced the actual propaganda. Or more accurately, multiple propaganda, where that of media investors such as Diab or al-Amin were no longer good enough for the military following the coup, or as Tamam remarked sharply about the military, they now took the approach of 'I am the market'.[203]

Conclusion

The overall findings of this chapter, which put forward a critical review of the political economy of the Egyptian media, suggest that an interest in controlling the media sector was present, as the literature and expert interviews have suggested and confirmed. The mainstream media have succeeded in strengthening the elites' economic and political discourses, as it dealt with them as 'systems of hegemony'. Control has been exercised since the era of Nasser's era (1952–70) and during Sadat's reign (1970–81), during Mubarak's tenure (1982–2011) – which witnessed the introduction and expansion of the private media until present – and al-Sisi's military rule (2014–present), which witnessed a shift in media ownership towards the military. There have always been legislative and conjectural changes depending on the political situation that the country was going through, such as Sadat's *Infitah* for example, where freedoms were slightly restored, however these were always minor and temporary. It has also been confirmed that the interest of the business elite in the private press has increased since 2004, which was associated with the introduction of Gamal Mubarak to the political scene. Legislation regarding the press in Egypt has always been complex and unclear, giving power to the state to control the industry since the 1950s, but since the late 1990s, however, legislation favoured the business elite and the press they own. The 'Unified Media Law' of 2017 brought even more state control over the press market. However, this control comes with less ambiguity than previous laws that prevailed since Nasser and Sadat's eras. Starting around 2016, the military stepped into direct and indirect ownership of media as a form of reinforcing hegemonic control over media content. The profiles of two editors-in-chief, Magdy al-Gallad and Yasser Rizk, in coordination with business tycoons Salah Diab and Mohamed al-Amin, also demonstrate the interest in control by the business elite over the media market in favour of the military elite in a mutually beneficial balance of power. However, under al-Sisi that balance has shifted towards full control by the military, as the business elite became merely submissive propaganda tools in military hands, while even the small margin of criticism that existed under Mubarak has disappeared. The military here appears to apply legal authoritarianism to give an impression of the rule of law, while the goal is restricting freedoms and controlling the economy through state capitalism.[204] In general, it could be concluded that the political economy of the Egyptian private media is highly controlled by the business elite in their own favour and that of the military, whether willingly or unwillingly. Hegemony has always existed ever since the foundation of the media market, but it was maintained and reinforced following the shock to the elites caused by the 2011 uprising. To achieve and maintain their hegemonic position over the economy of Egypt, the business and military elites engaged in significant and direct support for the 2013 military coup and full propaganda regarding military rule until today.

A Political Economy of Egypt's Distorted Advertising Market

Advertising is obviously a form of media, and as discussed in Chapter One, media are commodified. Mosco argues that the commodification of media content, audience and labour is the entry point from which to begin to theorize the political economy of communication. He defines commodification as the process of transforming goods and services, including communication, which are valued for their use, into commodities which are valued for what they will bring to the marketplace.[1] In this sense, the support of the business sector for particular media outlets, over others conveying opposing political messages/ commodities, is not surprising. In this vein, Hardy argues that advertising is the leading ideological agency for capitalism as it plays a role in promoting consumerism and possessive individualism. He finds that critical political economists of communication have gone even further in their understanding of advertising as a form of media that requires attention to its economic as well as its ideological importance. In this context they are addressing the nature and implications of advertising as a support mechanism for media.[2] This requires the study of the economic dimensions of advertising, in terms of how it functions in the production, circulation and consumption of goods and services, the study of the political dimensions, in terms of how it is organized and regulated, and the study of symbolic dimensions, by exploring the contribution of advertising to the production of meanings, social relations and material practices.[3]

Despite the distortions in Egypt's advertising market, which will be discussed later in this chapter, revenues remain an obviously crucial factor in the business. Not necessarily for media outlets, as a supposedly essential part of the market, but mostly to the advertising agencies. There is a lack of any accurate valuation of the advertising market in the country, in line with the lack of statistics in many other fields. However, Hisham gave an estimation of the market at large for the period he was leading *al-Masry al-Youm* in the mid 2000s, of almost EGP 3 billion (a little more than US$ 0.5 billion in 2005),[4] while this figure has most probably been growing over the years, at least until the military's takeover. Herman and Chomsky argue that advertising plays a powerful role in increasing the concentration of capital among rivals that focus with equal energy on seeking advertising revenues. They explain this using the example of a market share and the advertising edge of a paper or a TV channel that will give it additional revenue to compete more aggressively and allow it to buy more saleable content. The disadvantaged rival must add expenses that it cannot afford in a process of diminishing market and revenue shares, which benefits the media with an advertising edge.[5] The power of advertisers over the media comes from the fact that they buy and pay for the content of which they are hence the patrons. In this way, the media compete for their patronage, developing specialized staff to solicit advertisers and having to explain how their content serves advertisers' needs.[6] Through the competition of the media to please advertisers and concentrate capital, radical media suffer from political discrimination by advertisers. Companies will always refuse to advertise with media they see as 'ideological enemies' or those they perceive as damaging to their interests.[7] This is a practice which is present in the Egyptian media market, but with significant differences. However, again, the model does not fully apply to the case of Egyptian media, regardless of the form. Although the media would obviously welcome advertising revenues, they will not shut down if they do not make a profit. As discussed in Chapter Two, media investors in Egypt do not particularly invest in their media projects for profit-seeking purposes.

Based on the assumption that the advertising market in Egypt is highly distorted and politicized, this chapter answers the question of how was the political economy of advertising under Mubarak restructured under al-Sisi? In answering this question, Egypt's advertising market under Sadat's *Infitah*, which continued under Mubarak, will be introduced. The case of the leading advertising agency under Mubarak, Tarek Nour Communications (TNC) will then be discussed. Finally, the chapter will shed light on the significant transformations in the advertising market under al-Sisi, by focusing on the partially owned and directly controlled agency of Synergy.

Neoliberalization and the introduction of a new advertising market

Advertising in Egypt is not new and it did not start with Western colonialism. Historically, *al-monadi*, the person who governors would assign to walk through the streets calling out official messages to the public, would also convey advertising messages paid for by merchants. *Al-misaharati*, the person who shouts out to wake people up late at night in the month of Ramadan to have their *sohoor*, the last meal before fasting, did a similar job until recently, and are probably still doing so in some remote villages in Egypt. They are also convey paid advertising messages from merchants during the other eleven months of the year. In the nineteenth century, *al-dallal*, the person who walked around carrying new supplies for sale or holding samples for pre-orders – mostly portrayed as a woman called *al-dallala* in literary work – used to announce the arrival of new wares for sale in the market and introduced buyers to sellers. The traditional touring puppet theatre of *al-aragoz* also advertised the sale of goods, as Relli Shechter discusses.[8] However, with rising European influence on Egypt and the beginning of British colonialism by 1882, and in parallel with the development of a press industry, advertising took a different path, similar to that in the West. Before the turn of the century, the press industry grew exponentially in response to the growth of the Egyptian economy and its integration with European economies following the opening of the Suez Canal. However, it was obviously targeting the literate population, which made them the main group of consumers to be targeted by advertising.[9] During the period from the First World War until the mid-1950s, Egypt's press industry underwent new developments, one of which was the introduction of illustrated journalism. This particular development took advertising to a new level of appeal and visibility in terms of targeting potential consumers. Additionally, those who controlled press advertising expanded to embrace other forms of the business of promoting commodities, such as posters and billboards. This expansion mostly remained in print, until the 1920s when commodity advertising in cinemas was introduced and finally the illiterate population of Egypt was included as a target group in mass advertising. This was a success, as the Egyptian cinema industry was growing, but mainly in cities, where most cinemas were located. Nevertheless, the illiterate of urban Egypt finally had access. Radio advertising also started in the 1920s. However, it almost ceased with the introduction of state-run radio in 1934, and only restarted in 1959 under Nasser. Television advertising began with the launch of al-Television al-Masry in 1960.[10] However, despite all these non-print developments, press advertising remained the most dominant compared to all other forms of advertising, until the 1970s. In May 1960, a new law was issued to organize the press, which included the advertising sector. Under the new regulations, the four largest state-run advertising agencies were created: Sharikat al-I'lanat al-Misriyya (the Egyptian Advertising Company), Wakalat al-Ahram lil-De'aya wal-I'lan (al-Ahram Agency for Promotion and Advertising), Wekalat al-Qahira (Cairo Agency), and al-Wakala al-Ifriqiyya al-Asiaweyya (the Afro-Asian Agency). These were by far the dominant players in Egypt's advertising market for at least the two following decades,[11] while al-Ahram remained a visible player until the fall of Mubarak in 2011.

The introduction of colour television, a little after the beginning of Sadat's *Infitah*, took, in the late 1970s, Egypt's advertising market to new heights, and ushered in significant technical advancements during the 1980s. This was not disconnected from Sadat's *Infitah* and the neoliberalization of the Egyptian economy. As discussed in Chapter Two, Sadat succeeded in winning the political battle against the Nasserists and enforced new measures to re-shape Egypt's political and economic model, opening it up for Western economies. In 1978, the Camp David Peace Accord was signed between Egypt and Israel, which in turn took Sadat's policies to an increased level of economic neoliberalization, with the support of the United States. Local businesses and competition from abroad created a new business environment in Egypt, where concurrently mediated multinational corporations adapted to local economic conditions and produced 'Egyptianized' goods. In response to Western producers eager to penetrate Egyptian markets, advertisers eventually developed their approaches to meet these multinationals' marketing expectations.[12] Shechter says that the state-run advertising agencies maintained the status quo and were not keen on transitions in their field.[13]

The new orientation towards the rapidly opening markets came mainly from the newly established Egyptian marketing firms along with Western companies seeking entry into Egyptian markets. Hence, the development of television advertising was set in motion in the private sector,[14] as state-run advertising agencies were slow to respond. These new private advertising agencies won the multinationals' marketing accounts. The most important among them was Wakalet Tarek Nour lil-I'lan (the Tarek Nour Advertising Agency) named after its founder, who later became an icon in TV advertising, as we will discuss further in the following section. In this sense, the private advertising agencies not only advertised Western goods in local markets but they were also a catalyst within the bigger plan of transforming the Egyptian economy into a neoliberal model and promoting consumerism among the local population as part and parcel of the *Infitah*'s neoliberalization process. However, growth in the private advertising market did not necessarily lead to a shrinking of the state-run market, at least not for the following nearly three decades. On the contrary, market neoliberalization led to an increase in the revenues of state-run press and broadcasters. This increase in revenues came from selling time and space to the private advertising agencies for their promotion of goods from abroad as well as locally manufactured commodities in the emerging private sector. These, however, were scaled at different rates, as advertisements of foreign commodities were charged higher than local ones. In parallel, the four previously mentioned state-run advertising agencies continued their usual pre-*Infitah* business of providing basic advertising services to local customers, mostly from the public sector, offering them low quality and cheaper services. In the mid-1980s, it was estimated that these agencies handled around a 50 per cent share of the advertising market.[15] This indicates that the market share of the private advertising agencies constituted a significant portion of the other 50 per cent of the market share at that time. This is due to the fact that, as discussed earlier, the state-run advertising sector remained mostly limited to the print press, while the private agencies were exponentially growing in broadcast commercials.

With the deepening of the neoliberalization process of the Egyptian economy in the 1990s and the 2000s further elaborate privatization and structural adjustment plans as discussed in Chapter Two, and the introduction of several new satellite television channels competing with the rise of Al Jazeera, the private advertising market continued to thrive and dominate – especially considering the reluctance of state-run media, which was gradually receiving less funding from the state and losing its readership and viewership to the rising private media. Advertising in the state-run media was on a downward slope from

around 2003, with the rise of private media.[16] However, profit-seeking in the
private media, supposedly from advertising revenues, as Mosco, Hardy, Herman
and Chomsky argue above, was not a dominant factor in these private
investments. For Egypt's business elite, the media is not always a directly
profitable business. It is a matter of providing a benefit to those directly in power.
Although politics and economics often seem to be intertwined, in the case of
Egyptian (and Arab) media investors it is apparent that profit cannot be the
overriding expectation. This is because of the distortions in the advertising
market and restrictions on editorial content, which have undermined the
commercial potential of media operations. Where economic motives are
involved, these are often related to media investors' other non-media businesses,
which can benefit from belonging to an empire that controls one or more
significant media projects. As for political motives, controlling a network of
media is a good way to demonstrate loyalty and thus curry favour with a country's
rulers,[17] whether civilian or military.

Today's Arab media have grown into large industries operating under state
control as well as the self-censorship of those who own them in order to either
preserve their advertising revenues, or alternatively to remain on good terms
with the authorities. Most Arab news broadcasters are controlled by totalitarian
governments that exercise great power over media organizations. Although it
is hard to see authoritarianism as a nurturing environment for commercially
vibrant media systems, the Arab region represents a rather unique case where
commercialization and 'liberalization' of selected media industries have gone
hand in hand with continuous state intervention and increasing self-
censorship.[18] This brought about the contradiction and distortion in the
already grown private advertising market in Egypt under Mubarak.

The above phenomenon forces the question of why, while there was little
interest in the profitability of private media, the private advertising market was
allowed to become profitable? The answer to this question lies in the fact that
the advertising market itself was not an open market to all competitors. It had
been politically decided since the *Infitah* who would have access to advertising
opportunities. Only a few favoured private agencies such as the Tarek Nour
Agency, now called Tarek Nour Communications (TNC), were given access to
advertising space in the state media and later in the private media, while it was
difficult for other private agencies to gain access. It was not actually a free

market, as was promoted by the state or TNC – a direct beneficiary of this privileged access. This, however, should not lead to an underestimation of the creativity of the private agencies in producing content that would appeal to the public, as discussed in the following section around TNC's success. Additionally, such success raises the question of the rationale behind the extension of the relationship, not only between the political or military elites on the one hand and the media investors on the other, but to the advertising agencies themselves, as a part of the political economy of Egyptian media under Mubarak. In this context, two factors should be discussed: creativity and favouritism.

We cannot assume that the private advertising market in Egypt is only dependant on connections to the ruling elites. Otherwise, the market would probably have remained state-run. Creativity was lagging in the public sector, while the *Infitah* and the following decades required vibrant, creative, appealing advertising content in line with international standards. This applied to both commodities imported into Egypt and locally produced competitor goods. Beshara, an interviewee for this study, said that advertisements in Egypt have leapt in growth and quality from the 1980s to this day. This was not only the result of a conscious decision by the ruling elites to fully support the advertising agencies; it was also the result of the creativity of those running the advertising business. Beshara added that the advertising market in Egypt today is highly successful and even better, content-wise, when compared with the American market for example.[19] Gehad said that the idea that an advertising agency has more market access than others in Egypt, whether state-run or private, is partially dependent on creativity and new ideas. Egypt has a wealth of talent when it comes to creating advertising ideas that stick in the mind.[20] Baraa emphasized the creativity and strength of talent in the advertising sector in the 1980s and 1990s, despite lower production budgets in comparison to Western advertising agencies. However, according to Nour, advertisements of today are less impressive despite advancements in technology and bigger budgets. This is probably because of the new agencies that joined the market, which are mainly owned by the military,[21] as will be discussed later in this chapter.

Favouritism, or being part of the political network that first supported Sadat and his *Infitah* policies and continued with the same line of politics under Mubarak, is the second factor in understanding the expansion of Egypt's distorted advertising market. Besides being creative – which is not necessarily something in the hands of the ruling elites, as discussed above – advertising agencies needed to be an ally and a proactive supporter of the subsequent regimes since Sadat in order to continue to have access to the growing sector. If we look at the American model, as an example, where advertising revenues are fundamental for the media, we will find the relationship between politics and advertising to be different from the case of Egypt. CNN, for example, has advertisers that pay for political content that supports a particular political party, which is in turn supported by private donors.[22] In Egypt there are two red lines that an advertising agency may not cross without the approval of the ruling elites: religion and politics.[23] Playing by this rule is the reason why some agencies exist and continue to grow, and why others do not. The model that existed from the *Infitah* until the 2013 coup entailed that the advertising agencies are allies to the ruling elites, which in turn control the media, state-run at first, and then both state-run and private. As a reward for this alliance, agencies have access to advertising space in the media. This also works the other way round, as advertising agencies provide the pro-government media with advertising deals in order to support them and their existence, and so it continues.[24] This is not to deny the presence of other relational factors beyond creativity and favouritism, such as corruption and bribery in the state-run agencies. It was revealed following the fall of Mubarak that the state-run al-Ahram agency engaged in significant corruption including the plunder of public assets and finances and expenditure on bribery by providing high value gifts to Mubarak and his family. This is alongside the constant pro-Mubarak propaganda from al-Ahram, both as a newspaper and an advertising agency.[25] Another reason for growth in profitability in the private advertising market, also related to favouritism, is the fact that public broadcasters were not very keen to increase their revenues yet were dependant on the public budget. In this context, a private advertising agency that is well connected to the ruling elite would charge a commodity manufacturer for example market price, while paying significantly lower than market price for the advertising space given to them by the state broadcaster.[26] This unequal access to advertising opportunities and profitability caused some private advertisers to grow and others not. All this combined in Egypt's advertising market, with the creativity of the agencies and favouritism by the ruling elites, gave rise to the private advertising market, particularly under Mubarak, as political propagandists.

Advertising agencies and political propaganda
under Mubarak

Before the private advertising agencies managed to take over the broadcast advertising scene in the 1980s and 1990s, state-run TV produced commercials for companies which sought such services. In many cases, this was simply a sheet with writing and drawing on it, very similar to press advertisements, manually rolled out live in front of a camera with a voice-over, and always the same orchestral background music. The extremely poor TV advertising industry existing then was so uncompetitive that any private advertising agency would appear in the market to be more appealing and succeed in attracting advertisers' and audiences' attention. However, the pioneering Tarek Nour benefited from certain circumstances that enabled him to become labelled 'the king of advertising'[27] over the other private agencies of that period. Nour's business is now called Tarek Nour Communications (TNC), however 'Tarek Nour' as a brand remains popular until today as a trademark of its own in the advertising world of Egypt and the Arab region, not only among advertisers or commodity manufacturers, but among the general public as well. On its website, TNC describes itself as 'not-your-average communications firm. A multifaceted powerhouse, we are the first communications firm of its kind in Egypt and widely considered to be the pioneer of advertising in the Middle East. We have launched numerous firsts in the region and paved the way for a generation of creative minds to shape our evolving field'. They also state that the group has fourteen companies in the areas of advertising, production, broadcasting and event management.[28] What the group says about itself on the website, in ostensibly an act of self-promotion, is in fact an honest presentation of the reality of their market presence and image.

Since TNC's remarkable reputation is very much based on the person of Tarek Nour himself, it is important to give a brief history of his background. Nour was born in el-Minya governorate in the south of Egypt. This is supposedly one of Egypt's poorest governorates, but it seems from Nour's personal history that he belonged to a privileged class. In his youth he moved to Cairo and became a member of The Mass, Egypt's celebrated 1960s pop band, which was an elite music group mainly performing gigs in upper class circles such as the el-Gezira Club.[29] Nour later travelled to the US to study advertising. When he returned to Egypt in 1973, he immediately worked for al-Ahram Advertising Agency. In 1978 (or 1979 in other sources) he founded Tarek Nour for Advertising.[30] In a few years Nour became famous as 'the king of advertising', as stated above. His company later developed into a conglomerate of several companies, amongst them Americana, a record company with a studio that in the 1990s changed its name to Africana Records, before it was absorbed into today's TNC group.[31] According to Relli Shechter, Nour's socioeconomic and cultural background might give the impression that he was producing 'Western-cloned advertising' for imported commodities in Egypt. However, Shechter argues against this assumption, seeing Nour as a 'strong advocate of culture-specific advertising'. Schechter says that Nour's agency, as well as others during the 1980s and 1990s, was in favour of 'advertising native'[32] while capturing the consumerist market growth of the *Infitah*. In that same period, the rising private advertising agencies took the lead in TV advertising, which distinguished them from state-run TV and even international advertising competitors trying to operate in Egypt.[33] Nour's early hit which placed him above all other advertising agencies, state-run or private, was netting the advertising campaign for the Swiss soft drink Schweppes, which had been introduced to Egypt in the early 1980s. His campaign, which was themed as *Ser Shwebs* (the secret of Schweppes),[34] was a masterpiece that is still remembered today in people's jokes, when hinting at secrets in social gatherings. Nour built up the audience's anticipation and made them wait for advertising breaks, and people even preferred the adverts over the actual screened TV content.[35] The formula was a combination of contemporary Egyptian pop music, dancing, and a catch phrase or a joke by a famous Egyptian star. In a way, Nour was emphasizing the commodity's novelty, while keeping it authentically Egyptian,[36] although Belal Fadl took a contrary opinion, describing (in a respectful way) Tarek Nour as a person with 'a very American style'[37] during his interview for this book.

Using an American style, however, was not surprising for that period, running from the beginning of the *Infitah* until Mubarak's fall, and particularly during the first two decades following Camp David. The US image was somewhat damaged after the invasion of Iraq in 2003. The market's neolibralization, as discussed in Chapter Two, was very US-oriented and supported by them. When talking about Nour, Belal said his reference is always the US. Nour would see something American and say 'Let's do something like this'. This is understandable given that Nour lived in the US, married an American woman, and openly embraced American culture.[38] He is a pragmatic businessman in the sense that he would market any commodity allowed by the state, even if it were the political opposition itself, or if it were against his own opinions or convictions.[39] Marketing political opposition does not appear to have occurred though. On the contrary, Nour engaged in political propaganda for Mubarak and the NDP, of which he was a member in the Policies Committee under Gamal Mubarak, as well as several ministries. These campaigns were seen as 'political marketing, the American way'.[40] As Belal recalled, Nour once called him on the phone after Belal's written 'aggressive' criticism about Nour's advertisements. Nour told Belal that the fact that he had been approached by the NDP to produce advertisements for them meant that he was a businessman; he also said that whenever the Muslim Brotherhood or a communist party might be allowed to engage in advertising, he would produce for them whatever they dreamt of.[41] However, what Nour promised Belal never happened. Apart from the fact that the ruling elites never allowed any form of advertising campaign for political opposition to take place, he was clearly adopting an 'anti-Islamist' and economically 'liberal' agenda.[42]

Nour's political campaign for Mubarak in the presidential elections of 2005 was a success. Not that Mubarak would have lost without Nour's propaganda, but it provided the public with a new image of Mubarak. Before that, Mubarak was the seen as a firm military man who sometimes tried to express a sense of humour. The humour part was always a failure, though, and not that frequent. Nour introduced him as a family man sitting with his wife, children and grandchildren. He made him talk in a more personal fashion, like an ordinary father. The campaign was a remarkable success both politically and business-wise, as it was an introduction to the normalization of political marketing in Egypt. Baraa said: 'Tarek's advertisements for Mubarak were brilliant. With his own voice narration, he portrayed Mubarak as both a great leader and a loving person, a person who, if we did not vote for him, there would be something wrong with us. He [Nour] presented a remarkable talent in that campaign.'[43]

Nour was equally successful publicizing Gamal Mubarak during his campaigns for the NDP in the parliamentary elections of 2005 and 2010. He was smart to avoid presenting the young Mubarak directly, similar to the way he campaigned for his father. In fact, he came up with a formula that portrayed the NDP as the power of some sort of revolutionary transformation or a 'modernizing' force, while associating these transformations with Gamal as the new head of the Politics Committee. Instead of using mainstream hollow nationalist or patriotic slogans that were very frequent in pro-government or pro-Mubarak propaganda of the past, Nour introduced the slogan *min ajleka ant*, which translates as 'for the sake of you', in the NDP campaigns, where Gamal's picture was sometimes, but not always, present. This public attention for the first time in the party's history of propaganda seemed personalized and 'real'. Nour's engagement in political propaganda under Mubarak, particularly in his last decade of presidency, and for Gamal and the NDP, and for the ministries, moved TNC upward in terms of status. First it had held the status of a successful advertising agency that was remarkably creative in popularizing the neoliberal transformation of the Egyptian economy, through making its newly introduced to the local market consumerist commodities popular among average citizens. Then TNC upgraded its status, becoming an openly political propagandist for Mubarak and his regime by directly advertising for their neoliberal politics – not only the commodities produced under their neoliberal system.

The 2011 uprising and the fall of Mubarak obviously came as a blow to Nour and the business elite. They had to respond to it for the protection of their interests and privileges, as explained in Chapters One and Two, as they had become a part of the counterrevolution along with the military. Nour, then an expert political propagandist, campaigned – as he had for Mubarak – also for the former military man and field marshal Ahmed Shafik, who ran against Morsi in the 2012 presidential elections. Neither Shafik nor Morsi were expected to be the final runners in a second round. Morsi was not a figure well known to the public, and Shafik was a friend of Mubarak and an ally of the military at that time. The pro-revolution voters were forced to support Morsi, even though they were not on the Islamist side of politics, and Shafik received the support of Mubarak sympathizers and supporters of the military. Shafik's voters did not appear very vocal at that time. The military chose to support Shafik as their candidate, as the former chief of General Intelligence, field marshal Omar Soliman, suddenly died before the first round of elections. Nour's campaign for Shafik was not necessarily the only reason for making him a final runner, as the military and Mubarak sympathizers were behind him, as just mentioned. However, just as Nour smartly portrayed Mubarak as the loving father in his 2005 campaign, and Gamal as the transformer of politics in the NDP's two campaigns of 2005 and 2010, he succeeded in portraying the almost unknown to the public Shafik as a modernist who would rescue the Egyptian economy from collapse and the country from the Islamic fundamentalism of the Muslim Brotherhood. Shafik received 48.27 per cent of votes, losing to Morsi by only about three per cent, as the latter received 51.73 per cent of votes. Although Shafik lost the election, no one can deny the fact that he received more than twelve million votes, while more well-known candidates such as Hamdeen Sabahi, Abul Monem Abulfotouh and Amr Mousa received far less votes. Tarek Nour's political campaign for Shafik played a significant role in this 'success'. Through its campaign, TNC confirmed its intention to continue its role as a political propagandist after Mubarak's fall, as well as being a dominant private advertising agency. However, the balances of political and economic power of the military were about to change after the coup, and in turn changed how the commercial-political propaganda game was played.

The military as advertisers under al-Sisi

Since the 2011 uprising, the private media have made it clear that they are in favour of the military and have continued as almost non-profit-seeking investments. Mohamed al-Amin, discussed in Chapter Two, who is also the founder of several media projects including the newspaper *al-Watan* and the CBC TV network, openly stated, before being pushed out of the market, that no TV channels make a profit in their early years and that it would be an achievement if a channel broke even after five years. However, he also openly stated that even if CBC started making a profit, this would be donated to charity.[44] In the advertising sector, TNC did not stop following the same alliance with power and as both advertiser and propagandist following the coup of 2013. It campaigned for al-Sisi during the presidential elections of 2014. However, TNC's role seemed far less significant, as al-Sisi, the leader of the coup, was already highly popular and supported by all the state's institutions, not only the military, but also the state-run media and the private media, as will be discussed in Chapter Five. Al-Sisi's victory appeared to be certain, whether with the support of TNC's campaign or not. The company continued to support the military through their entertainment TV channel al-Qahira wal-Nas, as Nour seemed to follow his pro-regime business model employed since the early days of Mubarak. However, 2018 was a year that witnessed the trimming of Nour's privilege and access to economic opportunity almost overnight, due to his connections with Ahmed Shafik.

The former presidential candidate moved to the UAE immediately after he lost the 2012 elections to Morsi, and decided to run against al-Sisi in the second presidential elections following the coup of 2018. Shafik was placed under house arrest upon his arrival to Egypt, and all other serious candidates were also arrested. Nour, who was known to be a person with good connections with Shafik, suddenly became a risk for al-Sisi and the military, even though he ran their presidential campaign in 2014. A media campaign defaming Nour was launched in the state-run and private media, now owned and controlled by the military. He was accused of undermining the 'values of the Egyptian family', and 'disfiguring the image of Egyptians' through the content he produced for his TV channel, and the need to protect the media and drama production from him was underlined.[45] Taking matters even further, the state started to retroactively investigate his corruption during the Mubarak era and succeeded in seizing some of his property.[46] This withdrawal of privilege from TNC was not necessarily due only to the military's fear of Nour's connection with Shafik. It was more due to the rise of the military themselves as media investors and their interest in stepping into the advertising business themselves, rather than mandating private agencies to produce their propaganda. This was in addition to, as discussed in Chapters One and Two, their plans to expand into the Egyptian economy, where no sector was immune from their interventions, including the media and advertising. Tamam's response to this issue was as simple as 'Why not?' According to Tamam, the military see the value added in any sector and decide to take over, as they did decades ago with 'producing pasta'. This is a combination of using an available space that is also another tool to influence, and is unsurprising.[47] Aseel discussed the simple logic behind this move, considering that the 'deep state' with its military and security institutions always looks for what is 'profitable and strategic' and takes over. In this sense, any newspaper or TV channel they control will be forced to make advertising deals with these agencies as a form of 'political loyalty'.[48] Those who did not conform with the new advertising business rules were punished. Baraka Advertising for example, which was a prominent agency producing several TV programmes and once engaged in producing a 'pro-revolution programme', was 'kicked out of the game', according to Tayseer.[49]

The defamation and accusations of corruption against Nour, 'the king of advertising', coincided with the rise of another star, Tamer Morsi, who is briefly mentioned in Chapter Two as the CEO of the Egyptian Media Group (EMG). Before the 2013 military coup there existed a sort of separation in the private media market between the business of content production (TV programmes, drama, cinema and other forms of content) and the advertising business. This separation was never complete, as Tarek Nour himself engaged in content production, through his al-Qahira wal-Nas TV channel and other projects. However, general observation shows that this was not the norm. EMG, as a media producer and the owner of most of Egypt's outlets available in the market, does have an advertising arm named Synergy. However, at some point in 2019, a company called United Media Services (UMS) acquired EMG and other media companies, among and in addition to the media companies previously acquired by the military from 2016, making it an even larger media conglomerate than EMG. Information about UMS and its year of foundation is very scarce and ambiguous. However, we know that it is also owned by the General Intelligence's Eagle Capital and, like EMG, also has Tamer Morsi as its CEO. It is worth noting that many sources now mix up the two names (EMG and UMS), as it is no longer that clear to the public which owns the other. However, this might be a deliberate ambiguity by the military to water down the idea of one big company that owns everything, and perhaps new names will appear in the future following the same logic. So, to recap the order of ownership again from Chapter Two, Synergy is 50 per cent owned by EMG, which is owned now by UMS, which is owned by Eagle Capital, which is in turn owned by the General Intelligence – which is a military entity.

Synergy was founded in 2003 by Tamer Morsi purely as an advertising agency. No connections can be found between Synergy and the military at that stage, except that Tamer Morsi was a supporter of Mubarak. A few years later Synergy entered the drama production sector, however, it remained a small player in both sectors until shortly after the coup. The chain of events leading to the sudden rise of Synergy began in November 2016, when Tamer Morsi sold the previously mentioned 50 per cent share of his then newly created Synergy Production to EMG.[50] Synergy Production was a bigger entity that owns his 2003-founded advertising agency Synergy. Then, later in February 2018, Morsi was appointed by Eagle Capital as the CEO of EMG,[51] which owns 50 per cent of his Synergy Production, which in turn fully owns Synergy Advertising. In 2018, UMS acquired EMG and several other media projects. This is the chain of ownership that we need to focus on when discussing transformation in the politics of advertising in post-coup Egypt. It would otherwise be distracting to talk in this section about all the activities and the web of media ownership, as the names of Tamer Morsi, Synergy, EMG, UMS and Eagle Capital among others are all acquiring media investments, through one or the other. However, in the end they all feed into the intelligence's Eagle Capital, or simply the military. For simplification, only Tamer Morsi will be mentioned – not any of the names of the companies that he owns or runs on behalf of the military – when discussing advertising here, as his activities in this sector are not limited to just one of his companies.

The academic literature available on Egyptian military ownership of the media is very scarce and is thus far non-existent when it comes to the military's advertising investments. This could be because the current changes in the advertising sector only started to take place in 2018. Literature produced by media watchdogs and the press shows that there are good relations between Morsi and al-Sisi's regime, which is clear through the choice of Morsi as both business partner and manager of several of the al-Sisi regime media projects,[52] one of which is advertising through Synergy. By 2019, Morsi had already started working on restructuring the TV channels owned by his companies 'for the sake of elevating the media message' based on the instructions of al-Sisi.[53] Also in the same year he announced that he was working on 'reconstructing the advertising market'.[54] This raises the question of the obsessive interest in both the media production and the advertising sector. This brings a risk to the military's media investment, as merging both sectors together in one portfolio might result in a similar scenario to that of the state-run media, which has not been profitable since its foundation in the 1950s. Hossam said that this was justified by the military's fear of a repetition of the 2011 uprising scenario, which the military associate with the marginal freedom that the media had during the last decade of Mubarak's rule. His opinion was that even if such investments are doomed to make losses, they will continue for the foreseeable future, saying that the military 'are facing an existentialist threat and their Gulf patrons will continue pumping money in these projects, as they believe doing so is their safety valve. However, it is not clear until when this Gulf money will continue flowing in'.[55]

This obsession with controlling all forms of media including advertising is also evident on a smaller scale, like taking over highway billboards from other advertising agencies without any permission from the legal owners or renters. In such cases these other advertisers tend not to make complaints against the military.[56] However, such confrontation between the military and private advertising agencies over the rights to billboards on Egypt's highways predates the acquisition of Synergy by EMG as this practice started in 2015 on Cairo's Ring Road, which was quickly appropriated by the military in violation of legal regulations that have existed for decades.[57] Baraa said that there are two reasons why the military is keen on entering the advertising arena, and not continuing with Mubarak's model where he depended on private agencies, such as Nour's TNC. The first assumption is that the military know that investors would prefer to hire the military as their advertising agent, given the 'positive image' they think the people have of the army. The military also thinks that this image is in contrast to that of other agencies in the country. This makes the businesses think that consumers trust advertised commodities, since the military 'trusts' and advertises them. The second assumption that Baraa cited as a reason for the direct involvement of the military in the advertising business, which works in parallel with the first, is the market edge that the military have, as it almost forces investors to advertise with the military with a percentage of their marketing budgets, and this has become a norm now. Otherwise, they might lose privilege in their relevant sectors, which the military already controls.[58] However, the advertising activity of the military does not stop at commercial levels, as it goes to direct advertising propaganda. In September 2019, Tamer Morsi through UMS finished producing a propaganda documentary series on Egypt called 'Egypt, a Piece of Heaven', which does not stop at promoting the country's ancient history for touristic purposes, but transitions into portraying today's 'achievements' under al-Sisi in what the series calls the 'pathway to the future'.[59]

Today's model of the advertising market in Egypt has introduced a new business formula that differs from the one that prevailed under Mubarak. Under Mubarak's neoliberal private sector friendly policies, the ruling elites delegated the private advertising agencies to do their propaganda work and let these agencies profit from privileged access to the market, depending on the level of their loyalty to the regime. Al-Sisi, in his militarized neoliberal economic model, is no longer interested in Mubarak's model and wants to directly control, not delegate. In this case the model has converted to 'in-house' political propaganda, which is in addition to the military controlling one more market, the advertising market, alongside all other markets that the military have expanded into since 2013. In this unprecedented militarized model, the military elite have become the content producer, its buyer as the broadcaster, as well as the advertiser of their own commodities and of commodities manufactured by others. They have become their own propagandists when needed. This Tamam strongly condemned from an economic perspective as their monopoly is doomed to fail, as 'they're producing and selling to themselves'. Additionally, the loss on an artistic and cultural level, according to Hisham, is huge, as Egypt's advertising, which once was an innovative rising 'world pioneer' is now in ruins, which is a problem beyond market distortion.[60]

Conclusion

The Egyptian media model poses a challenge for CPE scholars like Mosco, Hardy, Herman and Chomsky, who all base their arguments on notions of profitability through advertising in the commercialized media. Despite the presence of a large private media market that looks vibrant, Mellor and Skovgaard-Petersen argue that these media investments are not profit-seeking, as they serve more as favours by the business elite to the rulers. This was made clear by major media investor Mohamed al-Amin when he publicly stated that his TV network did not make a profit, and that if it did some day, he would donate the revenue to charities. This does not necessarily rule out the concept of profitability among either media content producers or advertising agencies however. The first makes a profit in non-media sectors, as a reward for the benefits they served to the ruling elites by creating their mostly pro-government media. The second – the advertising agencies – make a profit through having privileged access to media space for their advertisements in both state-run and private media, as a reward for pro-regime political propaganda, whether through encouraging consumerism among the public in the neoliberalizing economy since the *Infitah*, or by producing direct propaganda, like that of Tarek Nour for Mubarak's presidential campaign of 2005, as one example.

The 2011 uprising and the fall of Hosni Mubarak came as a blow to the business elite, who the media investors and the advertising agencies were members of. They responded by quickly taking a counterrevolutionary position through siding with the military against the uprising. This could be observed in the increase in investments in the private media market by the business elite following the uprising, and campaigning for pro-military political figures by the advertising agencies. This reflected a temporary continuation of the political economy model of advertising under Mubarak, in which privately owned agencies benefitted from allying with the ruling elite in their neoliberal model. However, this balance changed after the 2013 coup, as the military further deepened its involvement in the Egyptian economy and expanded their investments to other sectors which they had not previously dominated, including the media and advertising. After pushing Mubarak's propagandists aside, a new model of militarized political economy of advertising was introduced under al-Sisi. This model is based on restructuring the advertising sector, from allying with the agencies to directly owning them, and in this way the military have become the propagandists of themselves. They have achieved this through a marathon of market acquisitions made through Eagle Capital, the commercial arm of the General Intelligence, which now owns the majority of Egypt's media businesses.

4

Social Media as a Political Space

Many national and international media outlets described the 2011 uprising in Egypt a 'Facebook Revolution'[1] and, somewhat less frequently, a 'Social Media Revolution' or 'Internet Revolution'. This over-simplification in labelling an uprising by its means of communication undermines the foundations of discontent among the population, which usually takes a long time to ripen, needs particular historical contexts to materialize, and requires the 'right' momentary sparks for events to break out and bring about a change in power structures. Communication is obviously essential between revolutionary actors and the masses in mobilizing for a revolt, whether through papyrus as was the case four millennia ago, or using the internet in the case of the Egyptian uprising of 2011. On the rising role of the internet as a medium for Egyptian content, Hisham Kassem said that in the 2000s, when videos of torture of citizens in police stations were posted online with minimum cost, this was a media hit that the traditional media could not compete with and this is why he decided to create a website for *al-Masry al-Youm*, as he had become aware by 2006 that the countdown for print journalism had already started.[2]

In a global contemporary socio-political context, the dot-com financial crash of 2001–2, when many thought that the internet had changed the very nature of capitalism, brought about the need for a more thorough analysis of the political economy of this medium.[3] However, regardless of optimism or pessimism concerning the internet and capitalism, Christian Fuchs argues that the internet is a form of contemporary media that needs to be critically studied, showing how the relationship between the internet and society is both 'shaped by and shapes societal antagonisms' in a capitalist society.[4] It is not a one-way direction of influence, as there are power groups such as governments and corporations wishing to influence societies through the internet, and segments of societies that wish to use the new form of media for autonomy and dissent, which is an anti-hegemonic and emancipatory bargain of power.

This political standpoint in itself is commercial, however, it differs from the commercialization of the traditional media discussed in Chapter Two. On the internet, users are content producers.[5] Without employing a permanent creativity, the hosts of content on the internet will run out of business and might cease to exist. This is a bargain of power that has existed in the blogosphere for around two decades, and is now the case of social media, despite all the hegemonic practices by both tech giants and governments. According to Jonathan Hardy, it is now well known that our data on social media, video streaming as well as personal communications are all subject to monitoring, management and exploitation by both the hosts and by governments.[6] For this reason, and that of the autonomy of the users as content producers, an approach of Political Economy of Communication (PEC) is needed when analysing the internet in Egypt as a political space. In such non-democratic states, the rapid increase of internet usage has provided an opportunity for expanding that political space, where the technology of the web seems, despite all hegemonies of corporations and governments, 'friendly toward democratic values'.[7]

This has indeed proven relevant in the role of the internet as a means of communication in the 2011 uprising. However, it raises questions about the degree of its importance in that year and its role in the 2013 military coup. Additionally, in following a CPE approach in analysing the role of the internet in Egypt as Mosco and Hardy would encourage, one should not forget to consider the fact that Egypt is not only a capitalist regime, but also a militarized hyper-neoliberal model of it, as discussed in Chapter Two. This hypothetically facilitates the regime's endeavours to control the internet as a political space and to monitor the public as consumers and producers of digital content.

The subject of the role of the internet in the 2011 Egyptian uprising has been studied thoroughly, and a wealth of literature analysing its phenomenon has been produced by many scholars and media experts. This chapter does not necessarily introduce a strikingly different conclusion to that taken by those scholars, however it serves two purposes in the context of this book. First, we cannot talk about the political economy of contemporary Egyptian media without contextualizing the topic by considering the role of the internet as a political space. This is both in parallel to the traditional media before 2011 and embedded within it after that. Second, it serves to introduce still relatively understudied recent political developments in Egypt within the online sphere which has served the military over the past couple of years in further reinforcing their hegemonic grip on the virtual public space, especially. This is under the assumption that the internet and social media are used as political spaces in Egypt, in accordance with which a CPE approach should be followed as Mosco, Fuchs and Hardy suggest, to understand the developments of events of the 2011 uprising and the 2013 military coup and the relevant developments that followed. Under such a promise, this chapter responds to the question: How did the internet change from almost being a blind spot under the rule of Mubarak, to Big Brother's territory under al-Sisi? With this focus, the chapter starts by discussing the introduction of blog activism and the internet as a political space in the 2000s. It will also discuss how this paved the way for the rise of social media as a 'revolutionary messenger' and controversy about the role that social media played in the 2011 uprising. It will then move to the introduction of the military as a social media content producer and the use of so-called 'electronic committees' and 'bots', which engaged in stirring social media debates and spreading disinformation during the 2013 coup period. Finally, following the success of the coup and having power settled in the hands of the military under al-Sisi, this chapter discusses the technical and legal changes that were introduced to the internet as an attempt to control the internet as a political space.

The internet as a political space prior to 2011

In his interview for this book, Belal mentioned how in the years before the 2011 uprising he imposed a condition on *al-Masry al-Youm* when agreeing his contract with them, which was not to publish his column online. His reasons for this were based on his dislike of online comments made under authors' articles. Belal commented: 'You write something and then you find people accusing you of saying the opposite of what you wrote, who swear at you and at each other'. However, following demand from the Egyptian diaspora, who had no access to the print edition of the newspaper, he agreed to have his articles posted online, with comments disabled. Today, Belal considers his opinion back then to be 'dinosauric', while ironically since the ban on his work in Egypt following the coup his life has become 'dependent on the internet' and without it he could have been 'finished'.[8] The internet has provided to Fadl, since 2013, and to many others since the early 2000s, a political space to which they were previously denied access. Whether facilitated by the internet or not, a political space serves as the window through which citizens of a country can offer input that can be received and taken into account by the authorities. A political space generally constitutes three spheres of activity for citizens: the ability to assemble, the ability to express themselves and the ability to participate in a free and fair electoral process.[9] However, since these three spheres have been limited in Egypt, the internet has turned into an alternative political space to some degree, as will be discussed in this section.

Olesya Tkacheva et al. justify this transition in most parts of the world due to the fact that people are attracted by the internet's affordability, speed, near infinite reach, and its multiplicity of forms, from hosting mainstream media to blogging and social media, where citizens are no longer conditioned to the sole use of printed content to be able to enjoy the right of access to free press.[10] In this sense, citizens have been able to engage with the internet in a variety of ways, from browsing to creating content through blogs. Creating and disseminating content is 'the highest degree of political activism' and is directly linked to freedom of expression.[11] However, in the 2000s the Egyptian state was slow to pay attention to this growing new political space.[12] Tamam thought that this lack of adequate attention by Mubarak's state was due to the internet being left as an arranged 'window for freedom', as they were a significantly small segment of the population anyway. This window would show Egypt from the perspective of foreign aid providers as moving towards democracy, while posing no threat.[13]

The year 2000 marked beginning of the use of the internet as a political space in Egypt, which witnessed the outbreak of the Second Palestinian *intifada*. Egyptian activists used email to share and disseminate news articles, pictures and videos of confrontations in the occupied territories. They also used email to share lists of Israeli commodities and names of international corporations that were supporting the Israeli occupation to be able to boycott them. This was in addition to sharing the names and news of those arrested in Egypt for their activities in solidarity with Palestine. They also used email to announce the dates and locations of political activities and demonstrations in support of Palestine in syndicates, university campuses and major squares.[14] These political activities during that year were replicated in 2003 with the American invasion of Iraq.[15] In parallel with increasing online activism in Egypt over the few following years, mobile phones – not yet smartphones – played a role as a means of communicating political news of both the *intifada* and the invasion of Iraq, and another in announcing the timings and locations of political solidarity events via SMSs.[16] At the same time, many activists started to realize the value of Voice over Internet Protocol (VoIP) as a means of making phone calls that the authorities could not at that time monitor, which was a significant leap forward beyond the reach of security.[17] Blogs, meanwhile, with their capability for providing text, pictures and videos for the public to view at any time, remained extremely valuable. According to Courtney C. Radsch, a blog in the 2000s is 'most often referred to as a reverse chronological, diary-like website typically maintained by a single user or small groups of like-minded and ideologically sympathetic individuals, primarily using open-source, web-based platforms like Blogger or WordPress.'[18] Beyond posted text material, blogging became a suffix attached to a variety of platforms, such as 'vlogging' for video blogging, typically on YouTube, and later, towards the end of the decade, 'mlogging' for mobile blogging.[19] However, earlier in the decade with the launch of the Yahoo! Groups service in 2001 and the spread of 'forums', a further spread of political news and engagement with blog contents was increasing. Yahoo! Groups provided another interlinked political space for discussing and debating current affairs and disseminating announcements of political activities on the ground.[20]

When studying the rise of the internet as a political space in Egypt one should be cautious about the degree to which it was influential among the public and not overestimate its influence. We should not forget that access to the internet by the general population, as mentioned earlier, was still limited. Internet access was almost exclusive to urban populations, particularly the bourgeoisie, and some segments of the middle class who could afford to buy computers and internet subscriptions. In 2000, less than 1 per cent of the Egyptian population had access to the internet.[21] Also during that decade not all blogs were purely political, despite some misconceptions of blogging during that era being like a training camp for the upcoming revolution. There was, for example, 'guide blogging' which could include a discussion about the process of the medical test for the obligatory military service, a topic not covered in books or newspapers.[22] Some blogged about individual hobbies, while others blogged about their feelings and diaries as completely apolitical topics.[23] Revolutions are unlikely to be the outcome of sudden organization or a response to grievances. They are rather the outcome of hard work on the ground by activists and grassroot organizers,[24] while the internet is not necessarily a condition for this to occur, as it plays more the role of a relevant means of communication.

In the Egypt of the 2000s, calling for protests and organizing political events did not initially take place in the virtual space of the internet. They were planned, discussed and agreed upon at physical meetings in venues belonging to political parties, syndicates and university campuses. Then came the mobilization phase, which took place outside internet fora, among the existing traditional networks of political, labour and student movements. Then finally came the role of the internet and SMS for mobilization and promotion of what had been agreed upon among the traditional political networks, to reach the general public. Thus, the process of mobilization in the 2000s was first planned on the ground and then valorized on the internet, rather than the opposite. Although many activists belonged to already organized political entities, there was actually no particular strategy for dealing with the internet as a political space, as it was mostly spontaneous.[25] 'Core bloggers' in the early 2000s were actually mostly blogging about personal subjects of interest, and happened to be in their twenties with an anti-establishment mindset[26] which more or less fitted the fluidity of the internet as a political space, not necessarily a space for organization, but one which could be used as a means for political communication, given the nature and leanings of these young bloggers. As Radsch describes them, 'several were self-described techies or "Linux geeks", while others just wanted to "try out" a new publishing medium. Several core bloggers worked in translation or technology-related jobs, and thus a natural affinity and predisposition toward technology facilitated their adoption of new communication platforms'.[27]

The trend in political activism in Egypt started slowly, focusing on local issues in addition to the regional ones of Palestine and Iraq. Issues of torture at Egyptian police stations and the constant renewal of the Emergency Law started to surface.

These were not necessarily issues that had been ignored in previous years, however they had not taken a central focus. For example, a protest would start in solidarity with Palestine or Iraq which was always met with the brutality of the riot police, and would prompt the protesters to shout out against the lack of freedom and police violence. In a similar kind of protest at Cairo University in April 2002, students chanted against Mubarak himself, which was extremely rare. The same thing happened in Tahrir Square in March 2003. However, the call for protests was always at least initially dedicated to regional issues.[28] Belal said that he saw the blogging phenomenon in the early 2000s as somewhat exaggerated. Reflecting on this opinion he thought this could have been due to his competitive professional attitude as a traditional journalist back then. He said: 'I wondered about these kids. I was from a slightly older generation and thought that what they were writing about was very similar to what I was writing in al-Dostour [an opposition newspaper discussed in Chapter Two], which seemed to have influenced their style.'[29] However later, Belal admitted that he started recognizing the names of 'brilliant' bloggers and 'excellent authors' such as Amr Ezzat, Ahmed al-Fakharany and Ayman Abdel Moaty, whom he did not see as a threat to his generation. He added: 'On the contrary, they inspired me and made me become more vital, and I started admiring the phenomenon.'[30]

The turning point in blogging came on 26 June 2004 during a protest on the International Day in Support of Victims of Torture in front of the Public Prosecutor's office. This was was a protest with a particularly local cause, not regional as the previous ones since 2000 had been. It had been unheard of to call for a protest against the police in the heart of the city centre of Cairo since the 1990s. It was not a coincidence that the organizers of the protest were the same leftist and human rights activists who had led the struggle for solidarity with Palestine and Iraq during the previous four years.[31] This structural change in discourse towards local issues coincided with a number of political initiatives and campaigns against the continued rule of Mubarak and the rise of his son Gamal and the obvious preparation for him to inherit the presidency from his father. Later, these initiatives united under the umbrella of *Harakat Kefaya* (the 'Enough' Movement), which organized its first protest on 12 December 2004, also in front of the Public Prosecutor's office.[32]

A few internet-related developments that occurred during the rise of *Kefaya*. The first involved improvements to the infrastructure of the internet and the IT sector that took place under Ahmed Nazif, first the Minister of Communications and Information Technology and then Prime Minister and enthusiast for Gamal Mubarak as future president and a 'modernizer' of Egypt. These advancements were not necessarily for reasons of increasing the living standards of average citizens, as they were more of an unavoidable necessary minimum level of infrastructure for any economy in the twenty-first century.[33] Before these technical advancements to the internet, Egypt had only a few bloggers in 2002, around thirty to forty in 2003, and maybe a hundred by 2004. However, shortly after, and coinciding with the appearance of *Kefaya*, a critical mass of Egyptians started blogging and self-identifying as a community. At that moment an Egyptian blogosphere became distinct from the more generic virtual community of bloggers worldwide.[34] As mentioned earlier, initially blogs were mostly personal or technical, and generally apolitical.

However, another development in the blogosphere was the result of the so-called 'Black Wednesday' on 25 May 2005 when thugs who had been hired by the NDP and organized by the Ministry of the Interior violently attacked protesters and particularly targeted female demonstrators and journalists in an unprecedented and shocking manner. Many of the victims were themselves bloggers. In response, these bloggers immersed themselves in dedicated political opposition and activism, and invited other apolitical bloggers to join them. Thus started the intensification of both political blogging on the internet and protests on the ground, both in coordination with the rising *Kefaya* movement[35] as a popular growing political umbrella. From that moment on, these bloggers started pioneering many of the tools of what is now a globally known 'cyberactivism tactical repertoire', leveraging the unique characteristics of the internet as a political space. As a result, blogs have become Egypt's primary vehicle for dissent and an alternative public sphere.[36]

Many bloggers also founded the movement of Youth for Change, which introduced new blood and new tactics to street protests, which were sometimes sarcastic in tone. One example was the organization of a 'sweeping protest', where protesters literally brought broomsticks and swept while chanting. The same movement played an important role in covering protests using photography and videos in an attempt to create alternative media and document police violence, which was ignored by both the state-run and private media.[37] The private media at that time were starting to enjoy a tactical small margin of freedom, as discussed in Chapter Two, however police brutality was not a topic they were easily allowed to cover.

On 6 April 2008, significant protests took place in the textile city of al-Mahalla. This was labelled later as *Ahdath al-Mahalla*, or 'the Mahalla Events'. It was a turning point in the scale of protest in Egypt, as there were casualties among protesters and Mubarak's picture was seen, both online and in the international media, being stamped underfoot by angry protesters. The relation between these events and the internet, particularly social media, is controversial and somewhat exaggerated. It is important to refer to the Mahalla Events here, as they are associated with the internet, but they will be discussed more thoroughly in the next section, which focuses on social media and the fall of Mubarak.

Regardless of the degree of significance of the internet as a political space, cyber activism seems to have contributed to the overthrow of a president who had held power for almost thirty years. Nevertheless, this was a process that occurred gradually over several years before finally culminating in the countrywide protests of 2011.[38] There might be a consensus among activists and political analysts on the importance of Egypt's blogsphere in the 2000s, but some of the mechanisms of this influence might not be sufficiently clear to them. On the one hand, the size of the population that had access to the internet in Egypt was relatively small: 12.75 per cent of the total population in 2005, and 18.01 percent in 2008.[39] On the other hand, on the days when blogs were covering political events, some sites had an excess of visits,[40] which is significant enough. Baraa says that blogs before 2011 were not as common as many might think, however, those who had their own blogs became very popular figures and were seen as 'very impressive persons', which was politically influential.[41] There is also another factor that facilitated these young bloggers' role as political players. Many had a family background of political involvement. Some of their parents had forged their way as human rights activists before the rise of the internet in Egypt. Alaa Abdel Fatah's father, Ahmed Saif al-Islam, headed the Hisham Mubarak Law Centre, and his mother, Laila Soueif, is a high-profile political opposition figure and professor at Cairo University. Manal Hassan's father, Bahey Eldin Hassan, is the co-founder of the Cairo Institute for Human Rights Studies. Nawara Negm's father, Ahmed Fouad Negm, was a prominent leftist revolutionary poet and her mother, Safinaz

Kazem, a prominent intellectual journalist.[42] This heritage of political charge in the history of families of some of these bloggers has obviously helped in both the turn to political blogging and in transferring know-how to the blogsphere. However, others such as Wael Abbas, who became an internationally renowned blogger mainly focusing on documenting torture and police brutality,[43] were not known to have such a political family background, despite the fame and status Abbas made for himself as a political blogger.

Hossam El-Hamalawy, who is also a prominent blogger known as '3arabawy', writes in his study on the relation between the internet and the 2011 uprising that the influence of various blogs arose from the type of their followers, not necessarily their numbers. It was the 'unofficial marriage' between blogs, as new media and the existing traditional media. This started to happen towards the end of the 2000s, when journalists working in Egypt and abroad started paying attention to the content of blogs. Similarly, international academics and foreign diplomats also started paying attention to the phenomenon. They passed the contents of blogs to their traditional audiences and to their governments, which led to millions knowing about these blogs inside and outside Egypt. The 'marriage' between the blogosphere and traditional media was further reinforced when some of these successful bloggers became traditional journalists themselves, while some traditional journalists started their own blogs to catch the wave.[44] This blurs the role of the internet, now intertwined with the traditional media, in overthrowing Mubarak.

While studying the internet as a political space in Egypt and blogging as a proactive political involvement, we must not forget the significance of the 'passive' political influence of the internet on those who simply just browse web content produced in Egypt or abroad. Badr thought that the most important influence that the internet had on him personally was access to knowledge about other peoples around the world. According to Badr, this made an 'enormous difference' between the generation that had access to the internet and the previous one that did not enjoy this sense of openness, regardless of political affiliation or understanding of freedoms. Badr said: 'Suddenly we had access to knowledge beyond what is written in schoolbooks or even other books that were not easily available, and if they were, they would be very outdated. This is an opportunity that was not available to previous generations. People did not know before that things could be done differently'.[45]

The work of Mohammed el-Nawawy and Sahar Khamis finds that blogs played a critical role during that period, along with other forms of media, in changing the map of Egyptian politics, as was obvious after 2011. However, we should be very careful not to overestimate this role or to frame it as a cause-effect relationship between blogging and political change.[46] This brings us to the conclusion that the internet has played a significant role as a political space, whether by producing or consuming political content, locally or internationally. In this sense, we cannot assume the degree to which this influence led to the fall of Mubarak in 2011. However, we cannot disregard the fact that the internet was there, and it was important alongside the already existing traditional mobilization strategies on the ground. To understand this influence, one should deal with the interconnectedness of the internet in enabling political potential, generating new public spheres, and developing contentious politics among the youth.[47] In all of these the Mubarak regime was too slow and too traditional to respond adequately to or successfully repress it, as it was almost a blind spot for them as the older generation.[48] The internet has opened the door for documenting violations that were not well documented previously, and has given the public the means to learn about these violations throughout the 2000s. However, the rise of social media towards the end of the decade was a turning point for the internet, which made it a popular political tool in the hands of the average citizen,[49] beyond the genius and dedication of bloggers.

Social media as a revolutionary messenger

The Mubarak regime continued to be too slow to respond or engage adequately with the growth of the internet as a political space, as discussed earlier, and by 2007 Facebook and Twitter started to become popular among the Egyptian youth as alternative or additional political spaces in intersection with the already existing blogosphere. Radsch justifiably considers all these forms of political expression, whether on now 'traditional' blogs or the rising social media, as part of the evolving blogosphere.[50] The advancements in telecommunications in Egypt towards the end of the decade, for economic reasons and to integrate with the global economy, and the increasing penetration of the internet and mobile phones, were important in transforming the dynamics of the blogosphere as it transitioned from depending on only the primary blogging platforms such as Blogger or WordPress, to blending in with more dynamic social media platforms such as Facebook and Twitter.

Many Egyptian cyber activists swiftly adapted these new platforms for political purposes, which, given their appeal and simplicity, encouraged a newer generation of youth to also become active online.[51] Fadl, although a relatively young but 'classical' journalist, as he described himself, admitted that he was 'impressed' by the capability of Facebook and Twitter in the mobilization and dissemination of political views.[52] Social media helped the earlier form of blogging, towards the end of the decade, to provide an outlet for further expressing oneself and connecting with others, who would then automatically broadcast directly to friends and friends of friends in what we know call 'sharing', which helps posts to be spread easily and quickly. The existing cyber activists boosted the expansion of blogging into social media, which spread their blogposts faster. However, back then, Facebook still had a real-name policy,[53] which was not mandatory with blogging. Many bloggers had famous pseudonyms such as 3arabawy, Zenobia and Sand Monkey. Twitter did not have such a policy and was therefore considered to be more secure among activists, as they were able to use their already well-established pseudonyms.

The name of the industrial textile city of al-Mahalla, mentioned briefly earlier, has been associated with Facebook since 2008. The mainstream story is generally that there was a call on Facebook by a few young activists such as Israa Abdel Fattah and Ahmed Maher for a general strike across the country on 6 April of that year. The response across the country was not significant, except among the workers of al-Mahalla, who responded positively, and the city clashed with the riot police for at least two days. This event was the beginning of the spread of the label 'Facebook activists' in local and international media. El-Hamalawy in his research rejects the narrative of al-Mahalla's turn of events as a Facebook phenomenon and criticizes the spread of the newly coined 'Facebook activists' label.[54] He argues that the story starts earlier with the workers of Mahalla Tex, the biggest textile factory in the country, who organized a large protest on 17 February 2008 demanding salary increases. On the same day they threatened to escalate this to a strike on 6 April. Then a few youths, among whom were Abdel Fattah and Maher, created a Facebook group in solidarity with the al-Mahalla workers and called for a general strike across the country on the same day. Tens of thousands joined the group in record time. On the day, the riot police occupied the factory and arrested labour leaders, and the strike was suppressed. As for the rest of the country, almost nothing happened as well, except for a few minor protests at the Lawyers Syndicate of Cairo, the factory of Kafr al-Dawar Tex, South Cairo Mills and a couple of universities. All were symbolic and short-lived. The Facebook call for a general strike failed both in al-Mahalla and in the rest of the country. The first work shift at Mahalla Tex proceeded almost normally on that morning. The course of events began to change in the evening of that day in al-Mahalla, where the people, not necessarily the workers, started to clash with the riot police around the factory.[55]

No one has a definitive explanation of what ignited of the clashes, but narratives range from a child, or sometimes a woman, being beaten up by the riot police. Another narrative centres on a rumour about the arrest of further labour leaders. The concrete result was that clashes lasted for about two days and Mubarak's pictures were trodden underfoot in front of the cameras of the international media. This in itself was big enough news and buried the fact that the Facebook call for a general strike had failed. The media, local and international, rushed to link the al-Mahalla clashes with Facebook, which has been considered a 'historical fact' to this day, while there was not a single strike in al-Mahalla or anywhere in Egypt on that day: just the angry poor of the city clashing with the riot police over an unidentified rumour. In fact, the workers' buses were attacked as they were leaving after their first shift on the day of the strike, as they were accused of betrayal. However, the Facebook activists continued to appear in the media, which encouraged many to call for other strikes following the false 'success' of 6 April. A large activist group, which later played an important role in the 2011 uprising, was even created, and took the date as its name: 'the 6 April Movement'. A general strike was called for on Facebook for 4 May 2008, Mubarak's birthday, and nothing happened. On 23 July nothing happened. Following another call on the first anniversary of the al-Mahalla events in 2009, nothing happened either.[56]

Regardless of disagreements about social media as an organizing space, social media continued to grow, integrating with the blogosphere, as a political space, and was gaining further popularity and more political content, including text, photography and videos, as well as growing in volume and reach. In

March 2009, Facebook launched its Arabic platform and a few months later, by early 2010, it had become the second most popular website in Egypt after Google. By that time, Facebook's membership had reached 2.4 million.[57] In parallel, the microblog Twitter (back then posts on Twitter were limited to 140 characters) had been launched in March 2006. This platform was more suitable for mobile phones, the use of which was also on the rise. As mentioned earlier, cyber activists were able to use their popular pseudonyms on this platform. Having no real-name policy on Twitter, in contrast with Facebook at that time, was helpful in to provide some camouflage for activists, encouraging them to send stronger messages. Since Twitter was not available in Arabic it did not gain popularity until 2008, when young tech-savvy cyber activists started using it for political content. Many were writing in Arabic transliteration using the Latin alphabet, which some called Anglo/Franco-Arab. Much of the communication on Twitter was among bloggers, and it was also used for quickly following news updates.[58] Twitter however remained much less popular than Facebook. By 2009, Twitter had only 3,000 users in the entire Middle East region, which increased to 40,000 by mid-2010[59] – which could be due to the lessons learned by Arab activists from their Iranian counterparts during the 2009 repressed uprising there, in which Twitter played an important role as a means of political communication. The 'hashtag' feature of Twitter was particularly different from other social media platforms, and Egyptian activists adapted it to their context. They used it to amplify their messages, frame their grievances and demands, and create public conversations on specific topics. Succeeding in making a hashtag trend could trigger amplification and attract traditional news coverage of the hash-tagged topic, which in turn would bring greater attention from key external actors, which finally was a key strategic goal for activists. This in itself brought activists in touch with the traditional local and international media and international rights groups, which was a tactic with the purpose of both protection and valorization when the authorities arrested any of those activists.[60] To wrap it up in numbers, right before the fall of Mubarak, in 2010, 21.6 per cent of Egypt's population had access to the internet, access to mobile phone subscription was at 85.38 per cent, and in early 2011 the country had about five million Facebook users and about 129,000 Twitter users.[61] This helped exceed the geographical limitations of political activism in downtown Cairo enabling it to spread across the country, and helped like-minded politicized young people communicate regardless of physical distance.[62] However helpful this was, internet access remained limited to those who were able to buy smartphones and high-speed internet ADSL instead of very slow dial-up subscriptions, which made the political trend largely limited to the youth of the middle and upper classes.[63]

A turn of political events took place on 6 June 2010, when a young man from Alexandria called Khaled Saeed was brutally killed while in police custody. The authorities concocted a story that he was a drug dealer. However, the coverup story backfired and caused public outrage when a picture of his corpse, with his face disfigured by obvious brutality, was shared on social media. Towards the end of 2010, a Facebook page called 'We Are All Khaled Saeed' was created by several activists, among them the Egyptian Google employee Wael Ghonim. The page played a key role in bringing attention to the tragedy and was instantly followed by tens of thousands of the growing Facebook population. It was also used to organize several small protests in different cities, which were documented and news of which reached the large number of the followers on Facebook, whose number was obviously much bigger than the number of protesters themselves.[64] At the same time, Mubarak's large security forces were not prepared or properly aware of the now-sophisticated strategies of the Egyptian activists in their mastered territories of the internet. Mass protests on 25 January 2011, Police Day, were called for on the page. The old-fashioned regime was left with only two choices: either to shut down the internet, or to allow it but use violence to crack down on the protests. The regime used both choices but exercised them clumsily and failed. The rest of the story and the huge literature written about it are a familiar by now.[65] However, it may be useful to consider the influence of the Khaled Saeed Facebook page and other opposition pages and Twitter accounts, not only from the aspect of the number of followers. We should consider the traditional media that followed these social media accounts and pages and how they passed their content on to tens of millions of readers and viewers inside Egypt and abroad.[66]

Tkacheva et al. argue that there was a symbiotic relationship between social media and the traditional media during the 2011 uprising. The traditional media reached a high percentage of the local population, in addition to the vast regional and international populations. This allowed social media to present a competing narrative of what was occurring on the streets versus the regime's narrative of events, which will be further discussed in Chapter Five. By 'informing' the traditional media, social media were able to influence the level of foreign pressure on the Mubarak regime and they were able to get their message across to the offline Egyptian population.[67] The events of 25 January were not as fully spontaneous as some might think and didn't solely occur because of a Facebook event. It was preceded by several meetings held by different political groups to discuss demonstrations and the slogans to be chanted on the day. The top demand was the sacking of the interior minister Habib al-Adly, not the 'fall of the regime'. Significant promotion of the event took place in the traditional media, local and international, which were the main players in spreading the word, while the role of social media was complementary.[68] What might have helped to charge the situation was the obviously false narrative of the Egyptian traditional media about the escalation of violence during the days that followed 25 January, which made people turn to social and international media,[69] such as Al Jazeera and others. This in itself still gives significant credit to social media,[70] despite the incomparably wide reach of the international traditional media – especially when the internet was shut down on 28 January, which outraged many more people.[71] Hanan Badr confirms that successful spill-over effects occurred from online media to mainstream media, thus reaching wider non-politicized audiences.[72] Revealing the brutality of the riot police is one example. One might reflect now, after a decade, and think that if the Egyptian regime had dropped the signal of a few satellite channels, most importantly Al Jazeera, rather than shutting down the internet, this could have weakened the uprising.[73] However, the pictures and videos that were shared on social media before the shutdown caused many people to join the uprising, and its role is thus undeniable.[74] All this was in addition to the fact that traditionally Cairo happened to be the hub of the Middle East for international media covering the region. A large number of correspondents are therefore always there, which was another reason for the attention of the international media.[75] However, according to Aljosha Karim Schapals and Zahera Harb, many international media did send their reporters four or five days before the event took place, meaning that news coverage was highly reliant on social media content.[76] Another element of the relative success of social media is that it acted as an electronic 'word of mouth', through sharing functions, apart from traditional or professional media, people usually passively share as they do in real life through word of mouth. This was particularly given the government did not provide an actual political 'sharing' space for the people.[77] Such a sharing tendency, however, was sometimes bordering on 'mass hysteria', according to Badr, as news of police violence was 'multiplied by a hundred' and posted live with an extreme sense of urgency.[78] Beyond the degree of political change on the ground, the fall of Mubarak led to further millions from the older generations of 'parents, aunts and uncles' buying smartphones and creating a social media accounts,[79] even if they did not have an email address before.

The portrayal of the 25 January 2011 uprising is relatively similar to that of the al-Mahalla events on 6 April 2008. Both portrayals insist that the events 'suddenly broke out' because of Facebook, as if there was no accumulation of years of economic, political and social discontent[80] as explained in Chapters One and Two. It was an extension to how Western media similarly reduced the 2009 mass protests of the Iranian Green Movement to a 'Twitter revolution'.[81] Tkacheva et al. hold a middle ground in the debate about the role of social media in Egypt's 2011 uprising and argue that even if bringing people onto the streets on 25 January was the only contribution of social media to the uprising, this still makes it key to the fall of Mubarak. They do not deny either that the broader political context played a critical role in facilitating the uprisings,[82] which is indeed a very critical role. However, this does not diminish the significance of the work of cyber activists who skilfully used the internet and social media as a political space to practice their right of opposition and then, from the early 2000s, as a means of communication to challenge a longstanding authoritarian regime. Downplaying the role of cyber activism and social media in Egypt is just as dangerous as overselling it.[83] In this context Belal admitted that he was fascinated by the role that social media played in the uprising, before he started realizing how 'annoying' it became after the uprising,[84] which is to be discussed in the next section, as the military quickly realized Mubarak's mistake of ignoring the internet as a political space, and then stepped in.

Militarizing social media: the business of e-committees

In the three-month period from July to September 2012, around eight million new mobile subscriptions in the MENA region were registered. This was

almost eight times more than the number of new-borns across the region in
the same period. During this time the overall number of mobile subscriptions
across the region reached about 990 million, which was almost double the
entire population. The region's rate of subscription growth for that year was
103 per cent, while the worldwide rate was 91 per cent, China was at 81 per
cent, and India at 72 per cent.[85] Within the same regional context, Egypt's IT
sector had also witnessed remarkable growth since the 2011 uprising until
recently. For example, the percentage of internet users by January 2020 had
reached 54 per cent of the entire population of more than 100 million, the
country had 92.7 million mobile phone subscriptions, which is about 91 per
cent of the population. As for social media, Facebook had 42 million users,
Instagram 11 million, Snapchat 6 million and Twitter 3.6 million. All are
expected to continue to grow.[86] Following the fall of Mubarak in February
2011, Baraa shared the observation that 'You could hear while walking in the
streets the word "Facebook" mentioned in conversations all the time. Many
people who never had a smartphone, including [people who were illiterate],
bought them and created Facebook accounts. Many had their names misspelled.
The military were aware of this trend and made use of it'.[87]

This leap in social media's spread across all strata of Egyptian society had its
own cultural, social, political and economic consequences on them. They were
no longer dependant on the Mubarak era traditional media mechanism, which
was mixed between state-run media and the business elites' media, as discussed
in Chapter Two. After the 2011 uprising, whether traditional media covered an
event or not, social media would cover it anyway. It even reached the point
where traditional media were forced to rely on social media to guarantee the
reach of their content to the public.[88] The army was not far from this as their
pages played a big role in shaping voters' opinions regarding the constitutional
declaration of March 2011, just two months after Mubarak's fall, a first attempt
to understand the power of social media.[89] This was a great success for them,
as they wished the referendum 'Yes' vote to win, and they indeed managed this,
with 77 per cent of votes supporting the constitutional declaration. It was clear
then that the fulfilment of Hardy's perception of the internet as a space which
is monitored, managed and exploited by hosts and governments[90] was starting
to materialize in Egypt. The military Facebook pages became many, but they
were also simplistic and inefficient. However, they worked well in terms of

attracting people's attention, especially social media newcomers from the poor and uneducated. Some were even announced the distribution of food such as meat, which is expensive in Egypt. The time and location of where the food would be distributed for free would be posted on their Facebook page, while asking some Facebook subscribers working for them to share the post, which would then go viral in a very short period of time.[91] In doing so, and among other changes discussed in previous chapters, the military were replacing Mubarak's regime, or at least the image of it, as the caretaker of the people, gaining more traditional social popularity, and social media followers.

One of the main differences between governance under Mubarak and that under the military following the fall of Mubarak, is that, according to Radsch, the latter are 'adept at using the internet as part of their repertoire of control',[92] which was almost a blind spot under Mubarak, as discussed earlier. From 2011, the internet as a political space has no longer been left for bloggers and their politically militant blogosphere and social media. Social media have quickly become a crucial political domain for the military and other political players, due to being part of the post-Mubarak daily social, political and economic life of Egyptians.[93] This expanding internet space has become an active environment for the military to seek to influence the public, partly by blocking content, and separately by flooding the internet with distracting or promotional content. Sometimes this is done through state-run Facebook pages, and other times through so-called *legān elektrōneya* (electronic committees),[94] referred to in this book as e-committees and will be discussed shortly. In today's world, with all its IT advancements, when an authoritarian ruling elite struggles to hold its grip over the public domain it may opt for selective content deletion.[95] For example, much of the content produced by TV channels such as those of the ONTV and CBC Network, among several others, was deleted from their YouTube channels and other social media accounts following the coup. However, the role of the e-committees remains more significant as a tool that the military frequently use to influence public opinion. This tool materialized once successive governments realized that they could no longer influence public opinion without utilizing social media. The solution they thought of in response was the creation of e-committees. The role of these is to control the narrative of public opinion, which is the same objective that traditional media were aiming at before.[96] Not only have the military and their post-Mubarak governments engaged in this, but political Islamists and other political groups also had their e-committees. The Islamists, for example, carried out organized attacks against public figures who were critical of Morsi and his rule from June 2012 until the coup in July 2013.[97] However, the use of e-committees by the military has been obviously on a much greater scale in comparison with any other political group. Generally, authoritarian governments and other political actors tend to manipulate the information available on social media in order to distort users' access to the political blogosphere, in its broader sense of the internet as a political space and distract them from accessing sensitive information.[98] According to Gehad, 'What happened after 2011 is that the political input [to the internet] has intensified. The messages were too many and contradictory. And after calling for [the ouster of] a dictator in 2011, instead the people called for supporting a military coup in 2013'.[99]

By 2012, the existence of e-committees as a business was already common informal knowledge. Undefined entities and high-profile individuals hired young people and tasked them to simply spread certain information on social media or to engage with certain posts. This did not necessarily deny the fact that sometimes a pro-military message was also spread through unpaid enthusiasts who could be Mubarak loyalists, genuine supporters of the military, or simply 'haters' of Islamists, who were all visible segments of an increasingly conflicted Egyptian society. However, regardless of the existence of voluntary pro-military disinformation workers, e-committees existed as a business at least from 2012, and probably earlier. Running up to the military coup, e-committees were almost turned into an industry, where real IT companies would hire young workers in halls filled with computers. They would be told to monitor certain social media accounts or certain public figures. There were big screens in these halls where texts are displayed to be copied and posted on the employees' accounts or as comments to particular posts by those who they were targeting. The average monthly salary for such a job, which was growing more organized over time, became EGP 1,500 or more,[100] more or less the unofficial minimum wage in Egypt at the time. According to Badr, the military learned from the social media strategies of the 2011 uprising and applied them in the 2013 coup.[101] The phenomenon significantly increased as opposition hashtags became more frequently attacked than previously, with identical posts and comments being posted mainly at the same time.[102] By 2020 the social media giants started to crack down on these activities in Egypt, which has become one of the world's top hosts of fake social media accounts.[103] It was revealed by Facebook that there are two major companies running this business in Egypt: New Waves and Flexell.[104] Both companies are specialized in 'marketing' and 'media production', which, as discussed in Chapters Two and Three, are now military-controlled sectors. This business, from its rise following Mubarak's fall until the coup, has managed to cause significant confusion in the public domain. Aseel made two comparative observations about this confusion. The first is that before the 2011 uprising the number of internet and social media users was rather small, which helped political messages to be specific and accessible in an uncrowded space. The second is that following the uprising, when the numbers became huge, the message was often lost.[105]

According to Zhuravskaya et al., government-sponsored posts do not necessarily aim to engage in meaningful arguments on social media, but mostly to try to 'manipulate the discourse through agenda setting and framing to change the tone and the topic of discussions'.[106] This framing has indeed influenced the Egyptian traditional media, which started to follow the trending frames on social media and to produce 'follow up' content, which aims to bring them more clicks.[107] This was a significant reverse of influence between the two forms of media following the 2011 uprising. The e-committees, whether directly in their social media sphere or indirectly through the traditional media that now follow their trends, were thus mostly engaging in two political activities. The first was the defamation of an opposition political figure, group, or unfavourable narrative. The second was the amplification of favourable opinions that they wished to set trending, hoping that this would influence and keep public opinion under control.[108] Tayseer, however, did not give great credit to social media in paving the way for the 2013 coup, as the Muslim Brotherhood government was already very weak and the traditional media was told by the 'deep state' to criticize and humiliate them, which was very effective.[109] Tamam, taking the opposite position, asserted that the social media, particularly its newly subscribed millions of 'mamas and papas', especially on Facebook, played a very important role in supporting the coup.[110] Aseel more or less agreed with this, but insisted that the support of the coup on the ground was 'honest and organic' and that the social media magnified it rather than created it.[111] Regardless of this, the manipulation of social media by authoritarian regimes is not necessarily an exclusive Egyptian phenomenon, as countries such as China and Russia – two examples of many – are known to engage in subtle manipulation of information through the distraction of users or the manipulation of search results, which can be more effective than blatant censorship. However, the use of social media as an instrument of propaganda and surveillance remains highly effective.[112] The human e-committees seem more convincing than the 'bots' ('robots'), which are digitally animated accounts, usually with numbers or gibberish names as handles, which the public is now growing aware of.[113] However, these bots are sometimes still useful in causing some hashtags to trend. The military-supported Tamarod Movement that called for the deposal of Morsi in 2013, besides being supported in the traditional media, also used e-committees for the same purpose. However, their content was still widely shared on social media by average citizens without necessarily being connected to e-committee business.[114] One of the most disturbing successes of the military in social media was convincing large segments of society to accept the 'massacre' of the Muslim Brotherhood protesters on 14 August 2013 (this will be discussed in detail in Chapters Five and Six), and further, to encourage the public to celebrate the event of this tragedy as a victory, with music and dancing.[115] However, despite such a dim outcome for the role of social media in 2013 and the violent suppression of opposition in the following years, Hanan Badr is optimistic that if the system opens up again, the social movements that were active before might re-emerge as political actors.[116] However, this might occur with totally new faces, as the original operators are tainted with fatal mistakes.

Intensifying e-surveillance post 2013

There is a particular structural characteristic of internet surveillance in Egypt that makes the process convenient for the military. TE Data, the biggest internet provider in the country, with about 75 per cent of the internet's market share, is the data communications and internet arm of the state-owned Telecom Egypt. This makes intercepting most citizens' communications, when not encrypted, an easy job.[117] In discussing the topic of controlling social media, Zhuravskaya et al. argue that social media provides much information about the attitudes and behaviours of the public and their local environments which can also be used to monitor them and the performance of local governors.[118] Through social media, the Chinese authorities have been effectively intercepting public discontent, potential protest, and the poor performance of local government.[119] In parallel to spreading disinformation over social media and influencing public opinion through e-committees, Egypt, since the fall of Mubarak and increasingly since the coup, is following a relatively similar path to that of China. In the end, digital censorship does appear to be at least partially effective.[120] The increase in digital surveillance following the coup in Egypt did not only censor the content the users posted online, but also their vocal conversations, as many phone calls of political activists were intercepted and found their way to the military-controlled traditional media.[121]

Despite the obvious power of the military over cyber activists and opposition online due to their ability to invest in surveillance technology and pay for e-committee activities, it remains unwise to totally disregard the side of anti-military digital manipulation. It is hard to assume that the military is completely successful in controlling and intercepting the internet as a political space in a country like Egypt today with such a large young population. Data shows that by January 2021 there were 59.19 million internet users in Egypt, which is 57.3 per cent of its 103.3 million population,[122] a proportion which is relatively high. Hisham paid special attention to this by pointing to the many people who were posting petitions on social media asking al-Sisi to 'help them feed their families' because of increasing poverty, while many others 'curse him' for the same reason.[123] This is despite the current presence of severe oppression and excessive e-surveillance.

Joey Shea and Alexei Abrahams studied what they call a 'battle on Twitter' between the Egyptian government and the opposition in relation to the protests that were called for in 2019 and 2020 by Mohamed Ali, a contractor who used to work for the military and then became a popular opposition figure from abroad. According to Shea and Abrahams, both sides engaged in significant 'coordinated inauthentic behaviour' on Twitter in response to the call for protests by Ali in September 2020.[124] For example, there were two trending hashtags, one pro-regime that said: 'Sisi defeats the international organization', and an anti-regime hashtag that said: 'The Friday of Anger 25 September', both of which trended in large numbers on 25 September 2020.[125] Considering the pro-regime hashtag, there was a spike of 173 tweets in a single minute at 5:18 am. There were also suspicious spikes in the number of accounts created in a single day: on 7 September and on 20 and 24 September, between forty and fifty accounts were created each day.[126] As for the anti-regime hashtag, there was also a 'suspicious spike of 503 tweets in a single minute at 19:38 on 24 September. There were also anomalous spikes in the number of accounts created in a single day: September 16th, September 20th and 24th, each had between 335 and 435 accounts created each day'.[127] However, the two researchers conclude that, generally, in most other cases, the Egyptian authorities do conduct many more operations with much higher sophistication than those of the opposition.[128]

Over the course of about ten years from the fall of Mubarak, the military have engaged in several forms of internet manipulation and censorship. Mostafa al-Sayed categorizes these into five interlinked forms of digital authoritarianism: censorship, disinformation, blockade, digitization of public services, and what he calls 'building a legal arsenal'.[129] Some of these concepts have already been discussed; now it is important to focus on two complementary aspects of these concepts: first, the heavy investment by the military in e-surveillance of the opposition, and second, building a legal arsenal to serve as a means of punishment for those intercepted under e-surveillance.

E-surveillance includes not only sophisticated technological forms of programming, but also online human surveillance. There are those who are tasked by the military to penetrate particular Facebook groups, not necessarily political ones, but which might include members who could be seen as suspicious by the authorities. Badr mentioned that 'informers' were found in a Facebook group that talked about whisky and in another that talked about dating. Informers in these groups took screenshots of what they saw, which could then be used later against any of these members.[130] Beshara said that the social media which ten years ago was a means of empowering the opposition, has turned into a tool used by the military to attack and defame them, turning it into a 'scary place'.[131] However, what remains more 'scary' than the human element of online surveillance, is the level of sophistication and intensification of investment in e-surveillance technology against activists, opposition and against civil society organizations.[132] To give a few examples of these investments, the military bought FinFisher spyware from the UK in 2011, ProxySG from the

US in 2013, Vortex and Cortex from France in 2014, Remote Control System from Italy in 2015, Amesys from France, via the United Arab Emirates, in 2017, Pegasus from Israel in 2018, and Sandvine and PacketLogic from the US also in 2018.[133] These are only a sample of what has been documented by a couple of watchdogs, which means that in reality there are probably many more. We are talking about a level of coordination between several states and spyware giants. These e-surveillance technologies can provide the Egyptian authorities with a spying edge in intercepting calls, SMSs, emails and chats, as well as video spying through the cameras of computers and smartphones. This spyware is also capable of analysing the content of information gathered, and monitoring social media and online public opinion. They can monitor what citizens browse online, they can impersonate the identities of targeted citizens, and they can control most existing operating systems of computers and smartphones including Windows, Apple, Android and iOS. This is all in addition to other spying activities.[134] According to Badr, everything in Egypt is being spied on, and if someone is not an 'important figure' then everything will be recorded and saved automatically without necessarily checking the content, until a time in the future it may be needed. Badr added that this even happens among members of the authorities because they spy on each other, as seen from the occasional leaks of officials' intercepted phone conversations.[135] This tells us that the intensification of e-surveillance investment by the military used on each other and their civilian partners in power is also used as 'bargaining cards' against each other.[136]

It is strategically important for an authoritarian regime such as Egypt's to 'legally' justify its oppression of freedom of expression. With the amount of information gathered through the e-surveillance technology discussed above, huge numbers of citizens are prosecuted for expressing critical views of the military and their puppet civilian governments. Immediately after the coup, the legal foundations of many of these political arrests were, at the least, flawed and unclear, if not in total violation of authoritarian Egyptian law itself. Soon after, the military engaged heavily in changing the existing laws and passing new ones in order to use them to prosecute dissent and make examples of it. This gave the military the chance to argue, both locally and internationally, that they are simply applying the law.

The rights to privacy of communication and correspondence do nominally exist in Egypt, even in the 2014 constitution (article 57), which is a product of the coup a year earlier. However, there is a relative absence of legal and judicial enforcement, which gives the military and their representatives the opportunity to violate these rights and freely access personal information, calls and all forms of communication between citizens.[137] The military have used existing authoritarian legal frameworks such as the Emergency Law of 1958, the Law of the Communication Sector Regulation of 2003, and the Counter Terrorism Law of 2015. They have all provided powers to all levels of authorities to violate citizens' freedoms and privacy when needed. This is alongside the changes in the media laws discussed in Chapter Two, which were intended to provide military control over the content produced in and for the traditional media. One interesting detail, within the frame of the new traditional media laws, is that any individual holder of a social media account who followers exceed 5,000 will be considered a 'media entity', and the media laws will apply to them.[138]

A further increase in the intensification of this legal arsenal through the introduction of what is called the Cyber Crimes Law came in 2018. This deliberately mixes legal surveillance of those who commit online fraud with online news and information sources that provide opinions and discuss social and political topics.[139] Punishments can vary from blocking these online sources, to fines and imprisonments, or all of these. Amr Hamzawy says that the law in its articles 27 and 34 which focus on the 'crimes' of 'web managers' and the 'criminal responsibility of providing electronic services', and the 'crimes of harming the national security' and 'harming social peace', all leave the door open for blocking online sources that provide opinions and ideas that contradict official ones. This, according to Hamzawy, enables the authorities to target online content producers based on elastic definitions, in addition to the laws previously imposed on the traditional media sector, which are all intended to 'put freedom of expression and the public space under siege'.[140]

The increased investment in e-surveillance in Egypt and the changes in the legal environment with the purpose of controlling the internet as a political space discussed above, which mutually support each other as two aspects of control, are not without international interest. Badr sourly accused the EU of hypocrisy, saying: 'The European Parliament gave us headaches in condemning human rights violations in Egypt, but is fine with European surveillance companies selling their products to the country'.[141] In the same line of hypocrisy,

Baraa discovered while working on a story that the Italian government uses Signal, an encrypted communication app, to communicate with its own embassy in Cairo,[142] fearing e-surveillance, while Italy is itself a source of spyware for Egypt. Multinational e-surveillance technology producers play a significant role in violating human rights in Egypt through the spyware they sell to the authorities.[143] The military are indeed trying to provide a legal framework for their violations in order to improve their image both locally and internationally. However, as Gehad concluded on the topic, there is 'nothing legal under a regime founded on a military coup', and this makes them fear the public and to intensify their control.[144] On the other hand, Badr said that the authorities are not that keen to follow their own laws which they keep introducing, as for example, they arbitrarily stop people in the streets and force them to open their phones to check them for political content, while those who try to refuse will be roughed up, as if the laws are not already on the authority's side.[145]

Conclusion

The first decade of the millennium in Egypt witnessed the growing use of the internet as a political space, in response to the absence of one which was active and inclusive. In coordination with physical tactics on the ground, young activists succeeded in creating a political blogosphere that kept growing towards the 2011 uprising, with several milestones and minor political events taking place even before. Disagreements remain about the degree to which this internationally recognized Egyptian blogosphere influenced the course of events. However, the solid understanding remains that it was influential in spreading awareness to a higher degree and creating mobilization to a lesser one. This was all while Mubarak's traditional regime was almost in a blind spot concerning the influence of the internet as a political space on the real-life political space. The rise of social media as a means of communication towards the end of the decade played a significant role in disseminating the content of the already well-established blogosphere to larger segments of the Egyptian youth who had become both producers and consumers of political content. Like the disagreements as to the degree of the blogosphere's influence on the course of events, particularly the 2011 uprising, social media are agreed to be an even more influential tool of disseminating political content, but not necessarily the cause of or the major influence on those events that led to Mubarak's fall, while his regime remained in the same earlier blind spot. The role of the traditional media, particularly Al Jazeera and other regional and international outlets, was crucial in arriving at the consequences of the 2011 uprising as disseminators and magnifiers of social media content. This is in addition to the essential role of social, political and economic grievances and the piling up of discontent over the years leading to the uprising. However, authoritarian regimes in the region remain prevalent, and they are becoming increasingly 'savvy' in enhancing their new media tools to their own advantage.[146] Since the fall of Mubarak, but more intensely since the 2013 coup, the military have actively engaged in filling the online void that Mubarak left behind and have clearly learned from his regime's 'mistakes'. The military overturned the balance in their favour in relation to the internet as a political space in a very short period of time. First, by investing in the e-committees business with the purpose of disinformation and influencing online public opinion. Second, and in parallel, by investing in e-surveillance technologies, which were mostly imported from 'established democracies'. As a punishment mechanism for those electronically surveilled and found 'guilty' of expressing their critical views, a 'legal arsenal' was introduced. Not only for the punishment of these voices, but also for making an example of them and discouraging others from trying to act similarly. This is in addition to trying to give a less damaged image of the military as the rulers of Egypt, locally and internationally, as human rights violators. The youth of Egypt, which constitutes the majority of the population, might have chosen silence, but relatively though, as there is an increase in the use of sour humour against the ruling elites in the digital space.[147]

The Fall of Mubarak and Morsi: A Review of News Coverage

The media carries out an important role in conveying political and economic discourses to the public across the world. Egypt's private media – and those who own it – are in no different a position. Journalists everywhere have developed countless ways to frame the news. The most commonly used themes include emphasizing conflict, the emotional aspect of a story, or grim economic consequences. These frames can promote a definition of a particular problem, causal interpretation or moral evaluation,[1] and thus influence debate and structure political outcomes. This chapter will show that news production is heavily influenced by the political and business interests of the owners of private newspapers.[2] Nevertheless, regardless of the influence of news coverage on the public, we still have to examine the issue case by case to learn how such influence prevails within certain news agendas. Each case has the potential to teach us how decision-makers – including members of the business elite in Egypt – formulate their responses to both the news agendas that they control and the public that they target.[3] In this context, Sahar Khamis finds that the 'hybridization, uniqueness, and complexity of specific media cases, as by-products of their specific historical, cultural, and political contexts', which allows us to evaluate each case based on its 'own unique features, indigenous qualities, and dynamic transformations'.[4] Within the same context, the instrumental character of media becomes obvious, not only when one investigates the relationships between the owners of the media and the ruling elites, but also when one considers the implications of the published material.[5] This goes in line with this book's approached to studying media, CPE, which places an emphasis on the unequal distribution of power, whereby such inequalities are sustained and reproduced. The concept of reproducing power is also important to understanding how the business elite and 'Mubarak's state' managed to survive the 2011 uprising and launch a comeback in support of the military in their coup of 2013.

The 'critical' aspect of CPE is usefully broad and encompassing, but it also has distinctive practices and values of critique in intellectual enquiry such as questioning, interrogating and challenging the adequacy of explanations of phenomena,[6] which are suitable for analysing news content in a country undergoing challenges between revolutionary and counter-revolutionary powers. Generally speaking, the vast domain of CPE stands out with its focus on studying a wide array of media influences on a society which play a central role in the successful maintenance of control and hegemonic consolidation.[7] This may be observed in the news produced during each period of focus in this chapter.

On 24 July 2013, *al-Masry al-Youm* published a news article with the headline 'Tamarod: Demonstrations on Friday to Mandate the Army to Stop Civil War'. It is clear that this headline and many similarly dramatic ones sent strong messages to the public. Hence, alongside following a critical approach in understanding the hegemony of Egypt's private media, framing analysis is a suitable and complementary approach to understand this type of content. Many scholars agree that framing analysis provides a direct and reliable interpretation of the role of certain media in shaping ideas and public views about current affairs, and also tendencies of responses to issues covered.[8] In 1974, Erving Goffman explained that frames are basic mechanisms of understanding what is happening in a society and trying to make sense of events that occur. This conceives the media as a tool used to form public opinion and determine individuals' trends and ideologies.[9] The press particularly plays an effective role in forming public opinion, where it has become a social necessity.[10] It has also been argued that journalists operate within a set of assumptions, or frames, which provide a way of organizing and filtering the information that they receive, and in turn they transmit this as news.[11] In news framing, a journalist might redesign an event in terms of using certain words, meanings and images to represent a window for recipients to see the world.[12] Or, in other words, journalists highlight certain parts of reality and restrict or tune down the rest of it while they are producing what they think is news. To sum this up, since frames constitute 'centrally organizing ideas or storylines that provide meaning to an unfolding strip of events',[13] they are essential for understanding the scope of this chapter, which examines the way in which the news media was 'telling the story' of the series of critical events from the uprising to the coup, in support of both of which millions marched on the streets, despite the contradictions in cause.

Following on from the foundational discussions and analysis of the political economy of the Egyptian media in previous chapters, this chapter takes a step back to the eve of the uprising in 2011 and provides a few snapshots of events and how they were covered in the news. This provides us with an applied understanding of the political, social and economic power relations discussed earlier in the book, between society, the civilian-military political elite, and the business elite, all in relation to news production. The chapter focuses on coverage of the private print press and starts by providing a news review of the first eighteen days of the uprising, which resulted in Mubarak's fall. It then introduces a review of major events and their coverage in the period immediately following Mubarak, which was directly under the rule of the SCAF in intersection with the Muslim Brotherhood's short rise to power. It then investigates the emergence of the Tamarod movement, which led popular support for the 2013 coup. In applying a framing analysis as discussed earlier, this chapter will then provide a study of the 112 days of news coverage around the period of the coup and discuss its findings.[14] In intersection with the success of the coup and the fall of Morsi and the Muslim Brotherhood, the chapter introduces one final news review that reflects on how al-Sisi was presented by the private press as 'the saviour', which brings us back to the conclusions of previous chapters regarding the military, who are now almost in full control of the public space, both physical and virtual.

A review of the coverage of the uprising and Mubarak's fall

As mentioned earlier, the first reaction of state media was to ignore and downplay the events of the uprising. When these events escalated further than could be manipulated by the state-media narrative, they switched to scare tactics. A short time after the failed tactical disappearance of the police from the streets across the country on the night of the 'Friday of Rage'[15] – 28 January

The Political Economy of Egyptian Media

2011 – the state media, television and newspapers heavily focused on the theme of chaos and what they called 'foreign agendas';[16] this did not work either. Many people organized themselves in neighbourhood watch groups called *legan shaabeya* (popular committees), which prevented this narrative of chaos while the police were absent. The 'foreign agendas' narrative, which focused on the idea that 'external elements' were behind all protests in order to 'burn Egypt',[17] also failed. Among the powers accused of involvement in the accelerating events were Israel, Iran, Hezbollah, Hamas, the EU, the US and some other randomly selected countries, which caused people to be unconvinced of the state's narrative.

Leila Fadel and Ernesto Londoño wrote that 'a day after pro-Mubarak forces were unleashed into Tahrir Square [...] inciting a bloody battle that left thousands wounded, *al-Ahram* reported on its front page that millions of government supporters had flooded the streets, grossly exaggerating their numbers. State television called the anti-Mubarak demonstrators "destabilizing" forces and accused foreign powers of instigating instability'.[18] The public very quickly ridiculed this narrative by spreading the joke that Egypt had finally succeeded in bringing Israel, Iran, the US, Hamas and Hezbollah all together. The private press however was challenged to find a convincing narrative that did not too obviously contradict with that of the state, and at the same time did not look unconvincing to its audiences. *Al-Shourouk*[19] and *al-Dostor* positioned themselves differently in comparison to most other private newspapers. They deliberately placed themselves far from the state media narrative during this period. Reda recalled: 'We survived all pressures after the first two days, where the main and only one pressure at that time [had been] Mubarak's regime, other pressures were loose. So, I guess we had the best time in that period'.[20]

As for *al-Masry al-Youm*, it had already enjoyed a significant margin for critical news allowed by the authorities since its foundation in 2004. This relative freedom, which had lasted for seven years prior to the uprising, had in turn developed a culture of relatively solid practice of (some) freedom among the journalists and editors working for the newspaper. This freedom was difficult to take away in order to force them to adopt the simplistic state narrative of news. However, it seems that the management – both business and editorial – applied some pressure and created some strategic distance from the breaking events in order to protect themselves from losing journalists and readers, on the one hand, and whatever remained of their connections with Mubarak's regime on the other.

On 24 January, the day before the planned marches that had been called for on Facebook, *al-Masry al-Youm* and *al-Shorouk* opened with lead stories about the discovery of evidence by the Ministry of the Interior regarding 'terrorist' connections to the bombing of All Saints church in Alexandria,[21] which had happened on New Year's Eve. *Al-Masry al-Youm*'s headline was 'Al-Adly Reveals: Clear Evidence that "Palestinian Islamic Army" behind "All Saints" Bombing'. Similarly, *al-Shorouk*'s headline on the same day was 'Suspect Behind the Planning of All Saints Church Bombing Arrested'. The story, however, failed to distract attention from the planned events of 25 January or from the motivation for the uprising spread from Tunisia to Egypt, despite the story's significance and the fact that it had been top news from the time that the bombings had occurred three weeks earlier, up until 25 January. However, these headlines still met both newspapers' expectations of introducing serious and well-presented news, while consciously keeping the planned protests at a low profile. It was however on the 25 January, and due to the failure of distracting the public from the planned protests the day before, that both newspapers raised the profile of the protests. *Al-Masry al-Youm*'s lead story was titled 'Early Rehearsal for the "Day of Rage", 12 Protests in Cairo and other Governorates Demanding Jobs, Wage Increases and Compensation'. *Al-Shorouk*'s leading headline was 'The Day of Rage', which was not intended as the actual 'Day of Rage' of 28 January but might have accidentally inspired the name. This type of headline did not ridicule the papers' audiences through not discussing the protests or ignoring them on the same day that they were planned to take place, but at the same time, they did not mention a word about torture or the police brutality which had led to the brutal death of Khaled Saeed, whose tragedy was a significant reason behind the planned protests. These lead stories show that the private press was keen to give space in their news agendas to the protests that the public were anticipating and paying attention to. They cleverly did so by tying the day's earlier small protests to purely economic demands, unrelated to police brutality.

On 25 January, the protest was massive. Instead of a few hundred, the numbers were at least in the tens of thousands. The protesters managed to storm into Tahrir Square, a fortress where no significant protests had been allowed for a very long time. As a result, the private press could no longer downplay the events. Nour said: 'Of course there were business and security power relations that affected the coverage during that time. The owners have their economic interests in addition to their security relations that serve those interests as well'.[22] In its reporting the next day *al-Masry al-Youm* insisted on sticking to the economic narrative. By doing so it did not produce false news, but it undermined the violence and police brutality. *Al-Shorouk*, however, was slightly closer to the reality of the street, although it was not as influential as *al-Masry al-Youm*, nor as well connected to the political and economic power groups. On 26 January *al-Masry al-Youm*'s leading story was titled: 'Warning: Thousands Protest against Poverty, Unemployment, High Prices, Corruption, and Demand Departure of the Government'. As for *al-Shorouk*, it ran with 'Angry Egypt in the Street'. The lead stories were again true and did not contain false information. However, they, especially *al-Masry al-Youm*, emphasized the same economic perspective of the events and continued to avoid police brutality or to mention casualties. They played the same game of Egypt's marginal media freedom since 2004 well, as discussed in Chapter Two, which gave them space to blame the government (the cabinet) but not Mubarak or those close to him.

The graphic pictures and videos that flooded social media on Friday 28 January, followed by the disappearance of the police all over the country towards the end of the day, brought a significant strategic change in the position of *al-Masry al-Youm* and *al-Shorouk* towards the breaking events and the political elite. On 30 January, *al-Masry al-Youm* led with 'Conspiracy by the Interior to Create Chaos', while *al-Shorouk* led with 'The People Advance and Mubarak Retreats'. For some reason, with these lead stories the two newspapers decided for the first time to take a clear position against the interior ministry, marking the beginning of their demonization during that period and for at least two years to come. This is in contrast to the position taken during the five days prior – especially in the case of *al-Masry al-Youm*, as we can see from their lead story. It seems that this was a 'decision from above' by the owners and their connections within the political elite, giving the green light to attack the interior ministry. Probably very few, such as Magdy al-Gallad, with their high-profile connections to the elites, can have access to such knowledge. It was clear from that day, judging from the published press, that the political elite had decided to abandon the interior ministry, reasoning that changing the minister Habib al-Adly and reshuffling its administration would do the job and the protesters would go home. However, this did not work, as the following days showed. The protesters' demands were escalating by the day in reaction to the state's violence and obvious state media manipulation.

By 1 February it was clear that *al-Masry al-Youm* remained a well-read newspaper and a relatively trusted source of news as a second option after social media and Al Jazeera. *Al-Shorouk* was also growing more popular, but it was also clear that there was a shift in connections and loyalties. By focusing on the development of the two newspapers' editorial policies, we can see that after taking a position against the interior and the government of Ahmed Nazif, who was loyal to Gamal Mubarak as discussed in Chapter Two, they started enjoying a stronger connection to the military. Wesam described this period, saying 'A status of political confusion prevailed, and no one knew where the events were heading. Hence the coverage was extremely neutral. However, soon afterwards control was regained, and coverage fell in line with whatever power might seem to be stronger than the other'.[23] It seems that the military used both newspapers, now trusted by an angry public, as a means of communicating certain political messages. This was clear when seeing the highly recognized Nasserist and pro-military intellectual Mohamed Hassanein Heikal[24] making it into lead stories in both newspapers on 1 February. He gave an exclusive interview to *al-Masry al-Youm* and a lengthy opinion piece for *al-Shorouk*. The former's lead headline was: 'Mohamed Hassanein Heikal in an Exclusive Interview for al-Masry al-Youm: It is Impossible for the Army to Shoot One Bullet at Citizens, and Placing Military Forces in Confrontation with the People is Suicide.' As for *al-Shourouk*, it led with 'Heikal Speaks About What is Happening in Egypt Now'. It is significant that besides Heikal being known as a Nasserist supporter of the military, he was a person who very rarely communicated with any sort of media, local or international, since the early 1980s. He was also openly critical of Mubarak and his policies. In turn, it was known in the media and political spheres that Mubarak did not like him, especially when Heikal had talked critically about him on Al Jazeera a few years earlier in his briefly broadcast high-profile TV programme *Ma'a Heikal* (With Heikal).

On 2 February both newspapers allowed themselves again to be messengers to promote calm on the streets. *Al-Masry al-Youm* led with 'Mubarak Promises

Not to Run for Presidency, Peaceful Transition of Authority, Changing [Constitutional] Articles 76 and 77, Investigating Who Caused the Security Chaos and Prosecuting the Corrupt'. *Al-Shorouk* briefly led with 'Mubarak: I Won't Run for a New Term'. Mubarak's decisions, which were part of his speech the day before, were introduced in a way to seem firmer and clearer than Mubarak's actual rather more flexible and loose promises given in the same speech. This shows that the two newspapers, besides being used again to convey a message to calm the people, both started to understand that Mubarak might not be taking decisions alone and that there might be stronger forces at work at that moment. At the end of the day, the newspapers maintained their image as trusted and engaged sources of news. This was not such a challenge at that moment however, as the state media then had already become the joke of the country.

As much as there was a shift by both newspapers in terms of their connections within the political elite and leaning towards the military while protecting their readership, it seems that by 3 February the editorial management of both newspapers realized – or were told – that Mubarak was about to fall for certain. Alaa said directly: 'Normally authorities are the ones determining editorial lines. However, during January [2011] the street interfered, and events escalated in a way that no one could have ignored. And newspapers were at times written following the authorities' standards, and at other times the streets', which was the main player at that time. And here came the confusion. This remained until the military and [some businessmen] took their decision to stand with the street against Mubarak's rule'.[25] On 3 February, *al-Masry al-Youm* led with 'Tahrir Turns into a Warzone, Homeland Demands Calm', while *al-Shorouk* led with 'Heikal Writes: First Complete Egyptian Revolution in Modern History'. Here, *al-Masry al-Youm* remained a messenger for the political and militarily elites. However, for the first time in ten days it clearly recognized the violence perpetrated directly by Mubarak's state. It also seems that they still used the fear tactic through pictures of buildings on fire and did not mention a word about how the military, alongside the riot police, used violence against protesters or how they allowed the attackers of the Camel Battle pass,[26] quite absurdly riding camels and bearing swords, to Tahrir Square to kill and assault protesters, who were already under siege imposed by the army. *Al-Masry al-Youm* did not mention any of these details and insisted on a positive portrayal of the military. Another delayed development in *al-Masry al-Youm*'s editorial policy was switching terms from *mothahara* (protest) to *milioneya* ('one-million' march) on 5 February. *Al-Masry al-Youm* led with 'New Milioneya Message: Departure First', and *al-Shorouk* with 'Egypt Changed'. This was the twelfth day of the uprising, by which time a number of *milioneyas* had already occurred following 28 January. The relatively less influential *al-Shorouk* had however mentioned the term earlier in a few news stories.

On 7 February, day fourteen of the uprising and long after hundreds had already been killed and thousands injured, another term of glorification was introduced. *Al-Masry al-Youm* started using the term *Shaheed* (martyr) for those killed during confrontations with the police and Mubarak's *baltageya* (civilian thugs). *Al-Shorouk*, as the voice of a publishing house, had the tendency to use short and poetic lead story headlines regarding the end of the eighteen-day protests. On that day, *al-Masry al-Youm* led with 'Egypt Prays for the Martyrs of Freedom', and *al-Shorouk* with 'Religion for God and the Square for All'. Yet another term was introduced on 8 February, labelling those in Tahrir Square and in other occupied spaces across the country as 'revolutionaries' instead of 'protesters'. *Al-Masry al-Youm* led on that day with 'The Revolutionaries of Tahrir Demand the Return of Stolen Finances', and *al-Shorouk* led with 'The Prosecutor Accuses Habib al-Adly of Deliberately Killing Protesters'. (This is similar to how 'casualties' were transformed by *al-Masry al-Youm* into 'martyrs' in the previously mentioned headline 'Egypt Prays for the Martyrs of Freedom'.) However, *al-Shorouk* on the same day led with a more professional headline, keeping the term 'protesters'.

It seems that the private press had suspected since the day of the Camel Battle that Mubarak would leave, and that the army was waiting to see the impact of this attack on the protesters in order to take a final decision regarding their old leader, hence the pragmatic private press knew who to ally with. Certainly, this was not Mubarak nor his close circle, or at least the part of it that was not on good terms with the military. Both *al-Masry al-Youm*, and *al-Shorou*k following that, knew their position. They maintained their high readership, while at the same time they worked to protect their owners' good relations with the military by glorifying them. At the same time, both newspapers, although *al-Masry al-Youm* to a greater degree, saw no harm in glorifying the uprising and its 'martyrs'. It was clear that the protesters were the winners for at least a week before Mubarak's exit from office, and it was only a matter of time. This does not contradict with the norms of the region, of which Egypt is an important part, where elites take political sides and define the uprisings and their outcomes in their own way in their respective state and private media.[27] In this sense, regardless of the archaic position of the Egyptian state media, the private media introduced a considerable challenge to the discursive hegemony of the authoritarian regime and fuelled a transformation,[28] even if it was within a framework of reshuffling power structures and adjusting alliances and meant changing the editorial lines day by day at a moment of uncertainty, as was the case with Egypt's private media, according to Tayseer.[29] These changing lines are what probably caused Hisham to evaluate the coverage of the newspaper he founded, *al-Masry al-Youm*, during these eighteen days as 'weak' although he admitted that there were a few good days.[30] In what appeared to be an announcement of a new era, on 12 February, the day following Mubarak's fall, both newspapers led with emotional home pages also glorifying the revolution and the military. *Al-Masry al-Youm* ran with 'The People Willed it and Brought the Regime Down' and *al-Shorouk* with 'And the People Won' in a large font.

A review of the coverage of the period following Mubarak's fall

Following the fall of Mubarak, it was expected that a fundamental change in the cultures of the managements of state institutions, as well as among those working for them, would occur. The need for this was clearer in the context of state media than that of other state institutions. The Ministry of the Interior and other ministries may have continued to operate after the revolution as they did before, at least with a lower profile, with almost the same hierarchies and lines of authority kept from the public. The state media, now directly controlled by SCAF through al-Sisi (unofficially though) who remained as the head of Military Intelligence,[31] continued its work in its tall cylindrical building on the Nile that is a monument and symbol of state centralization, with its transmissions and hence its opinions in full view.[32]

The private media, however, quickly turned 'revolutionary', in the sense that they adopted the narrative that the uprising had been necessary to bring down Mubarak, the 'corrupt tyrant'. This was a position that most of them did not take, or did not clearly take, until the moment when his ouster appeared unavoidable a few days before it was announced on state television on 11 February 2011. The private media, and later the state media, were challenged by constant coverage from outlets like Al Jazeera, which had cameras with almost 24/7 live broadcasting from Tahrir. Al Jazeera also ran live commentaries by high-profile figures like the pan-Arab nationalist Azmi Bishara and the Islamist and pro-Muslim Brotherhood scholar Yusuf al-Qaradawi, who were both very critical of Mubarak and his legacy, and were also based in Doha. Their job, and that of other figures, was to keep the momentum of the uprising going. They both managed to draw the attention of audiences with secular and religious backgrounds towards a unified goal.

Social media also helped shape the private press coverage as these outlets could see clearly how ordinary people were talking about the uprising outside the traditional media. Additionally, interviews by Western media such as CNN and the BBC (to a much lesser degree in comparison with Al Jazeera's intense live coverage) with so-called 'media darlings'[33] and young English-speaking Egyptians such as Gigi Ibrahim, Mohamed Waked and many others, who were all prominent activist faces, forced the Egyptian media to take notice and follow suit. *Al-Masry al-Youm* and other private newspapers hired bloggers and popular social media figures for their newly established social media departments soon after Mubarak's fall, and even gave them fixed columns to write weekly opinion pieces in traditional print format.

This section will focus on the editorial lines of *al-Masry al-Youm* and *al-Watan* (launched in May 2012 and quickly becoming a top newspaper) following Mubarak's fall, looking at a few headlines from 2011 and 2012, when Egypt was directly ruled by the SCAF, until the beginnings of Morsi's rule, which was also shared with the SCAF. As mentioned earlier, this chapter will later provide a deeper analysis of the whole period (112 days) of the Tamarod campaign against Morsi leading to the 2013 coup and Morsi's fall.

As mentioned in the previous section, *al-Masry al-Youm* started the new era of post-Mubarak Egypt with the emotional headline: 'The People Willed it and Brought the Regime Down'. This was similar to almost every other private and even state-run newspaper in the country. They all anticipated the rise of the Muslim Brotherhood to power, especially after the military gave them the green light. Ihsan said: 'Some changes happened with the arrival of the Brotherhood as a ruling power. Most newspapers made significant shifts, especially the state-run ones, which provided the brothers with support, since they had become the rulers'.[34] This does not mean that the period following Mubarak's fall was clear and editorially settled with a new and confident news agenda, however. The year 2011 was confusing to almost every media outlet, as they had to consider re-drawing editorial red lines and power loyalties. *Al-Masry al-Youm* was a complex example of this confusion, given its importance as a highly influential and widely circulated newspaper that also had strong connections to different power groups in the country. However, there were a few settled themes, considering their editorial agenda: the promotion of 'stability', the notion that 'the revolution is over', and the concept that the army was 'the people's protector' were all dominant themes following the fall of Mubarak. The newspaper led on 15 February with 'The Army: Workers' Protests are Dangerous for Egypt'. This was four days after Mubarak's ouster. The newspaper was promoting taking a position against workers' protests among the public. This was a message that worked in favour of both the military and the business elites with which the newspaper had strong connections. It even gave a negative name to the workers' protests calling them 'factional protests', when it led on 20 February with 'Three from the Previous Regime Behind Escalating Factional Protests'. In this lead story, and through undisclosed 'informed sources', the newspaper pushed a conspiracy theory and the demonization of workers engaging in protests. *Al-Masry al-Youm* associated these with figures from the old regime, which at that moment was a symbol of 'evil'. Unsurprisingly, the three names behind the so-called 'factional protests' were never mentioned or disclosed later. On 20 March, the newspaper then led with 'The Day of Democracy, Tearing Down the Illusions of Tyranny'. With this, the newspaper was pushing the notion that the uprising was 'successful and already over'. This was the day after a referendum on the first constitutional declaration,[35] which was clearly a plan to protect whatever was left from the old regime. The editor decided that 'full democracy' had then been achieved. The newspaper totally disregarded military and Muslim

Brotherhood propaganda, pushing the people to vote 'Yes' – which they both succeeded in achieving.

As mentioned earlier regarding the editorial confusion of 2011, *al-Masry al-Youm* was clear in its position towards the military as the top political controller in the country, and towards the business elite that the newspaper's owners represented, or at least those who did not have overly open connections to Mubarak's regime. However, there was obvious confusion regarding the 'old' and the 'new' guard, discussed in Chapter Two, and how to distinguish between them, or to what degree the newspaper was free to publish critical or scandalous news about them. On 30 March, the newspaper led with 'Sources: Nazif and Ibrahim Suleiman to be Prosecuted within Hours'. It was a clear and easy editorial move for *al-Masry al-Youm* to run with this headline on that day. Prime Minister Ahmed Nazif and Housing Minister Ibrahim Suleiman both belonged to the new guard, Gamal's close circle of business-political support that the army decided to abandon and hold responsible for the wrongdoings of Mubarak's regime. Here the undisclosed 'sources' appear again; interestingly the newspaper knew in advance about their arrest, which is a sign of coordination with the military, the only institution in control of the country by that time.

Similar stories were published during this period, giving extensive news space to the shameful arrests of members of the new guard before they happened. The army seemed to be giving the media the chance to be present at the arrests in exchange for excessive coverage, sending a message to the public that 'there is no place for corruption in new Egypt'. This worked well, and the public were satisfied with the direction of change for a while. A month later we can notice a subtle but important editorial difference in covering the same topic of the corruption of Mubarak's elite. On 5 April, the newspaper led with 'The Revolution's Demands on the Way: Asset Freezing of the Big Three', and on 12 April, with 'Al-Sherif Detained for 15 Days for Investigations, Mubarak and his Two Sons Notified of Investigation in Sharm Al-Sheikh'. The two lead stories concerning the arrest of business and political figures in relation to corruption cases were significantly different from those relating to figures like Nazif and the group loyal to Gamal. This time they belonged to the old guard, which was closer to Mubarak than to his son and had no direct connection with inheriting his father's rule. It seems that the army had no intention of sacrificing the old guard as had happened previously with the new guard, who were greatly and deliberately shamed in the media in general and *al-Masry al-Youm* in particular. However, the old guard arrests came as the result of mounting street pressure on the military. It clearly appears, while looking through the news published about the old guard, that the newspaper did not know about their arrests from their so-called informed sources, as was the case with the new guard. The newspaper was also careful not to scandalize them in the same way. They simply followed the street's beat in this kind of story without attempting to make news hits. The private media's following of the street beat indicates its status of disorientation, or sometimes freedom, if we compare the periods before and after Mubarak's fall. Reda described this as 'A huge difference. All power structures who [were] always trying to control the press were gone. So, I think, with more than twenty years [of experience] in the field [I would say] that it was the golden age, no red lines, no forbidden subjects, no one was sacred'.[36] *Al-Masry al-Youm* then freely chose not to conduct any special coverage or provide classified information about the old guard, and simply to just reflect the street's response of disrespect towards these figures and the happiness at their arrests. By doing so, the newspaper continued to win the street's confidence in their editorial line and the way they covered news 'in favour' of the public and their uprising. This was happening without making the military or other remnants of Mubarak's regime too angry, as a precautionary tactic, since it was an unpredictable period.

Later in 2012, the editorial positioning of Mubarak as an ousted and imprisoned figure, and the Muslim Brotherhood and Morsi became clearer in the newly-founded and Egypt's richest newspaper, *al-Watan*. The newspaper appeared cautiously loyal to Mubarak, and hostile to Morsi and his Brotherhood, while the army was always praised. As a loyalist to Mubarak, the newspaper was carefully reprising a positive image of him and his family. The editorial line seemed to be anti-revolutionary. *Al-Masry al-Youm*, however, continued to sound 'revolutionary'. It was a rather difficult task to re-build Mubarak's reputation, as this entailed a big risk of the newspaper failing its goal of being a dominant and mainstream news outlet. However, *al-Watan* very quickly succeeded in becoming the second most circulated newspaper in the country after *al-Masry al-Youm* – according to Egyptian media circles, rather than from official figures, which are unreliable.

On 30 *May al-Watan* published 'Mubarak's Trial: The President's Cook: I feel Sad for His Excellency' and on 5 June 'Mubarak's Health Deteriorates … Medical Source: "He has Turned into Skin on Bones"'. In both headlines published just after the launch of al-Watan, the newspaper is clearly, but carefully, drawing an image of Mubarak as a sick old man who should be mercifully forgiven. It seemed like the newspaper was attempting to create sympathy among its readers. Interestingly, the editors mention Mubarak using the term 'former president', not 'ousted president' as most other private newspapers including *al-Masry al-Youm* did. Promoting a positive image of Mubarak was not an easy task, especially in 2012, when his ouster and the memories of his regime's oppression and violensce were still fresh in people's minds. *Al-Watan* was highly criticized for its position towards Mubarak and was labelled a *foloul* (remnants [of Mubarak's regime]) or anti-revolutionary newspaper. Therefore, the editors every now and then attempted to prove otherwise by publishing something negative about Mubarak to counter the paper's counter-revolutionary image. On 31 May, *al-Watan* published 'Mubarak's Trial: A People Winning and a Tyrant Waiting'. By doing so, the newspaper was acting as if it were on the side of the uprising in response to mounting accusations of being pro-Mubarak and anti-revolutionary. They thus called him a 'tyrant' in this rare piece. Interestingly, these tactics worked, and people continued to buy the newspaper until it reinforced its position as a top news source in the country, which other media would, in turn, use as a source.

From another perspective, the editorial line of *al-Watan* was clearly against the Muslim Brotherhood. Today's style guide for the newspaper no longer refers to the Muslim Brotherhood by name. The paper literally calls them *al-Irhabeya*[37] (the Terrorist [Group]). However, in 2012 this was still impossible, since the group were still in power. Nevertheless, from the beginning and even under the Brotherhood's rule, *al-Watan*'s editorial agenda focused on two themes regarding the Muslim Brotherhood, which were to ridicule and to demonize them. In terms of ridicule, on 24 May *al-Watan* published: 'The Brotherhood to a Voter: If You Don't Vote for Morsi, God Will Take Back Your Motorbike', and on 20 July it published: 'Brotherhood Songs: No to Love, No to the Wife, Yes to Morsi'. These two headlines appear to make the Muslim Brotherhood seem exaggeratedly ridiculous and backward. Interestingly, this worked, and the newspaper saw its readership increase, and TV talk shows started quoting their news, and the Brotherhood, in any case, were not acting politically in favour of the uprising or the public's expectations. While resentment of their rule was growing, many readers found this kind of story appealing. In terms of *al-Watan*'s demonization of the Muslim Brotherhood, on 31 July the paper published 'Khalid Youssef: The Brotherhood is More Capitalist than Ahmed Ezz and Will Do Worse to Us than Hitler Did', and on 11 August, it published 'The Brotherhood Continues with Terrorism ... Pro-Shater [Facebook] Page: Al-Watan is Next'. These two headlines illustrate the second strategy of building and magnifying fear among the public towards the Muslim Brotherhood by demonizing them. The newspaper used public figures, politicians and artists who were known opponents of Mubarak or at least who did not have a clear association with him in order to convey a message of fear and demonization in their own words, not the newspaper's.

Regardless of aggressive news manipulation and bias in the private Egyptian press, some research shows that the press did cover the political sphere substantially in the months following the uprising, and crossed some of the boundaries that had formed under the previous authoritarian regime of Mubarak. Newspapers such as *al-Masry al-Youm* readily responded to the dissolution of 'red lines' with a sharp rise in coverage of topics that had been formerly off limits. Opposition protests that reflected this growing public sphere were indeed recorded and disseminated in the press.[38] However, the media and journalists also became partially responsible for the incomparably worse situation than before Mubarak's fall in several ways. They heated and radically polarized public opinion during the period under Morsi. Egyptian public opinion, once united in an anti-authoritarian movement against Mubarak, left the consensus behind and rallied behind antagonizing camps. It seemed as if the ground rules of democracy were ignored. While Islamists disrespected the secular political players, the latter showed contempt for elections and the peoples' vote whenever that favoured Islamist parties, parliaments or presidents.[39] Controlling this divided landscape became a major political dilemma between the different political forces in Egypt. The extremely polemic tone adopted by journalists, of being reverential towards their 'ideological friends' and scathing towards their 'ideological enemies', extended to the dissemination of all kinds of rumours and misinformation, creating great confusion among the public. From this perspective, the emergence of an aggressive radical/oppositional style of journalism against the Muslim Brotherhood can be explained more as an expression of 'collaboration' with the traditional political and military elites than a deliberate strategy to critically 'monitor' the new regime of the Muslim Brotherhood.[40] This in itself was one of the biggest services the private media provided to the military and their takeover of the entire political sphere in the months to follow, going further even than their already dominant position.

The emergence of Tamarod[41]

'Thank You for Rebelling! The 30 June Revolution Succeeded Thanks to You.' This was the only text that could be found on the Tamarod (Rebel) movement official website (tamarod.com) for about a year after the coup of 2013. No forms, arguments, explanations or demands could be found. In fact, the data and information that had existed on the movement's website before the coup was deleted straight after it succeeded. Now the website itself no longer exists and the domain name is currently on offer for sale.

Firstly, to introduce Tamarod: this was an opposition youth movement founded on 26 April 2013, initially to 'withdraw confidence' from Morsi and to call for early presidential elections. The movement had the original idea of inviting ordinary citizens to sign an official petition of 'withdrawal of confidence', aimed at attaining a large number of signatures. The objective was to gather sufficient signatures that would outweigh the total votes Morsi had received in the 2012 presidential elections. The campaign was planned to end on 30 June, the first anniversary of Morsi's presidency. Its co-founder and spokesperson Mahmoud Badr – later a military-supported public figure – declared that the movement had managed to collect 22 million signatures calling for the withdrawal of confidence, which was around 10 million more than the number of votes Morsi received in 2012. Not a single attempt to investigate this figure has been documented since it was official announcement by the movement on 30 June.

In addition to the expected vocal criticism and hostility against Tamarod by the Muslim Brotherhood and their supporters since its launch, it was observed that following the 3 July military coup, non-Islamist voices of suspicion and criticism started to be heard across the country and the region accusing the movement of having been staged and funded to facilitate the military coup that quickly followed.[42] Later, two of the movement's founders were selected to join the committee tasked with re-writing the constitution, which only reinforced these suspicions. In a story published by France24 – Arabic Service on their news portal on 26 June 2013, four days before the big day, reporter Houssein Emara copied the following passage from the movement's Facebook page:

> We [the Egyptian people] are obliged to rebel given the country's deterioration economically and politically following the arrival of the Muslim Brotherhood Group to rule the country with their president, Mohamed Morsi, who has disturbed all balances of justice and completely ignored the revolution and the Egyptian people's will, as if the revolution did not happen. The picture is now clear to the whole world that the Egyptian regime has moved from one gang [Mubarak's] to another, and that the revolution has failed to achieve its goals and failed to fulfil the dreams of those who sacrificed for it in order to have a home that enjoys national independence, freedom and social justice, after the revolution has become controlled by traitors.[43]

As with their website, the above Tamarod Facebook page no longer exists. While many other Tamarod pages have mushroomed over the internet, none of them has this specific passage. However, it is easy to find this exact text on other websites through a Google search. It may be that the movement had to remove such an idealist and democracy-promoting campaign from their website and Facebook page(s). After all, what happened merely three days after 30 June was the exact opposite of what they had called for or promised to achieve.

During his tenure, Morsi took several actions (such as his supra-constitutional declaration in November 2012 which he quickly withdrew) that fuelled the discontent against him and the Muslim Brotherhood. Such actions made him an easy target for most political groups, revolutionary and counter-revolutionary, except for a few sympathetic Islamist ones. The Salafist al-Nour Party was strongly in support of Tamarod. Later, the party's position against the Muslim Brotherhood became clear as they allied with the army, supported the coup and provided it with religious legitimacy. Ahmed Abdo, one of

Tamarod's leading co-founders, told France24: 'The movement will head to the High Constitutional Court in order to submit those signatures, demand it to withdraw confidence from President Mohamed Morsi, and announce running early presidential elections'. He also added that this would be according to Article One in the Egyptian Constitution [ironically written a few months earlier by a committee largely dominated by the Muslim Brotherhood], which states: 'The people are the source of authority'.[44] Abdo explained that the movement had a large legal team that included Khalid Ali – a former presidential candidate with a revolutionary background – and headed by the President of the Lawyers' Syndicate, Sameh Ashour, in order to observe all legal procedures of the campaign and guarantee smooth dealing with the High Constitutional Court and 'examining signatures' authenticity'.[45] However, this supposed plan – which was promoted before 30 June – was never implemented or even mentioned following the coup. This puts the legitimacy of Tamarod and – and the legitimacy of the announcement of having collected 22 million signatures – in serious question

Looking collectively at the respondents' opinions in this book to the issue of Tamarod, they seem to have valid disagreements in their judgement as to the movement's relation to the army. One way or another, there seems to be consensus in terms of noting a certain connection between Tamarod and the military. However, they differ in their expression or assumptions regarding what this connection was like or when exactly it started. Ihsan offered his strong opinion that the Tamarod movement was totally controlled from the beginning, saying: 'I believe that it was highly supported financially and organizationally by factions of the deep state: police, intelligence, businessmen and media'.[46] All are directly and indirectly controlled by the military, as discussed in earlier chapters. Tamam clearly opined that Tamarod is 100 per cent manufactured, 'does not have one ounce of goodwill', and that they are the creation of whoever was behind the coup. Tamam, however, also added that this does not contradict the fact that people who went out on 30 June to support 'these kids' genuinely believed in them.[47] Although Aseel could not confirm that Tamarod was a 'conspiracy' from the beginning, they agreed that the mass support Tamarod received was also genuine, due to the deteriorating political situation and the mistakes of the Muslim Brotherhood, which the military used to their advantage.[48]

Reflecting on the complex issue of Tamarod, albeit cautiously, the scenario of full military control over Tamarod from the beginning of their campaign seems impossible to be sure of. More careful thought might lean towards seeing Tamarod as a movement that was somehow assumed or used by the military following its success in creating popularity among the public. Alaa and Reda were also very clear in denying the possibility that Tamarod was controlled by the military from the beginning, and they believed that it later fell under military control.[49] In support of this point of view are a few news stories that were published mainly during May and early June 2013, within approximately the first month following the movement's birth. The first was by *al-Watan* on 12 May with the headline: 'Cairo University Students Remember the Revolution's Martyrs and State Security Arrests Tamarod Members'. The second is by *al-Masry al-Youm* on 22 May with the headline: 'Two Tamarod Members Detained for Four Days for Assaulting 8 Policemen in Sadat Metro Stop'. The third is again by *al-Watan* on 6 June with the headline: 'Tamarod is Offered to Meet with the Interior Minister and Responds: We Won't Sit with a "Murderer"'.

Based on the responses of experts in this book and the above selection of stories, I suggest that coordination between Tamarod and the military started at some point after the first week of June, three weeks before the 30 June mass protests occurred. Here we have to remember that the Ministry of Interior was controlled by the Supreme Council of Armed Forces (SCAF) since Mubarak's fall, who openly and directly appointed several interior ministers one after the other. Therefore, having Tamarod members targeted by the police and refusing to sit with the then Minister of Interior (Mohamed Ibrahim, who later fully supported the movement) are all signs that the military – at least not until the end of the first week of June 2013 – did not communicate or directly coordinate with Tamarod. Hence, the control of, or at least the coordination with, the movement could not have happened from the beginning. Nour also did not believe it was controlled from the beginning, saying: 'I am not sure of that. Some rumours say that it was a pure revolutionary movement [and] then some security body used it to topple Morsi. Others say that it was totally controlled by the military since the beginning. In all cases, it was used by the military to get rid of the Muslim Brotherhood, at least that is how I see it'.[50] To this day, it is debatable the degree to which Tamarod was a civilian façade for the military coup, but it is agreed that they indeed made it a wildly popular success, or as Hisham put it, they were the Trojan Horse of the coup,[51] regardless of how it started.

News framing of the coup and Morsi's fall[52]

Operating under the shadow of the aforementioned ties between the business and political elites, both civilian and military, within the private press market, Egyptian journalists struggled to incorporate facilitative normative roles in their daily practices after Mubarak's fall. According to el-Issawi and Cammaerts, the radical-oppositional role against the Muslim Brotherhood government suited them better, following which most Egyptian journalists re-assumed their traditional collaborative role in the service of the ruling military elite. Their role was understood as the need to liberate themselves from the dictates of the official discourse as well as from the interference of media owners. However, again this was not realistic due to the lack of a tradition of investigative reporting, well-founded professional skills, and the presence of a legacy of reverential journalism. As such, Egypt's private media cannot be evaluated as free or independent media.[53] In this context, and in order to trace the evolving relationship between the private press and Tamarod, this research has analysed headlines from *al-Masry al-Youm* and *al-Watan* in the period from 26 April 2013 (Tamarod's launch in Tahrir Square) until 15 August of the same year (the day following the Rab'a Events, where at least hundreds of Morsi supporters were killed by military and police forces). In this study, which was published at the end of 2019, 337 news stories by *al-Masry al-Youm* with the keyword 'Tamarod' were chosen from the newspaper's online archive, and another 345 from *al-Watan's* with the same keyword and same timeframe. A first reading of these headlines was initially applied to see what message(s) they might frame to the readers, and it was found that there were two major themes that are highly repetitive. Many of the headlines would spread 'fear' of the Muslim Brotherhood, violence and/or chaos, while others would 'promote' Tamarod and/or the army as a saviour or a solution. Here are a few examples:

> Tamarod: We Collected 22,134,465 Signatures for a Withdrawal of Confidence from Morsi
>
> Tamarod Distributes Flowers to the Police and Army in Sharm al-Sheikh

In the first headline above, published on 29 June 2013 by *al-Masry al-Youm*, we can see directly the repetition of a Tamarod statement without questioning or investigating any facts. Even the body of this news item did not contain any mention of fact-checking or suspicion regarding the 22-million figure. This remains a claim that has never been confirmed or investigated to this day. Nour comments on this, saying: 'All that I recall is reports on how fast [Tamarod] was spreading, and the number of signatures it was collecting'.[54] This headline can be portrayed as the celebration of an early victory ahead of 30 June which was the date on which mass protests were called for by Tamarod, in promotion of the 'powerful' movement. In the second headline, published on 4 July 2013 by *al-Masry al-Youm* as well, the newspaper not only promoted Tamarod and the army, but indirectly promoted the – since January 2011 – highly demonized police.

Islamist-Related Plan for Fighting Tamarod on 30 June

Tamarod: Demonstrations on Friday to Mandate the Army to Stop the Civil War

On the first reading of the sample the theme of fear was clearly present, whereby it appeared that the nature of the news produced regarding Tamarod would have a high tendency to cause fear among readers in relation to thoughts about what the Muslim Brotherhood represented as a 'violent group', based on the editorial line, and what would happen if Tamarod failed to bring their rule down. The above two headlines from *al-Masry al-Youm*, the first published on 9 June and the second on 24 July, are two examples of many within the 112 days' sample wherein fear of the Muslim Brotherhood was promoted among readers. The second headline portrays the army as the only solution, otherwise the country would supposedly drown in a civil war. I argue that many of the news items produced in this period by *al-Masry al-Youm* regarding Tamarod were aimed at making the reader feel scared of the Muslim Brotherhood and Islamists in general (the fear frame) and instilling in the reader a hope for the success of Tamarod as a lifeboat (the promotion frame). *Al-Watan* was not so different from *al-Masry al-Youm* in relation to the position that they both took towards Tamarod, the army and the Muslim Brotherhood. Regarding the promotion frame, *al-Watan* outweighed *al-Masry al-Youm* in the polishing and support that they both provided to Tamarod. The language and editorial position of *al-Watan* were more overtly in favour of the movement.

Tamarod: New Videogame Ends with 'Game Over, Morsi'

Al-Gallad: Tamarod Has Become a Global Model for Peaceful Protest. Al-Watan is as Old as the Revolutionary Tide

In the first headline, published on 21 June, *al-Watan*, in its promotion frame campaigning for Tamarod, went beyond the idea of mainly positive news. They went for what journalists loosely term 'sexy news', something that should attract significant public attention. The above-mentioned video game was in fact poorly designed and did not create significant attention as a game, in comparison to how it was portrayed by the article. *Al-Watan* did not take the time to properly produce the story but quickly made a big headline out of the game's launch. No proper information or any quotes were provided from those who might have played it. This sarcastic piece by *al-Watan* was part of a media trend of satire against the Muslim Brotherhood. The most successful example, and by far the leading one, was el-Barnameg TV show by Bassem Youssef, who was at that time known as the Jon Stewart of the Middle East and was very popular. Adel Iskandar says that the rapid decline in the Muslim Brotherhood's popularity can be comprehended through understanding the role that satire played, both online and in mainstream media.[55] Moving to the second headline, published by *al-Watan* on 3 July, does not need a complex analysis or explanation, as no biased news agenda could possibly be more biased than this. The chief editor of the newspaper, Magdy al-Gallad, stood next to Tamarod's co-founder Mahmoud Badr in the newsroom, telling the readers in a televized press conference that Tamarod is a 'global model', and that '*al-Watan* is as old as the revolution'. Many journalistic professional standards and ethics were disregarded by the editor of the newspaper himself.

Brotherhood Rehearsal of 30 June: The Brotherhood in Armed Attack against Tamarod in Alexandria – the People Fight Back, Destroy their Office

Tamarod on the Republican Guards Incident: The Brotherhood is Pushing Egypt for Civil War

The fear frame in *al-Watan*'s headlines was applied relatively similarly to the use of the frame in *al-Masry al-Youm*, however with stronger language. In the first headline above, published on 14 June, *al-Watan* exaggerated a clash that occurred in Alexandria (not officially investigated by security) and took a demonizing and overtly anti-Brotherhood position. Details of this news story were anecdotal and one-sided at best. As for the second headline, published on 9 July, again the alleged spectre of the Muslim Brotherhood bringing the country to the brink of civil war was raised, although it was Brotherhood members who were actually the ones killed by the military in that specific incident (which is known as the 'Republican Guards Events'). The first reading of the sample confirmed that the second reading should have the purpose of spotting the two frames of 'promotion' and 'fear', whenever found in any of the 682 headlines of the examined sample.

A brief analysis of the results of the second reading and examination of the frequencies of the mentioned frames follows. Regarding al-Masry al-Youm's 337 articles on Tamarod published during the 112 days under focus, it was found that 197 of them (58.46 per cent) promoted Tamarod (the promotion frame) and eighty-one articles (24.03 per cent) aimed to cause fear among the public (the fear frame). Regarding al-Watan's 345 articles on Tamarod published in the same period with the same keyword, it was found that 221 of them (64.06 per cent) promoted Tamarod (the promotion frame) and seventy-seven articles (22.32 percent) would cause fear among the public (the fear frame). Of both newspapers' 682 examined articles, it was found that 418 of them (61.29 per cent) promoted Tamarod (the promotion frame), and that 158 articles (23.17 per cent) would cause fear among the public (the fear frame).[56] In their news content, both newspapers seem to have engaged in a polishing process of Tamarod and the military, and the demonization of the Muslim Brotherhood.

On 2 July, Morsi was forcibly disappeared by the military and taken to an undisclosed destination; details about his removal remain unknown. The two newspapers have arguably acted as PR campaigners for Tamarod and al-Sisi, however that was clearly not the case at the beginning of this period. Nevertheless, later, the movement and the military appeared in the two newspapers' content as the only solution to the threat of a 'civil war'. As Alaa commented, Tamarod grew due to the militarization in the media against the mistakes of the Muslim Brotherhood. The movement itself even held press conferences in newspaper offices, with *al-Watan* leading this trend.[57] A notable theme in most responses is the Muslim Brotherhood's political failures as a reason for Tamarod's success in addition to the press support the movement received.

A review of coverage of al-Sisi as 'the saviour'

Fear of 'chaos' and 'civil war' and the Muslim Brotherhood's exaggerated religious authoritarianism in the media show how the military, through the business elite's media, was dealing with daily news production. This control peaked during the 112 days of Tamarod, while swiftly preparing the public to accept, and even want, the army and al-Sisi to step in and 'protect' the people and the country from the 'danger' of the Muslim Brotherhood. As discussed earlier in this chapter, Tamarod was converted after its probably independent beginnings, into a Trojan Horse that brought the military and al-Sisi to the centre of the picture and put them again at the top the Egyptian state and the political sphere after about two-and-a-half years of almost sharing power with the Muslim Brotherhood, or at least pretending to do so. The editorial agendas of the private press, mainly *al-Masry al-Youm* and *al-Watan* as examined here, did not change in relation to the military as an entity above criticism. One different new element introduced to editorial policy was al-Sisi as a representative of the military, a future leader and a 'saviour' from the 'dangerous' Muslim Brotherhood. He was carefully and gradually promoted in an emotional way by the press, which was successful with the public, and to which they responded positively and asked the 'hero' to step in and run the country and to bring safety. Going through the responses of the interviewees regarding the manufacturing of al-Sisi as a leading figure, they more or less agreed that both newspapers were highly biased in his favour as a person, a defence minister and a president. Nour, for example, believed that the presentation of al-Sisi in the press was completely biased, and still is, in terms of its defence of him and anything he does.[58]

Reading through more than one thousand headlines which carried al-Sisi's name during the 112 days of Tamarod, it was found that *al-Masry al-Youm* and *al-Watan* generally portrayed him under four major themes while covering and promoting the Tamarod movement. The first was the theme of 'the average minister appointed by the Muslim Brotherhood', which appeared at the beginning of the Tamarod period. It was not yet clear what future was waiting for al-Sisi. Under this theme, *al-Watan* on 30 April published 'Morsi and al-Sisi to Launch Projects Executed by the Armed Forces Tomorrow', while *al-Masry al-Youm* on 22 May published 'Morsi, Qandil[59] and al-Sisi Receive the Liberated

Soldiers[60] in Almaza Airport'. The second theme was of 'the powerful apolitical military man', which was also prominent alongside the first theme and for slightly longer. This theme served al-Sisi's reputation well, as it portrayed him as a man with 'high values' who stands above political interests. Under this theme *al-Watan* on 5 August published 'Sources Close to al-Sisi: The Colonel Will Not Run for Presidency and Sees Egyptians' Love for Him as the Greatest Authority', while *al-Masry al-Youm* on 4 July, the morning following the coup, published 'Al-Sisi, The Young Leader Who is Aware of the Army's Boundaries in the Political System'. The third theme was 'a beloved icon', which was a result of sensational content concerning well respected figures in Egyptian society who enthusiastically support him, and other ordinary citizens who exaggerate their 'love' to him in sensational ways. Under this theme *al-Watan* on 14 July published 'Foad Negm:[61] Al-Sisi Reminds Me of Abdel Nasser and He Knows Where "Satan is Hiding his Son[62]"', and *al-Masry al-Youm* on 26 July published 'Al-Itihadeya Palace Podium: A Woman Gives Birth to a Baby Boy and Calls it al-Sisi. Al-Beblawy[63] Joins the [pro-Al-Sisi] Protests'. The fourth theme is 'the saviour', which grew after the fear frame became prominent. Under this theme, *al-Watan* on 11 May published 'Al-Sisi Warns: Don't Play with the Army. It's my Honour to be a Humble Servant of the People', while *al-Masry al-Youm* on 23 June published 'Al-Sisi Decides to Treat the Child Injured in al-Mahalla Clashes[64] at Maadi Military Hospital'.

Alaa argued that at the beginning, the coverage of al-Sisi's personality was indeed average. To some extent, as a minister of defence under Morsi, he did not receive significant media attention. However, after 30 June, he took the 'maximum attention of the press. And later as president, the private press never criticize him, however, they do not superficially portray him as 'holy' as the state newspapers do'.[65] *Al-Masry al-Youm* and *al-Watan* gave almost identical treatment of al-Sisi's character in the news. However, given al-Gallad's higher profile connections with the elites – military, civilian politicians and businessmen – *al-Watan* was ahead of *al-Masry al-Youm*'s news agenda when it came to access of information, as shown by the frequent appearance of 'undisclosed high-profile sources' during this period, who were always used to send messages to the public through both newspapers. A news story published on 21 February 2013, almost three months before the creation of Tamarod, with the headline 'Electronic Campaigns with the slogan "al-Sisi President for

Egypt". The Brotherhood: This is Playing with Fir',[66] implied that *al-Watan* and its well-connected chief editor might have known that the then average military figure of al-Sisi would receive a higher status in the near future. *Al-Watan* was indeed ahead of all other newspapers with more intense and more sensational news. Other journalists joked that their newsroom gave the impression of being more of an operations room for promoting al-Sisi. Reda and Wesam expressed their firm belief that this was all an early planned media campaign for al-Sisi. Reda particularly commented that this was nothing more than a public relations campaign and not news,[67] which Wesam affirmed, saying that the media dealt with al-Sisi as if he were already the president of the country.[68] This was an assumption that could be clearly seen in the headlines as shown above, where the private press engaged in obvious propaganda for al-Sisi, the president to be, and indeed have continued to do ever since.

Conclusion

Having taken a critical approach in understanding a political phenomenon through questioning the media as an attack of money and power, and in turn, as a structure that the elites use to dominate a society,[69] this chapter has reviewed the news produced by Egypt's top two newspapers, *al-Masry al-Youm* and *al-Watan*, during the period from Mubarak's fall in 2011 until the military coup and Morsi's fall in 2013. This chapter has considered a sample of news media content in the light of the economic, political, and social structural changes that were discussed in the previous chapters. As we know now, the support for Tamarod in the press quickly turned into a widely supported military coup against an elected president and his government. This chapter cautiously leaned towards the position that the Tamarod movement was not necessarily created by the military, however it was clearly used by them as a façade to promote the military among the public using the private press. Through doing so, the military managed to re-conquer the political space that had earlier been briefly shared with the Muslim Brotherhood following Hosni Mubarak's fall under the pressure of the 2011 uprising. The Tamarod campaign paved the way for the reinforcement of the military as direct rulers, and thus ultimately it represented the counter-revolutionary.[70] Supported by expert responses, this chapter has presented a study of framing analysis as an empirical investigation of the business elite's private press support for the 2013 military coup. As discussed earlier, many scholars agree that framing analysis provides a direct and reliable interpretation of the role of certain media outlets in shaping ideas and public views about current affairs, and also tendencies of responses to covered issues.[71] In this light, it is concluded that the framing of 'fear' (of the Muslim Brotherhood) and 'promotion' (of the military as a saviour) showed that the Egyptian press actively sought to create a basis of popular support for the removal of Morsi by the military. It was also concluded that the business elite's private press had played a pivotal role in reinstating the military at the top of the state hierarchy through preparing the public to expect and potentially accept the 2013 military coup as legitimate and necessary, while raising the figure of al-Sisi as 'the saviour' of the country.

The Military as Media Producers: Politics and Drama on al-Sisi's TV

On 4 July 2013, one day after Mohamed Morsi was deposed by the military, Adly Mansour, the president of the Supreme Constitutional Court, was appointed by the military as the interim president of Egypt. On 8 June 2014, Abdel Fattah al-Sisi started his first presidential term having successfully won the presidential election. However, as discussed in earlier chapters, al-Sisi had been, practically speaking, the actual ruler of Egypt since the coup, and, as portrayed by the media, the 'saviour' of Egypt even earlier. Since the coup, the overly militarized state seems to be sensitive to two clear facts. First, that it is a state founded on a military coup, which is legally problematic regardless of violating the very basics of a constitutional democracy that Egypt internationally claims to be. Second, they have repeatedly engaged in killing thousands of civilians, mostly supporters of the unlawfully deposed democratically elected president. These elements of legal vulnerability cause the military, through the media they directly and indirectly control, to proactively attempt to legitimize their violence against the Muslim Brotherhood and ultimately those who attempt to criticize the military's narrative of events. The military also produces media content that reinforces their version and vision of political, social and economic discourses in a form of military propaganda, which involves a good deal of anti-Brotherhood obsession.

This chapter focuses on power relations in governing the production, distribution and exchange of resources, as well as problems of control and survival,[1] during and after the coup. Autocratic rulers envisage media regulation and censorship not to prevent the concentration of media but to curb political opposition and foster a submissive public.[2] The year 2011 caused the business elite and the military to experience fear: fear of being prosecuted, at least, for all the corruption and favouritism under which they had flourished during the thirty or so years that Mubarak was in power. Because of this fear, and their desperation to survive the uprising and transform this fear to their favour, they did all that they could to make the 2013 military coup work. Their response to the uprising and support for the coup, however, may have gone too far. Most Egyptian media outlets went to extremes to support the post-Morsi military regime, with a few individual exceptions trying to maintain some degree of balance. Overall, radio and television were replete with patriotic songs and talk shows glorifying the military. For weeks following Morsi's deposal, the Egyptian state television as well as most private TV channels ran a banner with the Egyptian flag that stated: 'Egypt Fights Terrorism', in reference to the confrontation between the army and supporters of Morsi. Few talk show hosts shied away from biased commentary and leading questions, and their carefully selected guests responded with exclusively pro-military answers. Facts were routinely mixed with opinions on these highly popular shows, which have become the main source of news for many Egyptians.[3] Fatima el-Issawi writes in this regard:

> The presenter Ahmed Moussa [briefly mentioned in Chapter Two], known to be vocal in his support for the military, claims to have received exclusive 'information' from [the military], warning his audience: 'The free army officers have decided that anyone suspected of killing a security member will be killed by them directly in the street. There is no need for courts anymore'. The statement of this talk show host, clearly advocating unlawful killing in the streets, is not a unique feature in Egyptian media today.[4]

In the above quote, el-Issawi gives a brief and dim image of the media in post-coup – or post-Morsi – Egypt. Open calls for violence against opponents, the Muslim Brotherhood or others, became the norm to the ears and eyes of media consumers of whatever format. This demonization not only targeted political opponents; it was simply opposed to all critical voices, including those of journalists. Since journalists do not wear uniforms to differentiate themselves according to political affiliation (only a vest with a 'Press' printed on the back), many of them, including pro-military journalists, have fallen victim to chaotic street violence by civilians, as will be discussed in detail later.

The instrumental character of the media is obvious, not only when one investigates the relationships between the owners of the media and the ruling elite, but also when one considers the content produced.[5] To follow a critical approach in understanding a political phenomenon would question the media as an attack of money and power, and in turn, as a structure used by elites to dominate a society.[6] This 'attacking' of the media is a system that functions to communicate messages and symbols to the general public, as put forward by Edward Herman and Noam Chomsky. The media's function, according to Herman and Chomsky, is to amuse, entertain, inform, and inculcate individuals with the values, beliefs and codes of behaviour that integrate them into the institutional structures of larger society. In a world of concentrated wealth and major conflicts of class interests, fulfilling this role requires systematic propaganda.[7] The 'consent' notion in Herman and Chomsky's work goes hand in hand with Vincent Mosco's understanding of hegemony, in which hegemony requires the exercise of power to maintain consent under changing conditions. Communication here plays a central role in hegemony as it is vital to the successful maintenance of control, as well as to the resistance and the construction of counter-hegemonies.[8]

In his study of Egyptian TV propaganda during and shortly after the coup, Osama Diab analysed the content of three major prime-time shows and came across interesting findings. The content of these shows introduced a form of 'Egyptocentrism' as an identity discourse aimed at attacking the Muslim Brotherhood.[9] However, since Egypt is a prominent Muslim country that cannot appear as anti-Islamic, the analysed content showed that the media used Islam in an attempt to 'beat the Brotherhood at their own game', which mostly revolved around the theme that the Muslim Brotherhood was adopting a 'wrong version/ understanding of Islam' and using it for their political goals.[10] This put the military in a delicate position, one in which they, through these TV shows, were stressing Egyptocentrism in their fight against the Muslim Brotherhood as an Islamist group, while appealing to the Gulf supporters of the coup, who also embrace Islamic rule.[11] Within this narrative and the vulnerabilities of the legitimacy of the military under al-Sisi, in relation to the media content they produce, this chapter first looks at the topic of freedom of expression, which is mostly only allowed against the Muslim Brotherhood. Then it considers the topic of violence against journalists, whether by police forces, the military, or by civilians who are known as 'Honourable Citizens'. Then, from a news and political content production aspect, the chapter discusses the demonizing of critical news outlets and the consequences thereof for the safety of journalists on the streets, as violence gets out of hand. Finally, the chapter closes with the restructuring of Egypt's regionally popular drama market and the involvement of the military in the production of the TV series, and considers the successes and failures of this endeavour.

Freedom of expression: only against the Muslim Brotherhood[12]

Chomsky and Herman show how the US government and the elite-controlled media waged a war against communism, communists and anyone that may have seemed sympathetic towards them in the early 1950s. This has had an influence on American political life to the present:

> Communism as the ultimate evil has always been the spectre haunting property owners, as it threatens the very root of their class position and superior status. The Soviet, Chinese, and Cuban revolutions were traumas to Western elites, and the ongoing conflicts and the well-publicized abuses of Communist states have contributed to elevating opposition to communism to a first principle of Western ideology and politics. This ideology helps mobilize the populace against an enemy, and because the concept is fuzzy it can be used against anybody advocating policies that threaten property interests or support accommodation with Communist states and radicalism. It therefore helps fragment the left and labour movements and serves as a political-control mechanism.[13]

The military elite in Egypt adopted almost the same approach and declared a media war against the Muslim Brotherhood and anyone that may have sympathized with or sounded slightly critical of the coup. A facilitative role emerged through various attempts to tell stories from different angles and to bring political opponents onto the same debate platforms. This was short-lived. As a result of the increased polarization of the political scene, ideological opponents of the military's media-supported political agenda were increasingly portrayed as the ultimate enemy: as 'terrorists' whose destruction is legitimate.[14]

We return again to Herman and Chomsky as they discuss the phenomenon of those who 'converted' from communism to the 'centre' and were elevated by the media in the United States as eyewitnesses, very similar to the phenomenon that took place in Egypt. Former 'radicals', mainly from the Muslim Brotherhood, suddenly 'saw the light' (a phrase Herman and Chomsky use) and were labelled as 'experts' and turned into stars all over the media. Former Muslim Brotherhood member Tharwat al-Kharabawy is a good example. Al-Kharabawy, a lawyer, was a leading member of the Brotherhood until he left it in 2002. His fame spread all over the country when his book *The Temple's Secret: The Hidden Secrets of the Muslim Brotherhood* (published in 2012) received extensive airplay in the private media in 2013, especially around the period of the military coup. Unsurprisingly, in addition to his excessively frequent appearances on private and state TV channels, he became one of *al-Watan*'s regular opinion writers with a fixed column. His job was to give a solid foundation to the portrayal of the Brotherhood as a dangerous cult rather than a conservative religious political group.

On the night of the military coup, Islamist TV channels such as Egypt 25, al-Hafez, al-Nas, al-Rahma, and later other lower profile channels, were all shut down. This happened during the televised statement of the military coup, read out by al-Sisi from a written document. It was a move by the military that indicated the kind of repressive regime they were going to introduce following the Brotherhood's fall. Almost three months later, on 25 September 2013, the Brotherhood's newspaper *al-Horreya wal-Adala* (Freedom and Justice – the same name as their political party) was shut down, its were office raided and all equipment confiscated.[15]

Having said all the above, this does not mean that the pro-Muslim-Brotherhood or Islamist media in general were 'innocent', as they did engage in pro-Morsi propaganda. Ultimately, it is almost all about hegemony and how much of a media voice a power-seeking group uses to maximize control over a society for the sake of gaining or maintaining power. The Muslim Brotherhood's spending on media and communication was estimated at EUR 417 million (exchange rate for 2013: 1 EUR = 9.6 EGP) in that year alone.[16] In the same period, pro-Brotherhood voices from the Islamist camp had indeed incited violence against secular figures; such attempts, however, were mostly very quickly condemned by both the Brotherhood and most other Islamist voices.[17] Noha Mellor in her book *Voice of the Muslim Brotherhood: Da'wa, Discourse, and Political Communication* lists the group's attempts to control the media, and on 9 December 2012 more than 200 journalists and presenters protested in Tahrir Square against what they called an Islamist attempt to control the Egyptian media. However, many of the participants were Mubarak loyalists and military supporters from the state media. Again, this is not to deny the

Muslim Brotherhood's attempts to control, or at least influence, the state media, and their significant expenditure on private media at the time.

The Muslim Brotherhood's media, and the support of other Islamist media for Morsi and those who were in his camp, may have induced the counter-revolution camp (both military and civilian elites) to maximize their own efforts to counter a pro-Morsi media discourse that they had overestimated. Eventually, the millions who marched in the streets against Morsi and the Muslim Brotherhood on 30 June, were overwhelming evidence that all the pro-Morsi Islamist media combined did not succeed in stopping the Tamarod campaign. Further thorough research is required to understand this failure. The massive success of Tamarod and the colossal failure of Islamist media on that day gave a strong signal to the military that they could push for a full military coup. Three days later, on 3 July, Morsi had forcibly disappeared, in a striking difference to Mubarak's case one-and-a-half years earlier, when he was moved to his residence in Sharm el-Sheik.

Here, examining the assumption regarding the issue of anti-Brotherhood media practices during the period of the coup, the experts interviewed in this book were asked the following direct question, to elicit a direct response, whether through agreement or disagreement: 'Freedom of expression has, for the most part, become a practice only allowed against the Muslim Brotherhood, not the ruling elites. To what extent do you agree or disagree with this notion?' The question was intended to determine whether the interviewee could, or could not, directly acknowledge bias against the Muslim Brotherhood. Alaa, Ihsan and Wesam all very briefly and directly expressed their strong agreement.[18] Nour, who also agreed with the notion, added that the media are 'even accusing them of false charges. While if it comes to [criticizing] the ruling elites, newspapers could be prosecuted under the accusation of publishing false news.'[19] Ihsan added that it has now become 'hard to find a big difference between private and state-owned press when it comes to coverage of the president [for] example. I [would] say that we are living in a monotone era.'[20] Following the military coup, Fatima el-Issawi managed to interview the almost unapproachable *al-Watan* editor Magdy al-Gallad for her research project 'Egyptian Media Under Transition', and writes:

> For Magdy al-Gallad, the editor-in-chief of *al-Watan* newspaper, presumably close to the military institution, it was not possible for liberal media to adopt

neutrality. He said: 'This is a battle we did not choose. We were portrayed as evils: The spiritual leader of the Brotherhood called us the media of shame, the newspaper's offices were burned . . .' [. . .] Beyond lobbying for views, the publication of 'confidential' documents is a powerful tool frequently used by national media in smear campaigns. *Al-Watan*, known for mastering this game, had published various allegedly leaked documents, such as suspicious bank accounts for senior figures in the Brotherhood leadership or tax evasion for business projects owned by them. [. . .] If the publication of leaked documents is not specific to the Egyptian media, the frequent use of these documents, with no independent channels to verify their content, exacerbated the political manipulation of media platforms. The fact that these documents are amplified, being re-published by news websites, the press and social media pages as well as being debated on talk show platforms, makes them a powerful political tool.[21]

In contrast to al-Gallad's position concerning his editorial agenda for *al-Watan*, which was very similar to *al-Masry al-Youm*'s, in relation to voices critical of the military, the *Telegraph* published a story on 9 July 2013 with the headline: 'Ahmed Assem: the Egyptian Photographer who Chronicled his Own Death'.[22] The article conveys how these critical voices were violently dealt with. The story, also published by several other local and international news outlets, gave details about Ahmed Assem, the Freedom and Justice journalist who filmed his own assassination by a military sniper during what is known as 'The Republican Guards Events', where tens of pro-Brotherhood supporters staged a sit-in were killed on 8 July. It was obvious from the video, which was uploaded to YouTube, that this was a violent attack by the military. The video is disturbing graphic evidence that anti-Brotherhood voices are encouraged and supported, while criticism against the military and their allies is not allowed – or even worse, silenced forever. Egypt has since then become one of the world's most hostile environments for journalists and one of their biggest jailors.

Violence against journalists: police and the 'Honourable Citizens'[23]

In addition to state violence against journalists at the hands of the military and police forces, there has always been control over journalists and the content they produce, as explained earlier. A tremendous degree of state and military control continued to be asserted over the media through an oppressive regulatory framework which imposed restrictions on critical news reporting. For instance, putting journalists on trial was not only a frequent practice under the Mubarak regime but it was also prevalent under Muslim Brotherhood rule, as well as continuing under the military to this date.[24] This has led to highly controlled news content that mostly corresponds with the military's narratives of events. Ahmed Assem's murder by an army sniper is symbolic rather than the norm, however. Violence against journalists more often takes other forms: being assaulted or sometimes killed in less sophisticated ways in the middle of a protest that might turn into a clash; being arrested and tortured; or being detained with or without a legal warrant. However, a more confusing form of violence against journalists is that practiced by so-called 'Honourable Citizens', which will be discussed below.

As a background to the phenomenon, in 2014, in its report about the coup, the Committee to Protect Journalists (CPJ), which is referred to in this section as a trusted source, ranked Egypt as number six on the list of worst jailers of journalists worldwide.[25] The real number is very difficult to trace, as many were unofficially detained for short periods, sometimes only for a few hours, and then released. Other arrests are simply not reported at all, especially those of freelance journalists, as they have no proper protection, either from the publications they contribute to or from the Egyptian Journalists Syndicate. However, for research purposes and due to the difficulty of accurately tracking down information on detained, assaulted or killed journalists, this book sticks with the CPJ's data on that period as a highly trusted source.

To start with an interesting quote, a CPJ report says:

> Egypt's Minister of Interior Mohamed Ibrahim said in a press conference on Monday that he was monitoring media reactions to the killing of demonstrators and said some journalists had insulted him with their reporting. When asked about the detentions and harassment of the press, the minister joked that he would have arrested all journalists, not just those covering the protests this weekend, according to news reports.[26]

When asked about violence against journalists in Egypt and whether it is 'organized', Nour admitted that this phenomenon exists and is indeed organized, saying: 'I see that they're targeted all the time, especially photojournalists as they can be easily distinguished.'[27] Interestingly enough, police violence did not discriminate between any type of journalist, whether working for critical news outlets such as Ona or the pro-military DotMasr. The police did not want any form of media presence on the streets while dealing with protests, which is evident in the following quote from the CPJ:

> Among the other journalists detained were DotMasr reporters Mohamed Wesam, Mohamed Amin, and photographer Ahmed Adel; Veto editor Mohamed Mahrous and photographer Moamen Samir; Ona News Agency correspondent Alaa Eddin Murtada; Masrawy news website photographer Alaa Al-Qassas; and Albawaba News website correspondent Iman Ahmed, according to JATO [Journalists Against Torture Observatory, an Egyptian NGO] and the Egyptian Journalists Syndicate. The groups said that all of those detained were later released. It is not clear if charges will be brought against any of them.[28]

Alaa generalized such police practices over a longer history saying:

> The police are clear: Don't cross your limits [as a journalist] or you'll be made an example of. The Brotherhood practiced the same actions, Mubarak did so before, and the current regime is [following] their footsteps. I don't see it as a new phenomenon. We [journalists] were and will remain targeted, as we're considered the eye that might see what shouldn't be seen.[29]

During Mubarak's rule and until the military coup, Western journalists were almost immune from police targeting. However, since the return of police forces to the streets following the coup, this rule ceased to apply, as the CPJ documented then: 'In a Twitter post, Orla Guerin, the BBC's Cairo correspondent, said her team was warned by a plainclothes police officer that they would be shot if they continued to film in the Ain Shams neighbourhood of Cairo, where police were looking for Muslim Brotherhood demonstrators.'[30] Reda admitted that the environment is hostile towards journalists, but dismisses the assumption that such violence is organized.[31] Ihsan almost leaned towards Reda's opinion.[32]

While looking at the phenomenon of violence against journalists in Egypt from a different angle, it is worth observing the rise in a particular type of violence by civilians who are commonly labelled as *al-Mowatenoon al-Shorafaa*, or the 'Honourable Citizens', as mentioned earlier. The early use of this label can be found in the statements of the SCAF directly after the fall of Mubarak in 2011. They used this term whenever they were announcing a political decision or addressing the public in an emotional explanation of some military move or a political position that they were promoting. However, the first use of the term in a negative context was during the violent Maspero Events on 9 October 2011. On that evening, the army clashed with protesters, who were mostly Coptic Christians, killing several of them. Peculiarly, the state television at the time called for 'Honourable Citizens' to 'defend the army' from protesters, when in fact it was the army attacking the protesters. Human rights defender Hossam Bahgat describes the events and says, 'What started out as a peaceful protest in Cairo turned into one of the worst massacres of Christians in modern Egypt.'[33] Nour agreed with the assumption that the term 'Honourable Citizens' was first used by the military and confirmed the link between this and violence against journalists, saying:

> The first time this term was used was by one of the SCAF's members. Since then each one used it in his own way. And yes, there's a link, either they [the Honourable Citizens] are volunteering their efforts, thinking that they're helping in assuring the country's stability, or they're pushed by security forces to keep them [journalists] away from the scene.

On the other hand, the news website Moheet, which published an investigation of the phenomenon of the Honourable Citizens, related the emergence of the term a few weeks earlier, prior to the SCAF statements, contradicting what most observers thought:

> The Tahrir sit-in in 2011 was a space for a conflict between the street vendors and the revolutionary youth protecting the squares from one side, against the Baltageya (thugs) and the ousted president's [Mubarak] lovers, who were attacking Tahrir from time to time in order to evacuate the square at any cost. During that period a new term appeared, used to refer to the thugs and others defending Mubarak and attacking the revolution, which was *al-Mowatenoon al-Shorafaa*, as pro-regime media outlets back then started to dictate the term to viewers.[34]

Regardless of when exactly the term appeared, an association with security forces and unexpectedness is always present in relation to these attackers. Reda said: 'This term is mostly used to describe people who work with the Interior

Ministry [and] they are ready to move when orders are received. These days, it is dangerous to do journalism in the street. You never know what is coming [your way]'.[35] What Reda said can be inferred from the CPJ's reports on violations against journalists in Egypt, not only by the police, but also by the volunteer Honourable Citizens:

> Sara Hashem, a reporter for the independent[36] daily *al-Fagr*, said in a YouTube broadcast that she was arrested near Tahrir Square while covering demonstrations. She said that police handed her to pro-government demonstrators after telling them she was an anti-government protester. One of them dragged her to the ground while others punched and slapped her, she said. In a statement broadcast on the *al-Fagr* YouTube channel, Hashem said she fainted during the attack and was briefly hospitalized. A video on the *Cairo News* website showed Hashem being taken away by what she later said were pro-government protesters, while screaming for mercy and saying she is a journalist.[37]

Interestingly, Ihsan and Wesam refused to comment on this issue. Ihsan laughed in reaction to the question and only said: 'Usually, this is only the beginning', referring to this type of violence. A few interviewees refrained from discussing this topic, possibly out of fear, since the topic is already well known and well discussed among journalists.

Demonizing critical news outlets[38]

Understanding the intense discourse of demonization of critical news outlets starts with understanding the relationship between Egypt and the Qatari-based Al Jazeera. The network was always a concern for all Egyptian governments under Mubarak, and it continued to be a concern under the military following the 2011 uprising, which Al Jazeera supported and covered heavily in a biased manner. When Mubarak once toured Al Jazeera's headquarters in Doha, he jokingly asked: 'All this trouble from a matchbox like this?'[39] Philip Seib says that for Mubarak, who preferred his news media to be compliant, Al Jazeera had caused plenty of trouble by fostering debate about topics that many in the region did not favour.[40] This view of Seib in 2005 is still valid today, and even more valid given how much bigger and more internationally influential Al Jazeera has grown. The growth of influence of this network, or news empire, led to a significant growth in hostility between Egypt and Qatar since Mubarak's era, and now other Gulf states share Egypt's concerns. The network was clearly in support of the 2011 uprising, and the Qatari rulers (Hamad bin-Khalifa al-Thani then, and now his son Tamim) chose to support the Muslim Brotherhood, with whom they had had a good relationship for years before the uprising. This complex and old conflict had violent consequences for the network's journalists, among other foreign and local journalists, during the period following the 2013 coup.

In the end, Al Jazeera is a politically charged project representing the interests and ambitions of Qatar with its own regional agendas and international power relations. This concern includes the US government, as WikiLeaks' classified documents have shown, where former CEO Waddah Khanfar was holding secret meetings with the US ambassador in Doha negotiating changing the editorial agenda and news content, to which Khanfar was surprisingly positively responsive.[41] Khanfar had to resign a few days after the leak of these documents. However, the critical voice of Al Jazeera that always angers Egypt's ruling elites continues to be the same.

One of the reasons for civilian violence against journalists is the demonization of any form of media with a critical voice against the coup. Although critical media tried to cover the other side of the story – state violence targeting the Muslim Brotherhood – this was understood by readers and TV viewers, especially back in that period, as sympathy towards the Brotherhood. Both state and private media accused critical media, whether local, regional or international, of being pro-Brotherhood, thereby stoking anger among the public against them. Therefore, when a clash or a protest took place, the Honourable Citizens and other enraged civilians incited by state and private media would attack journalists at random. These angry civilians, however, were unable to distinguish between their targets, putting at risk journalists representing all forms of media, whether for or against the military coup. In some cases, journalists from the pro-military media, such as the case discussed in the previous section of Sara Hashem from the pro-military al-Fagr, would fall victim to random civilian violence against journalists.

The phenomenon of significant violence against journalists started with increased demonizing of the Doha-based Al Jazeera channel and its Cairo-based channel Al Jazeera Mubasher Misr. Al Jazeera showed a different side of Tamarod, the military and the Brotherhood that did not match with the image that the military propagated. Images of graphic violence against pro-Brotherhood protesters were shown and anti-coup figures were hosted on their programmes. In response, the now pro-military media such as *al-Masry al-Youm* published a story on 14 August 2013 with the headline: 'Al Jazeera, Channel of "The Coup Against Professionalism"', and earlier on 21 July *al-Watan* published: 'Yousef al-Houseiny: The Qatari Al Jazeera Zionist by Excellence'. As we can see in these two headlines, the private press promoted this demonization. At the beginning, the anti-Al Jazeera campaign worked well, as anti-Brotherhood protesters responded angrily – in line with the discourse of the private press (and the state-run as well). Protesters started chanting against Al Jazeera in their protests, and this soon escalated into physical attacks on the channel's crews. Following such success in demonizing Al Jazeera, which made it impossible for their crews to work on the ground, the authorities and the private press began following the same pattern against any other media with a critical voice.

Regarding this, Nour said: 'There are relations between private newspapers and security bodies which affect their editorial policies in this regard. So they either publish what they're told by those security services or try to defend the regime by attacking Western media in order to convince the readers that everything is OK.'[42] Later, on 2 September 2013, and after it had already become clear to media observers that the press-hostile environment was growing more dangerous and chaotic by the day, top global media freedom watchdog Reporters Without Borders (Reporters Sans Frontières – RSF) issued a report titled: 'Heavy Toll on Journalists in Two Months Since Army Takeover'. The report documented different forms of violations against journalists by the military, the police, pro-military protesters and also pro-Brotherhood protesters. The report also documented incitement against critical media outlets that were attempting to provide any picture of the situation on the ground that differed from the military's narrative of events. The report mentioned that a total of five journalists had been killed, eighty had been arbitrarily detained, and at least forty news providers physically attacked by the police or by pro-Brotherhood or pro-military protesters: 'Several journalists sustained gunshot injuries, while the security forces were dispersing pro-Morsi sit-ins on 14 August. They included Asma Waguih of Reuters, Tarek Abbas of *al-Watan*, Najjar Ahmad of *al-Masry al-Youm*, Mohamed al-Zaki of Al Jazeera and an Associated Press journalist'.[43] As we can see from the names of these news outlets, both security and protesters did not distinguish between the types of journalist, attacking pro-military and other news reporters alike.

Within the context of chaos in the streets – with attacks and retreats between pro-Brotherhood protesters on one side and the military, the police and pro-military protesters on the other – it came as no surprise that civilians reacted violently against the demonized journalists and their media. Reda said: 'So many [of the private media] volunteered to do such a thing [demonization of Western media] even without [being] asked to do so'.[44] However, the masses were not able to differentiate between journalists according to the Egyptian media's classification of pro-Brotherhood versus pro-military. Obviously, it was impossible, and any journalist could fall victim regardless of affiliation, as reports have documented.

The other aspect of understanding violence against journalists as a result of demonization of critical media – and mainly any media that did not follow the military's narrative of events – can be garnered from how the military-controlled state officially and openly dealt with critical media, as documented then by the State Information Service (SIS), which wrote in a statement: 'Egypt is feeling severe bitterness towards some Western media coverage that is biased towards the Muslim Brotherhood and avoids shedding light on violent and terrorist acts that are perpetrated by this group in the form of intimidatory operations and terrorizing citizens'.[45] In a country like Egypt, which is in almost full control of major media outlets, when a statement like this is issued against media in the context of violence and chaos against one side, the other side might violently react, which is in fact what then happened. This was because the pro-military masses were already exaggeratedly fearing the Muslim Brotherhood, thanks to the military-controlled media. All this happened while many journalists found themselves subject to attacks on the streets as they were simply attempting to do their jobs.[46] Yet after a while, the chaotic wave of street violence against journalists softened. Alaa explained the process of demonization after the coup saying: 'Newspapers deal with them [critical media] by piece. Those who write positively about us are made a good example of, and whoever takes us as an enemy, we make a bad example of'.[47] In this sense, the street violence against journalists became less visible the following years, however, what prevails now is the silence of fear.

Military monopoly over the TV drama business

It apparently was not enough for the military to control the narrative of news, both verbally and physically, as well as the content of other non-news programmes in the media they owned or controlled. They decided to bring these narratives to the production of entertainment content for television. Egypt had long been known as the 'Hollywood of the Middle East',[48] and many governments have historically taken advantage of its cinema and TV drama productions. Throughout most of the twentieth century, the film industry has been among the country's main exports to almost all Arab countries, where their populations have become familiar with the Egyptian dialect. This has provided the country with cultural influence and a propaganda tool.[49] King Fuad I (r. 1917–36) played newsreels promoting himself before features were shown, and Nasser later made sure that the monarchies were negatively portrayed.[50] The production of TV drama for both local and regional markets has continued since then and has been no less used as propaganda. The production of TV drama has always intensified in its high season during the month of Ramadan, as this is the time when advertising revenues soar and viewership levels escalate.[51] All Egyptian presidents used the cinema and drama production with more or less the same interest. However, al-Sisi seems to have been overly obsessed with controlling the entertainment industry even by historical Egyptian standards.[52] According to Badr, the military does not only want to be in control of the country politically, economically and socially, they also want to be in control culturally. 'They not only want to control what you think, but also how you think' – in a way similar to the brainwashing 'military education' course which is now mandatory at Egyptian universities.[53] TV drama is the military's way of guaranteeing that the public is 'convinced' of their political narratives, and not only consenting due to fear of their power.[54] TV drama is more important to the military than cinema, since more people can afford to watch and for several hours everyday, which makes its characters more influential in every house.[55]

Recalling the structural changes in the media and advertising markets discussed in Chapters Two and Three, following the 2013 coup the military acquired most of the companies in the media market in order to control almost all produced and consumed media content. The Egyptian Media Group (EMG), or whatever its current umbrella name (it keeps changing), is owned by Eagle Capital, an investment company owned by the General Intelligence Service. EMG in turn became the buyer of many media companies in the areas of cinema, drama, advertising, broadcasting, and the press, among other media fields. In February 2018 Tamer Morsi was appointed chairman and managing director of EMG, which became the largest media bloc in Egypt between 2016 and 2019. Sinergy, which was founded by Morsi, was, in 2016, 50 per cent acquired by EMG, and later became, as one of EMG's arms, the country's biggest producer of TV drama, and produced fifteen Ramadan TV series out of the twenty-three that were produced during 2019.[56] Baraa said ironically: 'Producing TV series now means Tamer Morsi',[57] which is practically the case. Not only in producing them, but also managing the channels that broadcast them, and the advertising agencies that sell their airtime. With such a level of market control, censorship, which had always been present in Egypt, has evidently reached a record high under al-Sisi. During Mubarak's time, a few films were marginally allowed to depict police brutality, government corruption, poverty and people's struggles, and homosexuality. These films and similar TV series from that period would be barred today.[58] The military believe these old films fed the 2011 uprising.[59] The military's open discontent and public announcement for this full control over the media was made clear in June 2017 through statements by the president and a number of government officials expressing displeasure with the content presented in Ramadan series and their desire to remedy the situation.[60] The military sees what happened under Mubarak, where there was a marginal freedom of media, as a 'cultural failure', as Ezzedine Fishere said to *The Economist*.[61] It seems that they have decided to fix this and to never allow it to happen again, as Mubarak's level of authoritarianism appeared too relaxed.

In 2017, al-Sisi issued three presidential decrees: numbers 158, 159 and 160, ordering the formation of the Supreme Council of Media Regulations (SCMR), the National Press Authority (NPA), and the National Media Authority (NMA). In January 2019, the NMA signed with Tamer Morsi, representing the military's

EMG, several protocols with the aim of providing 'better and advanced content on Egyptian television screens', to be executed within five years.[62] Adding to these vague protocols, Morsi said in a statement to the media, 'The work has started now to restructure the channels of the group [EMG] in order to uplift the message of media and draw a better future, in light of what the President of the Republic has demanded as a necessity for the media to fulfil its rule of developing the country'.[63] EMG and its several media arms appeared to be redrawing the rules of the TV drama market by owning production tools, TV networks and advertising agencies. This additionally weakened its competitors, as it managed to cancel four shows after their production had already begun, including a TV series being made with the powerful superstar Adel Imam.[64] The situation has further worsened for producers as state institutions have made it more challenging to issue script approvals, which has become more difficult than ever before.[65] This in addition to the new reality that production companies are no longer allowed to sell their work to more than one channel, each channel is allowed to air a maximum of four series, and the broadcasting rights cannot exceed EGP 50 million (about EUR 2.6 million in 2019 rates). The TV drama industry is estimated to bring in about EGP 4 billion (about EUR 210 million) in revenue during Ramadan, all of which, in the 2019 season, went almost entirely to EMG.[66] This came as a severe economic blow to many TV drama producers, who are now either out of the market or working as subcontractors for EMG, under its conditions concerning revenue and content. The TV drama market has become distorted, to the extent that Baraa describes it as: 'the army has become the producer and consumer at the same time'.[67]

It is not surprising, and is in fact fairly apparent, that the military carried out all the reorganization of the media production sector to control the content consumed by the public. As an example, a TV series such as *The Choice* is meant to glorify the military and al-Sisi, and defame the Muslim Brotherhood. *The Swarm* particularly glorifies the air force in a story about a strike that killed forty militant Islamists, however without mentioning the seven innocent civilians killed in the operation. Both TV series are produced by Synergy, which is owned by EMG, and both are headed by Morsi.[68] Apart from the technically high quality production of *The Choice*, which is historically unusual for a state-sponsored propaganda piece in Egypt, Beshara said that the production was definitely an undeniable success and 'almost all Egyptians watched it and cried'.[69] In today's controlled TV drama production, policemen are no longer corrupt, and military men have become 'superheroes' like those in the textbooks of the 'national education' courses taught at high schools,[70] while suspicions around NGOs are magnified.[71] None is allowed to provide a narrative other than the military's, as 'they know better', which is as paternalistic as the military usually is.[72] However, not all TV series are as successful as *The Choice*. They all, to different degrees depending on the plot, have to depict the police and army as brave and heroic in the face of supposed threats to national security through poorly implemented action sequences, among other themes. EMG on behalf of the market and the SCMR on behalf of the state decide on the themes to be tackled, which always hold echoes of al-Sisi's speeches, which is clear in various scenes.[73] The military rely on repeating their themes in these TV series, and directly controlling the drama market helps with this.[74]

One of the military's other mechanisms is to order screenwriters to write certain scripts and have them produced under close supervision, where actual members of the armed forces are present on set and interfere in most details while shooting. This evidently results in striking similarities between several TV series.[75] As for media ethics and professionalism, these are unsurprisingly bluntly violated. For example, in the case of *The Choice*, there is the character of Hesham Ashmawy, who was a military officer who in real life joined militant Islamists in Libya after the 2013 coup and then was captured and hanged in March 2020. In coordination with the EMG TV channels for the purpose of promoting the episode of his execution, the military leaked videos of Ashmawy's real execution, which was against Egyptian law and any professional media standards and ethics. *The Choice* became the most-watched TV series during the 2020 Ramadan season.[76] The violations and control mechanisms do not stop there, as they go even further to the physical freedoms of artists themselves. In the period from February to August 2018, the authorities arrested or prosecuted an Egyptian poet, a prominent pop singer, a playwright, a belly dancer and several actors and filmmakers, solely for their work. All were summoned either by the Supreme State Security Prosecution (SSSP), which oversees terrorism cases, or the military prosecution unit.[77] Drama production in Egypt has become a business executed by 'direct order', where the military produce, the Censorship Authority mechanically approves, and in some cases al-Sisi himself might evaluate scripts before production.[78] Beshara said that this is actually a problem even to the military themselves, as the 'voice influencing the public opinion has become monotonic', which does not suit the public mentality of today. Beshara added that this type of propaganda might influence older generations, from fifty and upwards. However, those who were children during the 2011 uprising do not identify with any of this.[79]

The success of *The Choice*, both in its production and in its popularity, is somehow exceptional. The military worked hard on coordinating all parts of its propaganda machine in favour of this TV series. However, the rest of Egypt's drama production since the military took over the entire media market has been less fortunate, both in volume and content. The historically regionally popular Egyptian television drama is witnessing an accelerated decline in favour of new regional competitors. Egyptian TV series are becoming less interesting than they were before the 2013 coup. This is in addition to rising competition from Syrian, Turkish and other dramas that are accessible, both via satellite channels and online, in and outside Egypt. This competition is not only in content, but even in production locations and facilities provided in other countries such as in Jordan, Saudi Arabia and the United Arab Emirates.[80] It is much easier to logistically manage productions in these countries now than in Egypt. It is ironic that some Egyptian TV actors now live in Saudi Arabia, as they have more work, and the environment there seems even 'less repressive' than Egypt,[81] which was unthinkable before. It has been reported that some productions in Egypt were halted for failing to acquire security permits for shooting, which are now mandatory in Egypt.[82] Since the coup, holding a camera on an Egyptian street, any camera including sometimes a mobile phone, has become extremely difficult. Egyptian television drama has almost become mainly a Ramadan habit that is not as common during the rest of the year. Beshara anticipated that if production continues to focus on the same themes, soon Egyptian viewers will abandon this 'out of touch with the street' drama for the other alternatives.[83] There is also another economic factor regarding the affordability of buying Egyptian TV drama in the Gulf counties, which are considered the most important export destination. Their TV channels are now suffering budget cuts due to austerity measures in response to the instability in oil markets and the endless war in Yemen. This is in addition to the fact that, as discussed in Chapter Two, the private media in Egypt has not necessarily been profitable since their beginnings under Mubarak, in order to fully depend on them to buy new drama. And even worse, Egypt has been suffering high levels of inflation since 2016,[84] which makes these TV series very expensive in local terms. One of the indicators of the regional decline of Egyptian drama is that Arab youth across the region have become now less familiar with the Egyptian dialect than their parents.[85]

To make things worse, for both the military and the market they seized, in early May 2019 United Media Services (UMS), the umbrella media company appearing in reports in alternation with EMG, made the poorly studied move of launching a paid streaming app called Watch It. In coordination with this, the military wished to prohibit the convention of broadcasting shows on YouTube for those who could not view them on satellite channels, which had previously been common. Free streaming apps such as EgyBest and others were blocked to allegedly mitigate 'piracy' and Watch It was granted a monopoly over the streaming market. This took place right before Ramadan 2019, as the military probably imagined that viewers would have no other choice than to use Watch It to satisfy their solid Ramadan social habits which is chiefly watching TV drama. While it is known that Egyptians' disposable income is low, the seemingly growing consumption of online content is slow in comparison to richer countries.[86] The results then were catastrophic for that season, as many did not wish to pay for such a service,[87] and those who did were confronted with significant technical failures of the poorly programmed Watch It app.

No one can deny the military's success in controlling the TV drama market and managing to produce content that sends their intended messages to the public. However, it is well documented that overall, the produced content has been failing in terms of its volume, quality and viewership. Beside the severe distortions forced upon the market, where the military play all the roles of the TV drama game from being the producers, the broadcasters and the advertisers, they have posed a significant threat, economically speaking, to the livelihood of about two million Egyptian workers of all specialties and long accumulated expertise, who contribute to and depend upon this industry.[88] Hisham described the TV drama market now using the more dramatic Arabic word *ḥarāb*, which means ruins.[89] The decline in the quality of content is an anticipated result of having the military as the only option in the drama market. This has been more recently realized and the military has been trying to fix this through subcontracting non-military owned production companies. As Badr said: 'they tried to control something bigger than they [were able to]'.[90] However, resorting to subcontracting will most likely fail as well, since the conditions are not in favour of the producers, the military and police themes are still persistently dominant, and the military need to continue reinforcing their fragile legitimacy as a state founded on a coup. In light of this existential challenge confronting the military, they are indeed still continuing with their thematic line of production with *The Choice II* which aired in Ramadan 2021, covering the Rab'a Massacre when hundreds of protesters from the Muslim Brotherhood were slaughtered by security forces in 2013, under the command of al-Sisi.[91] This event was widely described as 'one of the world's largest killings of demonstrators in a single day in recent history'.[92] Yet as expected, the heavily broadcast TV series was produced from the perspective of the 'heroic police'.[93] Showing no sign of foreseeable change, the military have already produced *The Choice III*, which was broadcast during Ramadan 2022.

Conclusion

Control over the Egyptian press in their coverage of the news has been the reality both during and since Mubarak's fall. There have always been changes depending on whatever political situation the country has been experiencing. Freedoms were sometimes slightly, but temporarily, restored, for example. As a continuation of the business elites' enforcement of hegemony through their private newspapers in favour of the 2013 military coup, this chapter found that freedom of expression then became a practice allowed only if used against the Muslim Brotherhood or in favour of their demonization. Entities such as Tamarod and the military were mostly above criticism, at least during the period considered in this research. Efforts by the military and its affiliates to silence dissent and shutter outlets associated with the Muslim Brotherhood have produced a media environment in which most public and private outlets are firmly supportive of the coup. Dozens of journalists were physically assaulted during the coup year by both security agents and civilians. The rise of violence by civilians against journalists in the public domain was at its peak in 2013, as documented by media freedom watchdogs and other media outlets.

So-called Honourable Citizens was the label loosely given to civilians who did not belong to any form of official authority but who committed acts of violence against journalists. Demonizing critical news outlets was an organized practice by the authorities and the business elite's press, which in turn fuelled the violence by civilians against journalists working for critical news producers, whether local, regional, or international. It was found that, especially during and after the coup, civilian violence against journalists spiralled out of control, given the randomness of the attacks and the fluid violent atmosphere, so much so that even pro-military journalists accidentally fell victim to such violence, in addition to the critical journalists against whom the private (and state) press – both controlled by the military – incited fear.

This excessive violence, perpetrated directly and indirectly by the military, alongside the question of the legitimacy of the military's rule following the coup to this today, have encouraged the military to resort to the drama market with the purpose of controlling public opinion through propaganda television drama, which has been a historical tool in the hands of several previous governments. However, this time the military have gone to an extreme level of control through buying and establishing most of the country's production houses, TV channels and advertising agencies, crowning themselves as the sole player in the TV drama market. They have indeed succeeded in magnifying their voiced narratives of events and unifying political, social and economic discourses presented to the public. They have also succeeded in silencing any different voices, even if just slightly different. However, they have at the same time caused an unprecedented decline in the historically powerful market, in relation to the volume of production, content quality, overall viewership and exports, which has left the gates open for other growing alternatives for the Egyptian and regional public to choose from, through other TV channels and via the internet.

Conclusion

The Egyptian media market witnessed significant changes under the leadership of both Mubarak and al-Sisi. Both eras have been neoliberally dominated, however each has its own characteristics. In discussing the media market under both presidents with military backgrounds, this book has studied how al-Sisi has succeeded in restructuring the media market so that it directly favours the military, in comparison to Mubarak's era, where there was an attempt to strike a balance between the interests of the business elite and those of the military. In studying this, the approach of Critical Political Economy of communication (CPE) was applied through conducting a qualitative analysis of several relevant topics. In studying Egypt's media market under Mubarak and al-Sisi, and the shock that it received in between – caused by the 2011 uprising – this book has focused mostly on hegemonic, and counter-hegemonic to a lesser degree, approaches to control the narrative of events.

The approach of CPE, as its name indicates, is to critically study the political economy of power relations and the socioeconomics that shape the communication of information from the mass media to its publics.[1] Jonathan Hardy and Vincent Mosco are two major scholars to whom this book has paid particular attention throughout with a critical approach to communication and has benefitted from their thorough approaches to understanding the political economy of media and how it relates to social change and power relations. Edward Herman and Noam Chomsky with their 'propaganda model' have also been important to this work as they helped the empirical understanding of the practice of control over the media from a CPE perspective as well. Although the works of these scholars have a Western or international focus, they were helpful and provided much insight in guiding the process of analysing hegemony in the Egyptian media market under Mubarak and al-Sisi.

Following the introductory chapter, the book commenced with a critical analysis of Egypt's media market by analysing the business elite and their political interests as well as the media landscape they dominate to their benefit and to that of the military elite. A critical qualitative analysis approach, using the literature covering Egypt's political economy in general and the media market in particular from the 1950s until the present, was applied throughout the chapters, as unavoidable connections and backgrounds to the book's focus on the period from 2011 to the present. Particular attention was paid to themes of hegemony imposed by the ruling elites, and political, economic and social changes that accompanied the processes of change enforcement. For example, the process of change under Nasser and the Free Officers Movement following the 1952 military coup and the building of a post-independence state; Sadat's *Infitah* and his approach to reinforcing his position by gaining support from the West; Mubarak's relatively similar approach to that of Sadat with some minor differences, and al-Sisi's excessive militarization of the economy and the existing media model of Mubarak, which had been largely dominated by the business elite. All these hegemonic policies and their relation to the media were critically discussed. All this has been embedded with the responses of Egyptian media experts who were interviewed for this book, all of whom, in different ways, have special access and experiences as influential media professionals who have provided significant portions of the daily news production in Egypt's media market before and after the 2011 uprising. The majority of these high profile experts (elite interviewees) were working for Egyptian media outlets, while the rest were covering Egypt for international media. Their strategic positions gave them awareness of the almost inaccessible and strategic side of the media industry that takes place behind closed doors.

By critically reviewing the Egyptian media market, this study concludes that an interest in controlling this market has always existed, as the literature and primary sources have suggested and confirmed. The mainstream media succeeded in strengthening the elites' economic and political discourses, as it dealt with them as 'systems of hegemony'. This control has been present since Nasser's era (1952–70), during Sadat's reign (1970–81), continuing through Mubarak's tenure (1982–2011), which witnessed the introduction and expansion of the private media until present, and then during al-Sisi's military rule (2014–present), which witnessed a shift of media ownership with this being largely taken over by the military. There have always been legislative and structural changes, depending on the political situation the country was passing through, such as Sadat's *Infitah* for example, when freedoms were slightly restored, however these changes were always minor and temporary.

The interest of the business elite in the private media from 2004 has been evident. This interest was associated with the introduction of Gamal Mubarak to the political scene. Legislation of the press in Egypt has always been complex and unclear, giving power to the state to control the industry since the 1950s. Since the late 1990s, however, legislation has favoured the business elite and the media they own. The Unified Media Law of 2017 increased state control over the press market. Starting around 2016, the military stepped into direct and indirect ownership of media as a form of reinforcing their hegemonic control over the content produced. Studying the profiles of the business elite as media investors and media executives (implementors) as editors-in-chief proved the interest in control by the former over the media market in favour of the military elite in a mutually beneficial balance of power under Mubarak. However, under al-Sisi that balance shifted towards full control by the military, as the business elite were reduced to submissive propaganda subcontractors in military hands, while even the small margin of criticism that existed under Mubarak disappeared. In general, the political economy of the Egyptian media is highly controlled by the business elite in favour of themselves and the military, whether willingly or unwillingly. Hegemony has existed since the foundation of the media market, however it was reinforced following the shock of the 2011 uprising. To achieve and maintain their hegemonic position over the economy of Egypt, the business and military elites engaged in significant and direct support of the 2013 military coup and full propaganda regarding military rule.

By studying Egypt's distorted advertising market, it can be found that the country's media model poses a challenge for critical scholars like Mosco, Hardy, Herman and Chomsky, all of whom base their arguments on notions of profitability through advertising in commercialized media. Despite the presence of a large private media market that appears vibrant, these media investments are not found to be dominantly profit-seeking, as they serve more as favours from the business elite to the rulers. This, however, does not necessarily rule out the concept of profitability among either media content producers or the advertising agencies completely. The former make a profit in the non-media sectors, as a reward for the favour they carry out for the ruling elites by creating and running the mostly pro-government media. While the latter, the advertising agencies, make a profit through having privileged access to media spaces for their advertisements in both state-run and private media, as a reward for pro-regime political propaganda, whether through encouraging consumerism in the neoliberalizing economy among the public since the *Infitah*, or producing direct propaganda, such as that by Tarek Nour for Mubarak's presidential campaign of 2005, as one example.

The 2011 uprising and the fall of Mubarak came as a blow to the business elite, members of which are both media investors and advertising agencies. They responded by quickly taking a counter-revolutionary position through siding with the military against the uprising. This could be observed in the increase of investments in the private media market by the business elite following the uprising, and campaigning for pro-military political figures by the advertising agencies. This was a temporary continuation of the political economy model of advertising under Mubarak, in which the privately owned agencies benefited from allying with the ruling elite in their neoliberal model. However, this balance has changed since the 2013 coup, as the military deepened its involvement even further into the Egyptian economy and expanded their investments to other sectors which they did not previously dominate, including the media and advertising. After pushing the Mubarak's propagandists aside, a new model of a militarized political economy of advertising under al-Sisi was introduced. This model was based on restructuring the advertising sector, moving from allying with the agencies to directly owning them, and thus the military became the propagandists of themselves. They achieved this through a marathon of market acquisitions by umbrella media companies owned by Eagle Capital, the commercial arm of the General Intelligence, which now owns the majority of Egypt's media and advertising businesses.

This study of the Egyptian media market could not be comprehensive without discussing social media as a political space, which has become a media game changer. The first decade of this millennium in Egypt witnessed the growing use of the internet as a political space, in response to the absence of an active and inclusive real one. In coordination with physical tactics on the ground, young activists succeeded in creating a political blogosphere that kept growing over time until the 2011 uprising, with several milestones and minor political events along the way. Disagreement remains about the degree to which this internationally recognized Egyptian blogosphere influenced the course of events. However, the solid understanding remains that it was influential in terms of spreading awareness to a high degree, and mobilization to a lesser extent. All of this happened while Mubarak's traditional regime was almost in a blind spot concerning the influence of the internet as a political space in real-life political space. The rise of social media as a means of communication towards the end of the decade played a significant role in disseminating the content of the already well-established blogosphere to larger segments of Egyptian youth who had become both producers and consumers of political content. As with disagreements regarding the degree of the blogosphere's influence over the course of events, particularly the 2011 uprising, social media is agreed to be an even more influential tool of disseminating political content, although not necessarily the cause or the major influencer on events that led to Mubarak's fall, whose regime remained in the same earlier blind spot. It was found that the role of the traditional media, particularly Al Jazeera and other regional and international outlets, were crucial, in terms of the ultimate outcomes of the 2011 uprising, as magnifiers of social media content. This is of secondary importance after the foundational role of social, political and economic grievances and the increasing discontent in the years leading up to the 2011 uprising.

Since the fall of Mubarak, but more intensely since the 2013 coup, the military have actively engaged in filling the online void that Mubarak left behind and clearly learned from his regime's 'mistakes'. The military overturned the balance regarding the internet as a political space into their favour in a short period of time. First, by investing in e-committees business with the purpose of disinformation and influencing online public opinion, and second, in parallel, by investing in e-surveillance technologies, which were mostly imported from 'established democracies'. As a form of punishment mechanisms for those electronically surveilled and found 'guilty' of expressing their critical views, a 'legal arsenal' was introduced. This was not only for the purpose of punishment of these voices, but also for making examples of them and discouraging others from trying to act similarly, alongside trying to provide a less damaged image of the military as the rulers of Egypt, locally and internationally, rather than as violent human rights violators.

Taking a critical approach to understanding a political phenomenon by questioning the media as an attack of money and power, and in turn, as a structure that the elites use to dominate a society,[2] this book reviewed the news produced by Egypt's top two newspapers, *al-Masry al-Youm* and *al-Watan*, during the period from Mubarak's fall in 2011 until the military coup and Morsi's fall in 2013, as applicable cases for the previously discussed topics. It looked at how the process of promoting Tamarod in the press quickly turned into a widely supported military coup against the elected president Mohamed Morsi and his mostly Muslim Brotherhood government. This book cautiously argued that the Tamarod movement was not necessarily created by the military, however it was clearly used by them as a façade to promote the military among the public through the private media. In so doing, the military managed to re-conquer the political space that was earlier briefly shared with the Muslim Brotherhood following Mubarak's fall. The Tamarod campaign paved the way for reinforcement of the military as direct rulers, and thus ultimately represented the counter-revolutionary. This study then concluded that the framing of 'fear' (of the Muslim Brotherhood) and 'promotion' (of the military as a saviour) showed that the Egyptian press actively sought to create a basis of popular support for the removal of Morsi by the military. It was also concluded that the business elite's private press had played a pivotal role in reinstating the military at the top of the state hierarchy through preparing the public to expect and potentially accept the 2013 military coup as legitimate and necessary, while elevating the figure of al-Sisi as the 'saviour' of the country.

This book also studied the political and entertainment content produced under al-Sisi's full military control of the television market. It was found that there was a continuation of the business elites' enforcement of hegemony through their private media in favour of the 2013 military coup. Freedom of expression was allowed only when expression was against the Muslim Brotherhood or promoting their demonization. Entities like Tamarod and the military were mostly above criticism. The efforts of the military and its affiliates to silence dissent and shutter outlets associated with the Muslim Brotherhood produced a media environment in which most public and private outlets were firmly supportive of the coup. Dozens of journalists were physically assaulted during the year of the coup by both security agents and civilians. The rise of violence by civilians against journalists in public reached its peak in 2013, as documented by media freedom watchdogs and other media outlets. So-called Honourable Citizens was the label loosely given to civilians who carried out acts of violence but who did not belong to any form of official authority. Demonizing critical news outlets was an organized practice of the authorities and the business elite's media, which in turn fuelled violence by civilians against journalists working for critical news producers, whether local, regional, or international. During and after the coup, civilian violence against journalists spiralled out of control, given the randomness of the attacks and the fluid violent atmosphere, to the extent that even pro-military journalists accidentally fell victim to the fighting alongside the critical journalists who were incited against by the private (and state) media, which were both controlled by the military.

This excessive violence, carried out directly and indirectly by the military, together with the question of the legitimacy of the military's rule following the coup, have encouraged the military to resort to the TV drama market to control public opinion using TV series as propaganda which has been a historical tool in the hands of several previous governments. However, the military have this time gone to an extreme level of control in buying and establishing most of the country's production houses, TV channels and advertising agencies, crowning themselves as the sole player in the TV drama market. They have indeed succeeded in magnifying their narratives of events and unifying political, social and economic discourses presented to the public. They have also succeeded in silencing any different narratives in the TV drama market, even if they differ only slightly. However, they have at the same time caused an unprecedented and disastrous decline in the historically powerful market, reducing the volume of production, the quality of content, overall viewership and export levels, which have all left the gates open for other growing alternatives for the Egyptian and regional public to choose from through non-Egyptian TV channels as well as the internet.

Overall, the Egyptian media market exists to serve the interests of the elites and maintain their political and economic privileges which are rooted in different eras in post-independence Egypt. This has been clear, whether it was in Nasser's developmental state, the early neoliberal model of Sadat's *Infitah*, the hyper-neoliberal model of Mubarak's state of balance between the military and a civilian business elite, or the militarized neoliberal model of al-Sisi. In striking similarity to Nasser's one media voice and Mubarak's neoliberalism, al-Sisi has succeeded in taking both elements to extreme levels of control and violent authoritarianism, unprecedented in Egypt's modern history. With an obsession of not repeating Mubarak's 'mistakes' – allowing relative power to a civilian business elite and a limited margin of media freedom under international pressure – al-Sisi has transformed the Egyptian state into a full military dictatorship,[3] where the economy and the media are directly run by the generals.

Reflecting on this book's findings and the insights of the interviewed experts, one might intersectionally remember the case of the Saudi and Kuwaiti media that exclusively broadcast Mubarak's statements and interviews after his fall in 2011. It is worth noticing that these statements were not first released through the Egyptian media, which should be the most relevant to the matter, especially that Mubarak never left the country following his fall from power. This kind of headline news was both regional, in Arabic, and international, in English and in other languages. Providing such exclusive coverage is highly politicized and intentional. It reflects the geopolitical agenda of the Gulf states for both Egypt and the region, presenting themselves as a platform for the counter-revolution, a topic that was not part of the focus of this book, but is still very important and requires further research. Qatar's Al Jazeera, which is highly influential from a global perspective, took the exact opposite position however, as discussed in earlier chapters. This goes in line with the concept of the transnationality of Daniel Hallin and Paolo Mancini in their models for comparing media systems,[4] which is unfortunately very difficult to apply to nondemocratic systems, although the concept remains applicable.[5] Reflecting on the concept of Hallin and Mancini, of linking the influence of media beyond national borders as a global phenomenon, and that of Jonathan Hardy and Vincent Mosco, that the media is used by the elites to maintain hegemony over societies, the problematic Egyptian media market should be addressed in both local and global contexts, if researchers or experts are seriously interested in tackling these problems. Egypt is a part of global neoliberalism, with national, regional and international overlapping characteristics. This is not separate from the media that it locally produces for either national or transnational consumption, which this book focused on. This global neoliberalism also applies to the media produced abroad and its influence on Egyptian audiences, whether intentionally or unintentionally. Hence, the Egyptian media are both local and global, national and transnational in all the three dimensions of political economy: the political, the economic and the social.

Under this understanding, most of the experts interviewed for this book agreed that the most important factors in the Egyptian media crisis today are the suppression of freedom of expression, the lack of independence, and poor professionalism. Concerning the first problem, the suppression of freedom of expression, Egypt has become one of the world's biggest jailors of journalists, as discussed in this book. With the absence of freedom of expression in the produced content, the media has become what Beshara called a 'media of the one voice'.[6] Control of what is to be said and what is not to be said has reached a peak, even by the standards of Mubarak's times, which were ironically better.[7] According to Hossam, with the lack of freedom 'there won't be journalism'.[8] The Egyptian media have turned into a means of mobilization of the public for the issues that the ruling elites, mainly the military, care about and want the public to care about too[9] – for example, the demonization of the Muslim Brotherhood, which has been the most dominant theme across all forms of Egyptian media content since the coup. What the country now has is 'directed media' with one voice, where many things that are happening in the country are talked about by citizens among themselves, but which never reach the media.[10] What makes this strikingly contradictory in the public awareness is that a few years earlier they temporarily tasted a sense of freedom, and it might still be difficult to forget.[11] The military are afraid of this 'taste of freedom', as they believe it was the 'mistake' that caused the fall of Mubarak, and the Gulf states are well aware of this both in Egypt and their own countries. This is in addition to their fear of the consequences of the crimes committed during and after the coup period. In this sense, the excessive military oppression of freedom of expression should be contextually understood as mutual fear, between society and its rulers, and fear of prosecution of the latter, if a window of freedom opens, regardless of how small it could be.

As for the lack of independence of the media, content has become remarkably similar in today's Egypt, as journalists are literally told exactly what to write or say.[12] TV content is now only representative of what the military wish to be the public opinion.[13] Additionally, funding of the media is a crucial factor in the issue of independence, and this is not exclusive to the situation in Egypt – it is a global problem or at least a challenge. With the absence of a separation between media investment, administration and editorial management, funding raises the challenge of maintaining media integrity.[14] Although the Egyptian media are not predominantly profit-seeking, the issue still challenges the integrity of journalists and media personnel whose incomes are only granted by a financially dependent media. In this context, Badr remarked that it has become difficult for journalists to have access to information, as 'people no longer trust journalists in showing the truth' given their relation to their current employers.[15] This in itself is problematic even to the regime itself, concerning the diminishing trust and interest of citizens in the media.

Ultimately, Egyptians do have access to the internet (even if silently) and they come across free media productions in other countries, they see governments under the pressure of their own media, and they also see other populations succeeding in democratically removing governments from power.[16] The public's lack of confidence in the monotonic media produced for them, even for those who support the military, is also problematic. Although one of the purposes of the controlled media is to create false narratives for satisfying the pro-military segments of the society, these very segments are actually aware of this. With this obvious lack of independence, the Egyptian media is not trusted even by the military supporters,[17] which is a compounded crisis in itself. The pro-military have even started watching Al Jazeera again, and sometimes the pro-Muslim Brotherhood media broadcast from abroad, just to have a glimpse of some alternative reporting, even though they still do not like these media.[18] This has caused the military to worry and increase attacks in the local media against foreign channels that tell the news with a narrative different to that of the military. Even with entertainment media content broadcasted through non-Egyptian outlets, the military are also trying in vain to control outlets such as Netflix and Shahid,[19] which is already a lost battle.

The previous two problems – freedom of expression and independence – may be directly linked to a set of national, regional and international geopolitical factors. However, the final problem that was discussed with the interviewees, the poor professional standards of Egyptian journalism, seems to be more internal than external. The Egyptian media have been suffering from this issue for long before the 2013 coup. There is an evident lack of fact-checking, respect for the rule of law, understanding of human rights values, and excessive sensationalism. The brief period of freedom between the fall of Mubarak and al-Sisi's coup was sometimes embarrassingly chaotic regarding media standards. Regardless of issues of media control or ideologies, according to Badr, even those who the youth were supporting as voices of dissent had 'zero professionalism'.[20] With the rise of social media, this has become even more seriously problematic, as the traditional media have tended to give the spotlight to social media stars in order to attract more audiences. Belal said that this in itself is not a problem in principle, 'otherwise we will be thinking like dinosaurs'. He explained that bringing social media stars to the traditional media should happen step by step, in consideration of established media ethics and professional standards, which is not the case in Egypt.[21] This is in addition to the military's current tendency to isolate experienced journalists with high ethical and professional standards, who by default refuse to be propagandists for the state, as many find themselves being detained or having to leave the country. This has caused a serious issue of 'deforestation of professionalism' in the Egyptian media market.[22] Although this has been a problem for years, probably decades, the situation of professionalism significantly deteriorated after the coup.

Looking at these three problems closely and thinking of solutions in the near future seems unrealistic to most of the interviewed experts. Badr believed that there was no solution for these problems and there was no bright future for the Egyptian media, and it might even get worse.[23] Hossam, less pessimistically in his tone, saw no horizon for reform in the Egyptian media as long as the same power structures continue to exist in the country.[24] He explained that the regime is as paranoid as the personality of al-Sisi itself, and this will continue to be the case until he is out of the picture. A military coup against al-Sisi or another revolution are both unlikely to happen soon. All experts agree that there is no foreseeable 'opening' in the near future. Badr both pessimistically and confidently explained this highlighting the fact that 'there is no safe exit for al-Sisi' and there will not be any similarly small window for freedom of expression to the one Mubarak opened in 2004.[25] In comparison with Mubarak, Badr added, 'al-Sisi is a man who committed a massacre, and he knows well what will happen if he is no longer in power'.[26] Arguably, once he is eventually out, regardless of how, there will be room for reform, whether marginal if his successor tries to slightly liberalize in order to absorb the public anger, or building an entirely new media market, if a revolution takes place.[27] In which case, Belal optimistically argued that many young media talents will take their rightful positions, however there will be a challenge in terms of providing them with the right training. He optimistically counted on the huge Egyptian population, which is mostly young and capable of providing such talents, when the time comes. In his precisely expressed opinion, the market only needs about 1,000 well-trained journalists to be given important positions, in which case they will manage to restructure the entire media.[28] Until this happens, whether after years or decades, several topics in the post-coup Egyptian media still need further and thorough updated research, among which are the topics of activist journalism, diaspora journalism (secular and Islamist), citizen journalism, and critical consumption of media content. This will fill in several gaps in the available literature, as well as perhaps providing guidance to the one-thousand talented young journalists who Belal is patiently waiting for.

Notes

Chapter 1

1 Magdy al-Gallad, "Al-ḥyāh ʿAla Aktāf Gamāl Mubārak" [Life on the Shoulders of Gamal Mubark], *al-Masry al-Youm*, 8 July 2009, https://www.almasryalyoum.com/news/details/1902511 (accessed 28 June 2021).
2 Denis McQuail, *McQuail's Mass Communication Theory*, 6th ed. (London: SAGE, 2010).
3 Magdy al-Gallad, 'Riḥlah fi ʿAql al-Sisi' [A Journey in al-Sisi's Mind], *Masrawy*, 20 January 2018, https://bit.ly/3gZUPic (accessed 28 June 2021).
4 Among the fifteen expert journalists interviewed for this book, both Belal Fadl and Hossam el-Hamalawy insisted on having their names revealed in the text. Names of the rest of respondents remain anonymized for security reasons.
5 Belal Fadl, interview by author, January 2021.
6 Hossam el-Hamalawy, interview by author, January 2021.
7 Sami Zemni, Brecht De Smet and Koenraad Bogaert, 'Luxemburg on Tahrir Square: Reading the Arab Revolutions with Rosa Luxemburg's The Mass Strike', *Antipode* 45, no. 4 (2013): 888–907.
8 The period is also mentioned in many media sources including *al-Masry Al-Youm* and *al-Watan*, as the 'June Revolution'. However, I call it 'military coup' throughout this study, since a democratically elected president was arrested, detained and months later appeared in a courtroom, while the major face representing these events was a field marshal, Abdel Fattah Al-Sisi, who is now the president.
9 Maher Hamoud, 'Hegemony and the Interest of Egypt's Business Elite in Post-Mubarak Press', *New Middle Eastern Studies* 9, no. 1 (2019): 115–32.
10 Jonathan Hardy, *Critical Political Economy of the Media: An Introduction* (Abingdon: Routledge, 2014), 3.
11 Archive-It, 'Egypt Politics and Revolution', https://archive-it.org/collections/2358?fc=meta_Creator%3AAl-Masry+Al-Youm (accessed 28 June 2021).
12 Vincent Mosco, *The Political Economy of Communication*, 2nd ed. (London: SAGE, 2009) and Hardy, *Critical Political Economy of the Media*.

13 Christian Fuchs, *Critical Theory of Communication: New Readings of Lukács, Adorno, Marcuse, Honneth and Habermas in the Age of the Internet* (London: University of Westminster Press, 2016), 215.

14 Hardy, *Critical Political Economy of the Media*, 35.

15 Hardy, *Critical Political Economy of the Media*, 36.

16 Matthew Loveless, Nael Jebril and Vaclav Stetka, *Media and Democratisation: What is Known about the Role of Mass Media in Transitions to Democracy* (Oxford: Reuters Institute for the Study of Journalism, 2013).

17 Hardy, *Critical Political Economy of the Media*.

18 Gillian Doyle, *Understanding Media Economics*, 2nd ed. (London: SAGE, 2013).

19 Maher Hamoud, 'Egypt's Military Coup of 2013: An Analysis of the Private Press in 112 Days', *New Middle Eastern Studies* 9, no. 2 (2019): 133–48.

20 Hardy, *Critical Political Economy of the Media*, 7–8.

21 Mosco, *The Political Economy of Communication*, 36.

22 Trish Morgan, 'Adorno and the Political Economy of Communication', *The Political Economy of Communication* 1, no. 2 (2013): 44–64.

23 Carola Richter and Bettina Gräf, 'The Political Economy of Media: An Introduction', in Nadja-Christina Schneider and Carola Richter (eds), *New Media Configurations and Socio-Cultural Dynamics in Asia and the Arab World* (London: Bloomsbury, 2015), 25.

24 Christian Fuchs, *Reading Marx in the Information Age: A Media and Communication Studies Perspective on Capital, Volume 1* (Abingdon: Routledge, 2015), 4.

25 Mosco, *The Political Economy of Communication*, 64.

26 Richter and Gräf, *New Media Configurations*, 32.

27 Morgan, 'Adorno and the Political Economy of Communication'.

28 Mosco, *The Political Economy of Communication*.

29 Juergen Habermas, *The Theory of Communicative Action: Volume 2. Lifeword and System: A Critique of Functionalist Reason* (Boston: Beacon Press, 1985), 375.

30 Kai Hafez, *Radically Polarized Publics and the Demise of Media Freedom in Egypt* (Copenhagen: University of Copenhagen, 2013), 8.

31 Edward S. Herman and Noam Chomsky, *Manufacturing Consent: The Political Economy of Mass Media* (New York: Pantheon Books, 2002), 1.

32 Herman and Chomsky, *Manufacturing Consent*.

33 Mosco, *The Political Economy of* Communication, 209, 210.

Chapter 2

1 Brecht De Smet, *A Dialectical Pedagogy of Revolt: Gramsci, Vygotsky, and the Egyptian Revolution* (Leiden: Brill, 2015).

2 Dina Matar, 'Contextualising the Media and the Uprisings: A Return to History', *Middle East Journal of Culture and Communication* 5 (2012): 75–9.

3 Mohamed Zayani, 'Media, Popular Culture and Contestatory Politics in the Contemporary Middle East', *International Journal of Media and Cultural Politics* 7, no. 1 (2011): 85–99.

4 Sahar Khamis, 'The Transformative Egyptian Media Landscape: Changes, Challenges and Comparative Perspectives', *International Journal of Communication* 5 (2011): 1159–77.

5 Samir Amin, *Theory is History* (New York: Springer, 2014), 70–71.

6 Amin, *Theory is History*, 71.

7 Also known as Black Saturday when a series of riots took place on 26 January 1952 burning and looting hundreds of buildings including the Cairo Opera House.

8 The defeat of Arab Armies of which the Egyptian was the largest, and the official beginning of Israeli occupation of Palestine.

9 Isam al-Khafaji, *Tormented Births: Passages to Modernity in Europe and the Middle East* (London: I.B.Tauris, 2004).

10 Amin, *Theory is History*, 71.

11 Ray Bush, 'Politics, Power and Poverty: Twenty Years of Agricultural Reform and Market Liberalisation in Egypt', *Third World Quarterly* 28, no. 8 (2007): 1599–615.

12 Joel Beinin, 'Labor, Capital, and the State in Nasserist Egypt, 1952–1961', *International Journal of Middle East Studies* 21, no. 1 (1989): 71–90.

13 Angela Joya, *The Roots of Revolt: A Political Economy of Egypt from Nasser to Mubarak* (Cambridge: Cambridge University Press, 2020), 237.

14 Also called the Tripartite Aggression, an invasion of Egypt 1956 by Israel, Britain and France with the aims of regaining Western control of the Suez Canal and to remove Nasser; the United States and the Soviet Union forced the three invaders to withdraw.

15 Timothy Mitchell, *Rule of Experts: Egypt, Techno-Politics, Modernity* (Berkeley: University of California Press, 2002), 43.

16 Joya, *The Roots of Revolt*, 237.

17 Amin, *Theory is History*, 71.

18 John Lewis Gaddis, *We Now Know: Rethinking Cold War History* (New York: Oxford University Press, 1998).

19 Amin, *Theory is History*, 76.

20 Charles Tripp, *The Power and the People: Paths of Resistance in the Middle East* (Cambridge: Cambridge University Press, 2013), 153.

21 In addition to Egypt's Sinai Peninsula, the West Bank and Gaza in Palestine, parts of Jordan and the Golan Heights in Syria were all occupied by the Israeli army.

22 Amin, *Theory is History*, 126.

23 Joya, *The Roots of Revolt*, 237.

24 Brecht De Smet and Koenraad Bogaert, 'Resistance and Passive Revolution in Egypt and Morocco', in Cemal Burak Tansel (ed.), *States of Discipline: Authoritarian Neoliberalism and the Contested Reproduction of Capitalist Order* (London: Rowman & Littlefield International, 2017).

25 Ali Sabri (1920–91) was an Egyptian politician of Turkish origin and one of the Free Officers' second row leaders.

26 Nadia Ramsis Farah, *Religious Strife in Egypt: Crisis and Ideological Conflict in the Seventies* (New York: Gordon & Breach Science Publishers, 1986).

27 Sadat's policy of 'opening the door' to private investment in Egypt in the years following the 1973 October War (Yom Kippur War) with Israel.

28 Bush, 'Politics, Power and Poverty'.

29 Joya, *The Roots of Revolt*, 237.

30 Signed by Sadat and Israeli Prime Minister Menachem Begin on 17 September 1978, following twelve days of secret negotiations at Camp David in the United States.

31 Adam Hanieh, *Money, Markets, and Monarchies: The Gulf Cooperation Council and the Political Economy of the Contemporary Middle East* (Cambridge: Cambridge University Press, 2018), 134.

32 Mitchell, *Rule of Experts*.

33 Farah, *Religious Strife in Egypt*.

34 Hanieh, *Money, Markets, and Monarchies*, 135.

35 Hanieh, *Money, Markets, and Monarchies*.

36 Sami Zemni and Koenraad Bogaert, 'Trade, Security and Neoliberal Politics: Whither Arab Reform? Evidence from the Moroccan Case', *The Journal of North African Studies* 14, no. 1 (2009): 91–107.

37 Founded by Sadat in 1978, considered a de facto single party with authoritarian characteristics within an officially multi-party system until its dismantling in response to the 2011 uprising.

38 Joya, *The Roots of Revolt*, 238.

39 Mitchell, *Rule of Experts*.

40 Tripp, *The Power and the People*, 156.

41 Ishac Diwan and Marc Schiffbauer, 'Private Banking and Crony Capitalism in Egypt', *Business and Politics* 2r0, no 3 (2018): 390–409, 407.

42 Joya, *The Roots of Revolt*, 238.

43 Joya, *The Roots of Revolt*, 240.

44 Joya, *The Roots of Revolt*.

45 Amr Adly, 'Mubarak (1990–2011): The State of Corruption', *Arab Reform Initiative* (2011): 1–19.

46 Hanieh, *Money, Markets, and Monarchies*, 141.

47 Hanieh, *Money, Markets, and Monarchies*, 173.

48 Ishac Diwan, 'Understanding Revolution in the Middle East: The Central Role of the Middle Class', *Middle East Development Journal* 5, no. 1 (2013): 1350004-1-1350004-30, 1350004-20.

49 Joya, *The Roots of Revolt*, 242.

50 Maher Hamoud, 'Editor's Letter: Egyptians between the Two Gamals (5 of 5): Sisi in Nasser's Suit, Sadat's Tongue and Mubarak's Fist, *Daily News Egypt*, 5 December 2013, https://dailynewsegypt.com/2013/12/05/egyptians-between-the-two-gamals-5-of-5-sisi-in-nassers-suite-sadats-tongue-and-mubaraks-fist (accessed 28 June 2021).

51 Hanieh, *Money, Markets, and Monarchies*, 2018, 135–136.

52 El- Hamalawy, interview.

53 Joya, *The Roots of Revolt*, 137.

54 Joya, *The Roots of Revolt*.

55 Yezid Sayigh, *Owners of the Republic: An Anatomy of Egypt's Military Economy* (Beirut: Carnegie Middle East Center, 2019), 19.

56 Sayigh, *Owners of the Republic*.

57 Sayigh, *Owners of the Republic*.

58 Sayigh, *Owners of the Republic*, 20.

59 Joya, *The Roots of Revolt*, 137.

60 Sayegh *Owners of the Republic*, 20.

61 Sayigh, *Owners of the Republic*.

62 Sayigh, *Owners of the Republic*.

63 Lawrence Joffe, 'Abdel-Halim Abu Ghazala: Egyptian defence minister with strong anti-communist views', *The Guardian*, 30 September 2008, https://www.theguardian.com/world/2008/sep/30/egypt (accessed 28 June 2021).

64 Wael Abul-Saoud, 'Jamilāt fi Malafāt al-Qadāya (2): Ḥasna' Misr al-Jadidah allai Ataḥat bel Mušīr' [Beauties in Court Files (2): Heliopolis Lady who Overthrew the Field Marshal], *al-Jarida*, 30 June 2014, https://www.aljarida.com/articles/1462359571481952800 (accessed 28 June 2021).

65 Sayegh, *Owners of the Republic*, 21.

66 Tripp, *The Power and the People*, 162.

67 Joya, *The Roots of Revolt*, 138

68 Hanieh, *Money, Markets, and Monarchies*, 249.

69 Sayegh *Owners of the Republic*, 22.

70 El-Hamalawy, interview.

71 Hanieh, *Money, Markets, and Monarchies*, 164.

72 Elke Grawert and Zeinab Abul-Magd, *Businessmen in Arms: How the Military and Other Armed Groups Profit in the MENA Region* (Lanham: Rowman & Littlefield, 2016), 34–5.

73 Hazem Kandil, *Soldiers, Spies, and Statesmen: Egypt's Road to Revolt* (New York: Verso, 2012), 234.

74 Tom Johnston McFadden, *Daily Journalism in the Arab States* (Columbus: Ohio State University Press, 1953), 2.

75 Noha Mellor, *Arab Journalists in Transitional Media* (New York: Hampton Press, 2011).

76 Noha Mellor, *The Making of Arab News* (New York: Rowman & Littlefield Publishers, 2005).

77 Founded in 1875, the most widely circulating state-run Egyptian daily and second oldest after *Al-Waqa'e Al-Masriya* ('The Egyptian Events', founded 1828).

78 Founded in 1954 following the July military coup using the facilities of Al Wafd Party's disestablished daily *Al-Misri* ('The Egyptian').

79 Founded two months before the 1952 July coup by *Akhbar Al-Youm* newspaper, which itself was founded in 1944.

80 Founded in 1956, issued by Al-Tahrir Publishing House along with *Al-Gomhuria* newspaper.

81 First aired on 4 July 1953 to the Egyptian population and later to the whole Arab World, Europe and North America.

82 Edmund Ghareeb, 'New Media and the Information Revolution in the Arab World: An Assessment', *Middle East Journal* 54, no. 3 (2000): 395-418.

83 Yahya Abu Bakr, Saad Labib and Hamdy Kandil, *Development of Communication in the Arab States: Needs and Priorities* (Paris: UNESCO, 1985).

84 Also called the May Events, a reshuffle of political power by Sadat on 15 May 1971 against the ultra-left faction of Free Officers who attempted to stage a military coup against him, while giving a speech on state-TV.

85 Hisham Kassem, interview by author, March 2022.

86 Munir K. Nasser, *Press, Politics, and Power: Egypt's Heikal and Al-Ahram* (Ames: The Iowa State University Press, 1979), and Munir K. Nasser, *Egyptian Mass Media under Nasser and Sadat* (Columbia: Association for Education in Journalism and Mass Communication, 1990).

87 Awatif Abdel Rahman, *Dirāsāt fil-Saḥafa al-Misrya wal-Arabya: Qadāyā Mo'āsira* [Studies in Egyptian and Arab Press: Current issues] (Cairo: al-Arabi, 1989), 33.

88 James Poniwozik, 'What You See vs. What They See', *Time*, 7 April 2003, http://content.time.com/time/magazine/article/0,9171,1004593,00.html (accessed 28 June 2021).

89 The newspaper of the Labour Party founded in 1978, which turned Islamist in 1986.

90 Founded in 1995 by a license from Cyprus, closed in 1998, relaunched as a weekly in 2005, and turned daily in 2007.

91 Fadl, interview.

92 Ahmed Bahgat is also the founder of Bahgat Group.

93 Mellor, *The Making of Arab News*.

94 Reda, interview by author, May 2015.

95 Wesam, interview by author, May 2015.

96 Amina Elbendary, 'TV Meets the Madding Crowd', *al-Ahram Weekly*, 14 June 2001: 14–20.

97 Ghareeb, 'New Media and the Information Revolution in the Arab World'.

98 Ahmed Al-Rawi and Adel Iskandar 'News Coverage of the Arab Spring: State-Run News Agencies as Discursive Propagators of News', *Digital Journalism*, (2021): 1–22.

99 Rasha Allam, 'From Flabby to Fit: Restructuring the Public Broadcasting System in Egypt' *Global Media and Communication* 17, no. 3 (2021): 297–320, 307.

100 Kassem, interview.

101 Ihsan, interview by author, May 2015.

102 Kai Hafez and David L. Paletz, *Mass Media, Politics, and Society in the Middle East* (Cresskill: Hampton Press, 2001), 8.

103 Nour, interview by author, May 2015.

104 Hanan Badr, 'Egypt's Media System: Historic Legacies and Blocked Potentials for Independent Media', *Publizistik* 65 (2020): 63–79, 73.

105 Alaa, interview by author, May 2015.

106 Rasha Abdulla, *Egypt's media in the Midst of Revolution* (Washington DC: Carnegie Endowment for International Peace, 2014), 4.

107 This section is partially based on a previously published article by the author: Hamoud, 'Hegemony and the Interest of Egypt's Business Elite'.

108 David Harvey, *The New Imperialism* (Oxford: Oxford University Press. 2003), 28.

109 Maha Abdelrahman, *Egypt's Long Revolution: Protest Movements and Uprisings* (Abingdon: Routledge, 2015).

110 Abdelrahman, *Egypt's Long Revolution*, 3–4.

111 Robert Entman, 'Framing: Toward Clarification of a Fractured Paradigm', *Journal of Communication* 43, no. (1993): 51–8.

112 Donatella Della Ratta, Naomi Sakr and Jakob Skovgaard-Petersen, *Arab Media Moguls* (London: I.B. Tauris, 2015).

113 Rodney Benson, 'Bringing the Sociology of Media Back In', *Political Communication* 21, no. 3 (2004): 103–25.

114 Timothy Cook, 'The News Media as a Political Institution: Looking Backward and Looking Forward', *Political Communication* 23, no. 2 (2006): 159–71.

115 Cook, 'The News Media as a Political Institution'.

116 Ihsan, interview.

117 Kai Hafez, 'Radically Polarized Publics and the Demise of Media Freedom in Egypt', *Égypte/Monde Arabe* 12, no. 1 (2015): 37–49.

118 Jakob Skovgaard-Petersen, 'An Introduction', in Donatella Della Ratta, Naomi Sakr and Jakob Skovgaard-Petersen (eds), *Arab Media Moguls* (London: I.B. Tauris, 2015).

119 Reda, interview.

120 Badr, *Egypt's Media System*, 74.

121 Skovgaard-Petersen, *Arab Media Moguls*.

122 Tourya Guaaybess, 'Broadcasting and Businessmen in Egypt: Revolution Is Business', in Donatella Della Ratta, Naomi Sakr, and Jakob Skovgaard-Petersen (eds), *Arab Media Moguls* (London: I.B. Tauris, 2015).

123 Nour, interview.

124 Herman and Chomsky, *Manufacturing Consent*, 1–2.

125 Alaa, interview.

126 Kassem, interview.

127 Kassem, interview.

128 Nasser, *Egyptian Mass Media under Nasser and Sadat*.

129 Nasser, *Press, Politics, and Power: Egypt's Heikal and Al-Ahram*.

130 Nasser, *Egyptian Mass Media under Nasser and Sadat*.

131 Toby Mendel, *Political and Media Transitions in Egypt: A Snapshot of Media Policy and Regulatory Environment* (Washington DC: Internews, 2011).

132 Nour, interview.

133 Hafez, 'Radically Polarized Publics'.

134 Maryam Wahid, 'Al-Khāriṭa al-Iʿlāmiyya al-Misriyya baʿda al-Thawra: Arqām wa-Tashrīʿāt wa-Qaḍāyā' [The Egyptian Media Map after the Revolution: Numbers, Legislations and Issues], *Al-Arabiya Studies Institute*, 12 February 2013, https://web.archive.org/web/20170509221740/http://www.alarabiya.net/articles/2013/02/12/265930.html (accessed 28 June 2021).

135 Alaa, interview.

136 Wahid, 'The Egyptian Media Map'.

137 Mendel, *Political and Media Transitions in Egypt*.

138 Ihsan, interview.

139 Wesam, interview.

140 Badr, *Egypt's Media System*, 63.

141 Allam, *Restructuring the Public Broadcasting System*, 317.

142 Mostafa Mohie, 'One, Two, Three, Four Media Laws: How Media Legislation in Egypt is Staging State Control', *Mada Masr*, 6 December 2016, https://www.madamasr.com/en/2016/12/06/feature/politics/one-two-three-four-media-laws-how-media-legislation-in-egypt-is-staging-state-control (accessed 28 June 2021).

143 Reda, interview.

144 Noha Atef, 'Pourquoi les radios locales disparaissent à Alexandrie?' [Why Do Local Radio Stations Disappear in Alexandria?], *Open Edition Journals*, no. 17 (2018): 238.

145 This section is partially based on a previously published article by the author: Hamoud, 'Hegemony and the Interest of Egypt's Business Elite'.

146 Kassem, interview.

147 Tayseer, interview by author, March 2022.

148 Tamam, interview by author, March 2022.

149 Youssef Abdel Kader, 'Man Howa Salah Diab?' [Who is Salah Diab?], *DotMasr*, 9 November 2015, https://bit.ly/2Tgdoph (accessed 28 June 2021).

150 Tayseer, interview.

151 Tamam, interview.

152 Tayseer, interview.

153 Sami Kamal Eddin, 'Mohammed Al-Amin: Milliārdīr 'Fulūl' al-Iʿlām' [Mohammed Al-Amin: Billionaire of the Media's 'Remnants'], *al-Ahrām al-ʿArabi*, 13 December 2012, http://arabi.ahram.org.eg/News/17973.aspx (accessed 17 November 2018).

154 Kamal Eddin, 'Mohammed Al-Amin: Milliārdīr 'Fulūl' al-Iʿlām' [Mohammed Al-Amin.

155 Kamal Eddin, 'Mohammed Al-Amin: Milliārdīr 'Fulūl' al-Iʿlām' [Mohammed Al-Amin.

156 Reda, interview.

157 Wesam, interview.

158 Nour, interview.

159 Nour, interview.

160 Alaa, interview.

161 Skovgaard-Petersen, *Arab Media Moguls*.

162 Sami Kamal Eddin, *Al-Ṣaḥāfa al-Ḥarām* [Forbidden Press] (Giza: Kayan, 2013), 43.

163 Good News, 'Magdy al-Gallad: 700 Alf Junayh Mukafaʾat Nehāyat al-ḫidmah min al-Masry al-Youm wa 200 Alf Junayh Rāteb Šahri fi al-Watan' [Magdy al-Gallad: EGP 700,000 End of Contract from *al-Masry al-Youm* and 200,000

Monthly Salary from *al-Watan*], 6 March 2012, http://www.masress.com/gn4me/4086359 (accessed 28 June 2021).

164 Tamam, interview.

165 Gololy, 'Magdy al-Gallad: CV', https://bit.ly/3dmuybV (accessed 28 June 2021).

166 Kassem, interview.

167 Tayseer, interview.

168 Kamal Eddin, *Al-Ṣaḥāfa al-Ḥarām*, 159.

169 Al-Gallad, 'Life on the Shoulders of Gamal Mubarak'.

170 Kamal Eddin, *Al-Ṣaḥāfa al-Ḥarām*.

171 El-Hamalawy, interview.

172 Yasser Rizk, 'Ayyām Lahā Tārīkh' [Days that have History], *al-Masry al-Youm*, 21 June 2014, http://www.almasryalyoum.com/news/details/468406 (accessed 28 June 2021).

173 Tayseer, interview.

174 Aseel, interview by author, March 2022.

175 Hafez, 'Radically Polarized Publics'.

176 Aseel, interview.

177 Magdy al-Gallad, 'Ana Sursār, wa Anta Ayḍan' [I am a Cockroach, and You too], *al-Watan*, 2 July 2015, https://www.elwatannews.com/news/details/762787 (accessed 28 June 2021).

178 Aseel, interview.

179 Mohamed Abbas, 'Al-Sisi: Abdel Naser Kān Maḥzūz' [Al-Sisi: Abel Naser was Lucky], *al-Masry al-Youm*, 5 August 2014, https://www.almasryalyoum.com/news/details/495094 (accessed 28 June 2021).

180 Reporters without Borders, 'Egyptian Media Group', https://egypt.mom-rsf.org/en/owners/companies/detail/company/company/show/egyptian-media-group (accessed 28 June 2021).

181 AFTE 2020, https://afteegypt.org/en/media_freedom-2/2020/09/27/20036-afteegypt.html

182 Sarah Ramadan, 'Who is to Conquer: Drama Production between the Private Sector and Intelligence Services', *Association for Freedom of Thought and Expression* (2020): 4–20.

183 Historically, there have been two competing intelligence entities in Egypt since Sadat: the General Intelligence, which is close to the presidency and friendly to the business elite, and the Military Intelligence, which is close to the Ministry of Defence, and obviously favours the military elite. Both, however, are run by military personnel. Al-Sisi was the head of the latter during the 2011 uprising and managed to win the historical competition once he became the president in 2014 by bringing his military loyalists in to the General Intelligence. We can say

today that there is therefore no longer competition between the two agencies, at least visibly, and that their political agendas – al-Sisi's own will – are the same.

184 Reporters without Borders, 'Egyptian Media Group'.

185 Ramadan, 'Who is to Conquer'.

186 Ramadan, 'Who is to Conquer'.

187 Ramadan, 'Who is to Conquer'.

188 Ramadan, 'Who is to Conquer'.

189 Ramadan, 'Who is to Conquer'.

190 Hossam Bahgat, 'Looking into the Latest Acquisition of Egyptian Media Companies by General Intelligence', *Mada Masr*, 21 December 2017, https://www.madamasr.com/en/2017/12/21/feature/politics/looking-into-the-latest-acquisition-of-egyptian-media-companies-by-general-intelligence (accessed 28 June 2021).

191 Bahgat, 'Looking into the Latest Acquisition of Egyptian Media Companies by General Intelligence'.

192 Bahgat, 'Looking into the Latest Acquisition of Egyptian Media Companies by General Intelligence'.

193 Reporters without Borders, 'Egyptian Media Group'.

194 Hamoud, 'Egypt's Military Coup of 2013'.

195 El-Hamalawy, interview.

196 El-Hamalawy, interview.

197 El-Hamalawy, interview.

198 Nour, interview.

199 Aseel, interview.

200 Tayseer, interview.

201 Tayseer, interview.

202 Nour, Interview.

203 Tamam, interview.

204 Badr, *Egypt's Media System*.

Chapter 3

1 Mosco, *The Political Economy of Communication*.

2 Hardy, *Critical Political Economy of the Media*, 135.

3 Hardy, *Critical Political Economy of the Media*, 137.

4 Kassem, interview.

5 Herman and Chomsky, *Manufacturing Consent*, 15.

6 Herman and Chomsky, *Manufacturing Consent*, 16.

7 Herman and Chomsky, *Manufacturing Consent*, 16, 17.

8 Relli Shechter, 'Press Advertising in Egypt: Business Realities and Local Meaning', *The Arab Studies Journal* 10, no. 11 (2002): 44–66.

9 Shechter, 'Press Advertising in Egypt'.

10 Shechter, 'Press Advertising in Egypt, 45.

11 Relli Shechter, 'Glocal Mediators: Marketing in Egypt during the Open-Door Era (Infitah)', *Enterprise & Society* 9, no. 4 (2008): 762–87.

12 Shechter, 'Glocal Mediators', 762.

13 Shechter, 'Glocal Mediators'.

14 Shechter, 'Glocal Mediators', 769.

15 Shechter, 'Glocal Mediators', 771–2.

16 Allam, *Restructuring the Public Broadcasting System*, 307.

17 Skovgaard-Petersen, *Arab Media Moguls*.

18 Mellor, *Arab Journalists in Transitional Media*.

19 Beshara, interview by author, January 2021.

20 Gehad, interview by author, January 2021.

21 Nour, interview by author, January 2021.

22 Beshara, interview.

23 Gehad, interview.

24 Badr, interview by author, January 2021.

25 Baraa, interview by author, January 2021.

26 Baraa, interview.

27 Al-Mal, 'Tarek Nour, Ḥayātuh, wa Qissat Najāhuh, wa Kifāhuh' [Tarek Nour, his Life, his Success Story, and his Perseverance], 3 August 2020, https://www.almaal.org/tariq-nour-s-life-and-success-story#i-6 (accessed 4 March 2021).

28 Tarek Nour Communications, 'About Us', http://www.tareknour.com/en/about-us (accessed 29 June 2021).

29 Samir Raafat, 'The Mass: From the 60's Music Scene', *Egy.Com*, 4 October 1997, http://www.egy.com/people/97-10-04.php (accessed 29 June 2021).

30 Al-Mal, 'Tarek Nour'.

31 Discogs, 'Americana A.A.V', https://www.discogs.com/label/639716-Americana-AAV (accessed 29 June 2021).

32 Shechter, 'Glocal Mediators', 778–9.

33 Shechter, 'Glocal Mediators', 780.

34 Tarek Nour Communications, 'Schweppes, Hassan Abdin 1983', *YouTube*, 2001, https://www.youtube.com/watch?v=tWLa1nhHfDU (accessed 29 June 2021).

35 Beshara, interview.

36 Shechter, 'Glocal Mediators', 780.

37 Fadl, interview.

38 Fadl, interview.

39 Fadl, interview.

40 Al-Mal, 'Tarek Nour'.

41 Fadl, interview.

42 Beshara, interview.

43 Baraa, interview.

44 Osama Diab, *'Prime-Time Nationalism: The Rational and Economic Underpinnings of the June 30 Nationalist "Hysteria"'* (PhD diss., Ghent University, Ghent, 2018), 86.

45 Mohamed Abu Awad, 'Tarek Nour wa-Tijārah bisomʿat al-Misriyīn' [Tarek Nour and Trading in the Reputation of Egyptians], *al-Youm al-Sabeʿ*, 3 June 2019, https://bit.ly/3hxmhmP (accessed 29 June 2021).

46 Akhbar al-Youm, 'Al-Baz: Somʿat Tarek Nour "ʿala al-Maḥak" wa Otālebhu be-Iʿlān Themateh al-Māleyah' [Al-Baz: Tarek Nour's Reputation is 'at Stake' and I Demand him to Declare his Financial Liability], 28 November 2018, https://bit.ly/3qyXToD (accessed 29 June 2021).

47 Tamam, interview.

48 Aseel, interview.

49 Tayseer, interview.

50 Reporters without Borders, 'Tamer Morsi', https://egypt.mom-rsf.org/en/owners/individual-owners/detail/owner/owner/show/tamer-morsi (accessed 29 June 2021).

51 Egypt Today, 'Tamer Morsi Appointed as new Egyptian Media Group CEO', 22 February 2018, https://www.egypttoday.com/Article/1/43531/Tamer-Morsi-appointed-as-new-Egyptian-Media-Group-CEO (accessed 29 June 2021).

52 Reporters without Borders, 'Tamer Morsi'.

53 Nevin Youssef, 'Hal Bāta al-Intāj al-Deramī fī Misr taḥta Saytarat al-Dawlah?' [Has Drama Production in Egypt Become under State Control?], BBC, 6 May 2019, https://www.bbc.com/arabic/middleeast-48178108 (accessed 29 June 2021).

54 Al-Wafd, 'Hiwār, Tamer Morsy: Iʿlām al-Misriyīn Tuʿīd Bināʾ Sūq al-Dirāmā wal-Iʿlān' [Interview with Tamer Morsy: EMG is Rebuilding the Drama and Advertising Markets], 14 May 2018, https://bit.ly/3gZx0Hs (accessed 29 June 2021).

55 El-Hamalawy, interview.

56 Besharah, interview.

57 Mohamed Tawfiq, 'Šarikāt al-Diʿāyah fī Misr Tantaqid Saytarat al-JayŠ ʿalā ʾIʿlānāt al-Turuq' [Egypt's Advertising Companies Criticize the Army's Control over Road

Billboards], *Al-Arabi al-Jadid*, 30 September 2015, https://bit.ly/36efrxj (accessed 29 June 2021).

58 Baraa, interview.

59 Egypt Today, 'UMS finishes "Egypt: A Piece of Heaven" documentary series', 30 September 2019, https://bit.ly/2UG4mCo (accessed 29 June 2021).

60 Kassem, interview.

Chapter 4

1 Olesya Tkacheva et al., *Internet Freedom and Political Space* (Brussels: RAND Corporation, 2013), 43.

2 Kassem, interview.

3 Hardy, *Critical Political Economy of the Media.*

4 Christian Fuchs, 'Information and Communication Technologies and Society: A Contribution to the Critique of the Political Economy of the Internet', *European Journal of Communication* 24, no. 1 (2009): 69–87.

5 Hardy, *Critical Political Economy of the Media*, 141.

6 Hardy, *Critical Political Economy of the Media*, 212.

7 Tkacheva et al., *Internet Freedom and Political Space,* 203.

8 Fadl, interview.

9 Tkacheva et al., *Internet Freedom and Political Space,* 4–5.

10 Tkacheva et al., *Internet Freedom and Political Space,* 2.

11 Tkacheva et al., *Internet Freedom and Political Space,* 6.

12 Badr, interview.

13 Tamam, Interview.

14 Hossam el-Hamalawy, 'Al-Internet wal-Thawrah' [The Internet and the Revolution], *Bawabat al-Ishteraky*, 24 January 2021, https://revsoc.me/politics/43522 (accessed 29 June 2021).

15 Tkacheva et al., *Internet Freedom and Political Space*, 59.

16 El-Hamalawy, 'The Internet and the Revolution'.

17 Badr, interview.

18 Courtney C. Radsch, *Cyberactivism and Citizen Journalism in Egypt: Digital Dissidence and Political Change* (London: Palgrave, 2016), 11.

19 Radsch, *Cyberactivism and Citizen Journalism in Egypt.*

20 El-Hamalawy, 'The Internet and the Revolution'.

21 El-Hamalawy, 'The Internet and the Revolution'.

22 Badr, interview.

23 El-Hamalawy, 'The Internet and the Revolution'.

24 Radsch, *Cyberactivism and Citizen Journalism in Egypt*, 10.

25 El-Hamalawy, 'The Internet and the Revolution'.

26 Radsch, *Cyberactivism and Citizen Journalism in Egypt*, 12.

27 Radsch, *Cyberactivism and Citizen Journalism in Egypt*.

28 El-Hamalawy, 'The Internet and the Revolution'.

29 Fadl, interview.

30 Fadl, interview.

31 El-Hamalawy, 'The Internet and the Revolution'.

32 El-Hamalawy, 'The Internet and the Revolution'.

33 El-Hamalawy, 'The Internet and the Revolution'.

34 Radsch, *Cyberactivism and Citizen Journalism in Egypt*, 11.

35 El-Hamalawy, 'The Internet and the Revolution'.

36 Radsch, *Cyberactivism and Citizen Journalism in Egypt*, 11.

37 El-Hamalawy, 'The Internet and the Revolution'.

38 Radsch, *Cyberactivism and Citizen Journalism in Egypt*, 10.

39 El-Hamalawy, 'The Internet and the Revolution'.

40 El-Hamalawy, 'The Internet and the Revolution'.

41 Baraa, interview.

42 Radsch, *Cyberactivism and Citizen Journalism in Egypt*, 12–13.

43 Badr, interview.

44 El-Hamalawy, 'The Internet and the Revolution'.

45 Badr, interview.

46 Mohammed El-Nawawy and Sahar Khamis, 'Blogging against Violations of Human Rights in Egypt: An Analysis of Five Political Blogs', *International journal of communication*, (2014): 1–18.

47 Radsch, *Cyberactivism and Citizen Journalism in Egypt*, 19.

48 Radsch, *Cyberactivism and Citizen Journalism in Egypt*, 10.

49 Beshara, interview.

50 Radsch, *Cyberactivism and Citizen Journalism in Egypt*, 11.

51 Radsch, *Cyberactivism and Citizen Journalism in Egypt*, 13.

52 Fadl, interview.

53 Radsch, *Cyberactivism and Citizen Journalism in Egypt*, 13–14.

54 El-Hamalawy, 'The Internet and the Revolution'.

55 El-Hamalawy, 'The Internet and the Revolution'.

56 El-Hamalawy, 'The Internet and the Revolution'.

57 Radsch, *Cyberactivism and Citizen Journalism in Egypt*, 15.

58 Radsch, *Cyberactivism and Citizen Journalism in Egypt*, 15–16.

59 Radsch, *Cyberactivism and Citizen Journalism in Egypt*, 16.

60 Radsch, *Cyberactivism and Citizen Journalism in Egypt*.

61 El-Hamalawy, 'The Internet and the Revolution'.

62 Gehad, interview.

63 Baraa, interview.

64 El-Hamalawy, 'The Internet and the Revolution'.

65 Tkacheva et al., *Internet Freedom and Political Space*, 71.

66 El-Hamalawy, 'The Internet and the Revolution'.

67 Tkacheva et al., *Internet Freedom and Political Space*, 70–1.

68 El-Hamalawy, 'The Internet and the Revolution'.

69 Beshara, interview.

70 Beshara and Baraa, interview.

71 Beshara and Baraa, interview.

72 Hanan Badr, 'Before the "Arab Spring": How Challengers Pushed Counter-Issues in Egypt's Hybrid Media System, *Media, War & Conflict* 14, no. 4 (2019): 522–41.

73 El-Hamalawy, 'The Internet and the Revolution'.

74 Beshara, interview.

75 Tkacheva et al., *Internet Freedom and Political Space*, 71.

76 Aljosha Karim Schapals and Zahera Harb, '"Everything Has Changed, and Nothing Has Changed in Journalism": Revisiting Journalistic Sourcing Practices and Verification Techniques during the 2011 Egyptian Revolution and Beyond', *Digital Journalism*, (2021): 1–19.

77 Gehad, interview.

78 Badr, interview.

79 Beshara, interview.

80 El-Hamalawy, 'The Internet and the Revolution'.

81 Schapals and Harb '"Everything Has Changed, and Nothing Has Changed in Journalism"'.

82 Tkacheva et al., *Internet Freedom and Political Space*, 70.

83 Tkacheva et al., *Internet Freedom and Political Space*, 71–2.

84 Fadl, interview.

85 Mohamed Fathi, 'Intišār al-Hawātef al-Maḥmūlah Yafūq Muʿadal al-Mawālīd fi al-Šarq al-Awsat' [The Spread of Mobile Phones Exceeds Birth Rates in the Middle East], *al-Masry al-Youm*, 11 December 2012, https://www.almasryalyoum.com/news/details/261478 (accessed 29 June 2021).

86 El-Hamalawy, 'The Internet and the Revolution'.

87 Baraa, interview.

88 El-Hamalawy, 'The Internet and the Revolution'.

89 Baraa, interview.

90 Hardy, *Critical Political Economy of the Media*, 212.

91 Hardy, *Critical Political Economy of the Media*.

92 Radsch, *Cyberactivism and Citizen Journalism in Egypt*, 332.

93 Radsch, *Cyberactivism and Citizen Journalism in Egypt*.

94 El-Hamalawy, 'The Internet and the Revolution'.

95 Ekaterina Zhuravskaya, Maria Petrova, and Ruben Enikolopov, 'Political Effects of the Internet and Social Media', *Annual Review of Economics* 12, (2020): 415–38, 430.

96 Besharaa, interview.

97 Fadl, interview.

98 Zhuravskaya et al, 'Political Effects of the Internet', 431.

99 Gehad, interview.

100 Walid Abbas, 'Al-Lijān al-Electrūneyah aw Sinā'at ad-Di'āyah al-Siyāsiyah fi Misr' [The Electronic Committees and Manufacturing Political Propaganda in Egypt], *Mont Carlo*, 29 September 2014, https://bit.ly/3tOuWra (accessed 19 November 2022).

101 Badr, interview.

102 Al-Arabi al-Jadid, "Lejān Elektrōneya Tudāfe' 'an al-Sisi, Ta'limāt 'am Tawāred Ḥawāṭer?' [Electronic Committees Defend al-Sisi, Orders or Telepathy?], 2 November 2017, https://bit.ly/361hZi8 (accessed 29 June 2021).

103 Al-Khalij al-Jadid, 'Al-Lejān al-Elektrōneyah fi Misr, al-Tanzim wal-Tamwil, wal-Mahām' [The Electronic Committees in Egypt: Organization, Funding and Missions], 10 March 2020, https://bit.ly/3dsRG8v (accessed 29 June 2021).

104 Katie Paul, 'Facebook Removes Two Middle East-Focused Fake Account Betworks', *Reuters*, 2 March 2020, https://www.reuters.com/article/us-facebook-gulf-idUSKBN20P2XH (accessed 29 June 2021).

105 Aseel, interview.

106 Zhuravskaya et al, 'Political Effects of the Internet', 431–2.

107 Badr, interview.

108 Beshara, interview.

109 Tayseer, interview.

110 Tamam, interview.

111 Aseel, interview.

112 Zhuravskaya et al, 'Political Effects of the Internet', 432.

113 Badr, interview.

114 Beshara, interview.

115 Badr, interview.

116 Hanan Badr, 'Social Movements and Social Media in a Post-Revolutionary Political Culture: Constitutional Debates in Egypt', in C. Richter, A. Antonakis and C. Harders (eds), *Digital Media and the Politics of Transformation in the Arab*

World and Asia. Studies in International, Transnational and Global Communications (Wiesbadan: Springer VS, 2018), 161–86.

117 Badr, interview.
118 Zhuravskaya et al, 'Political Effects of the Internet', 432.
119 Zhuravskaya et al, 'Political Effects of the Internet'.
120 Zhuravskaya et al, 'Political Effects of the Internet'.
121 Baraa, interview.
122 Simon Kemp, 'Digital 2021: Egypt', *DataReportal*, 11 February 2021, https://datareportal.com/reports/digital-2021-egypt?rq=egypt (accessed 29 June 2021).
123 Kassem, interview.
124 Joey Shea and Alexei Abrahams, 'Disinformation Wars in Egypt: The Inauthentic Battle on Twitter between Egyptian Government and Opposition', *Just Security*, 26 October 2020, https://www.justsecurity.org/72961/disinformation-wars-in-egypt-the-inauthentic-battle-on-twitter-between-egyptian-government-and-opposition (accessed 29 June 2021).
125 Shea and Abrahams, 'Disinformation Wars in Egypt'.
126 Shea and Abrahams, 'Disinformation Wars in Egypt'.
127 Shea and Abrahams, 'Disinformation Wars in Egypt'.
128 Shea and Abrahams, 'Disinformation Wars in Egypt'.
129 Mostafa el-Sayed Hussin, 'The Sisi Firewall: Cyber-Suppression Strategies and the Future of Cyberspace in Egypt', *Arab Center for Research and Policy Studies*, (2020): 1–6.
130 Badr, interview.
131 Beshara, interview.
132 Mohamed Taher and Marwa Fatafta, 'Misr: Tārīḫ Tawīl min Morāqabat al-Internet wal-'Itisālāt' [Egypt: A Long History of Surveilling Internet and Communications], *Access Now*, 6 October 2020, https://bit.ly/3y5L8EJ (accessed 29 June 2021).
133 Taher and Fatafta, 'Egypt: A Long History of Surveilling Internet'.
134 Taher and Fatafta, 'Egypt: A Long History of Surveilling Internet'.
135 Badr, interview.
136 Baraa, interview.
137 Taher and Fatafta, 'Egypt: A Long History of Surveilling Internet'.
138 Hussin, 'The Sisi Firewall'.
139 Amr Hamzawy, 'Qānūn Jarā'em Taqniyat al-Ma'lūmāt, 'Istikmāl Ḥisār Ḥoreyat al-Ta'bīr 'an al-Ra'y fi Misr' [Cyber Criminal Law: Continuing the Siege on Freedom of Expression in Egypt], *al-Quds al-Arabi*, 3 December 2018, https://bit.ly/35Y3MT5 (accessed 29 June 2021).
140 Hamzawy, 'Cyber Criminal Law'.

141 Badr, interview.

142 Baraa, interview.

143 Taher and Fatafta, 'Egypt: A Long History of Surveilling Internet'.

144 Gehad, interview.

145 Badr, interview.

146 David M Faris, 'New Media and Democracy in the Arab World', in *International Encyclopedia of the Social & Behavioral Sciences* (2nd edn) (Amsterdam: Elsevier, 2015).

147 Adel Iskandar, 'Egyptian Youth's Digital Dissent', *Journal of Democracy* 30, n. 3 (2019): 154–64.

Chapter 5

1   Entman, 'Framing: Toward Clarification of a Fractured Paradigm'.

2   Ratta, Sakr and Skovgaard-Petersen, *Arab Media Moguls*.

3   Benson, 'Bringing the Sociology of Media Back in'.

4   Khamis, 'The Transformative Egyptian Media Landscape': 1159–77.

5   Richter and Gräf, 'The Political Economy of Media': 32.

6   Hardy, *Critical Political Economy of the Media*.

7   Mosco, *The Political Economy of Communication*, 209–10.

8   Pippa Norris, Montague Kern and Marion Just, *Framing Terrorism: The News Media, the Government and the Public* (Abingdon: Routledge, 2004), Paul D'Angelo and Jim A. Kuypers, *Doing News Framing Analysis: Empirical and Theoretical Perspectives* (Abingdon: Routledge 2010).

9   Armand Mattelart and Michèle Mattelart, *Theories of Mass Communication: A Short Introduction* (London: SAGE, 1998).

10 William Gamson, 'Media Discourse as a Framing Resource', in Ann N. Crigler (ed.), *The Psychology of Political Communication* (Ann Arbor: University of Michigan Press, 1998).

11 Nicholas Abercrombie and Brian Longhurst, *Dictionary of Media Studies* (London: Penguin, 2007), 94.

12 Gaye Tuchman, *Making News: A Study in the Construction of Reality* (New York: Free Press, 1978).

13 William Gamson and Andre Modigliani, *The Changing Culture of Affirmative Action* (Greenwich: JAI Press, 1987), 143.

14 Hamoud, 'Egypt's Military Coup of 2013'.

15 'Rage' was a name given by protesters on that day who were angry at the police because of their brutality on Tuesday 25 January.

16 A term often used by Egyptian elites fighting against unexpected or uncontrollable change as a part of fear tactics, which increases xenophobia.

17 A term often used in the controlled media as another fear tactic that predicts chaos and destruction.

18 Leila Fadel and Ernesto Londoño, 'Egypt's State-Run Media Starting to Shift from Pro-Mubarak Coverage', *The Washington Post*, 9 February 2011, http://www.washingtonpost.com/wp-dyn/content/article/2011/02/09/AR2011020906234.html (accessed 29 June 2021).

19 A prominent newspaper founded in 2009 and published in Egypt and several other Arab countries.

20 Reda, interview.

21 An attack on a church in Alexandria on Saturday, 1 January 2011. Twenty-three people who were attending a new year service, were killed, and some ninety-seven were injured. Nobody was brought to trial, while various unfounded reports claim that Mubarak's Interior Minister Habib Al-Adly was involved in the bombings.

22 Nour, interview.

23 Wesam, interview.

24 Born in 1923, an Egyptian journalist who worked for seventeen years (1957–74) as the editor-in-chief of the top state newspaper *Al-Ahram*, and has been a commentator on Arab affairs for more than fifty years. He articulated the thoughts of Nasser earlier in his career and has been a member of the Central Committee of the Arab Socialist Union.

25 Alaa, interview.

26 On 2 February 2011, security officials were witnessed bribing ordinary citizens into attacking protesters in Tahrir Square with knives, swords and guns, while riding camels and horses.

27 Al-Rawi and Iskandar, 'News Coverage of the Arab Spring': 1–22.

28 Carola Richter, Indira Dupuis and Hanan Badr, 'Media pushing for political transformation: A comparative analysis of issue contestation in Poland before 1989 and Egypt before 2011', *The International Communication Gazette* 83, no. 4 (2021): 326–46.

29 Tayseer, interview.

30 Kassem, interview.

31 Tayseer, interview.

32 Maurice Chammah, 'The Scene of the Crime: October 9th, Maspero, and Egyptian Journalism after the Revolution', *Arab media and Society* 15 Spring (2012): 1–20.

33 A celebrity who is especially popular and who receives frequent and very favourable attention in the news media.

34 Ihsan, interview.

35 A measure adopted by the Supreme Council of the Armed Forces of Egypt (SCAF) on 30 March 2011 after it passed through a referendum on 19 March with a 'yes' majority vote of 77.2 percent.

36 Reda, interview.

37 The Muslim Brotherhood was banned and listed as a terrorist group by an Egyptian court ruling in 2014.

38 Noha Rayman, 'Is the Egyptian Press Ready for Democracy? Evaluating Newspaper Coverage as an Indicator of Democratization', *Arab Media and Society* 17, Winter (2013): 1–28.

39 Hafez, 'Radically Polarized Publics and the Demise of Media Freedom in Egypt'.

40 Fatima el-Issawi and Bart Cammaerts, 'Shifting Journalistic Roles in Democratic Transitions: Lessons from Egypt', *Journalism* 17, no. 5 (2016): 549–66.

41 Hamoud, 'Egypt's Military Coup of 2013'.

42 Al-Arabi al-Jadid, '70 Daqiqah Tasrībāt: Al-ʾImārāt Mawalat "Tamarod"' [70 Minute Leaks: The UAE Funded Tamarod], 1 March 2015, https://bit.ly/3hg3dco (accessed 29 June 2021).

43 Houssein Emara, 'Harakat Tamarod al-Misreyah, Man Hom wa Mādhā Yorīdoūn?' [Egypt's Tamarod Movements: Who are They and What They Want?], *France 24*, 26 June 2013, https://bit.ly/3xhOt3m (accessed 29 June 2021).

44 Emara, 'Egypt's Tamarod Movements'.

45 Emara, 'Egypt's Tamarod Movements'.

46 Ihsan, interview.

47 Tamam, interview.

48 Aseel, interview.

49 Alaa and Reda, interview.

50 Nour, interview.

51 Hisham, interview.

52 This section is partially based on a previously published article by the author: Hamoud, 'Egypt's Military Coup of 2013'.

53 El-Issawi and Cammaerts, 'Shifting Journalistic Roles'.

54 Nour, interview.

55 Iskandar, 'Egyptian Youth's Digital Dissent': 154–64.

56 Hamoud, 'Egypt's Military Coup of 2013'.

57 Alaa, interview.

58 Nour, interview.

59 Prime Minister of Egypt under the presidency of Morsi.

60 Soldiers that were kidnapped by a militant group in Sinai in 2013.

61 Egyptian satirical poet (1929–2013) who reflected on Egyptian life and inspired generations of the young to push for change.

62 An Egyptian proverb referring to a smart person who knows all secrets and how to handle them.

63 Later to become the first Prime Minister.

64 These clashes were between Supporters of Tamarod and others of the Muslim Brotherhood.

65 Alaa, interview.

66 Hany al-Waziry, 'Hamalāt Elektrōneyah Tarfaʿ Šeʿār "al-Sisi Raʾīsan li-Misr", wal-ʾIḫwān: "Laʿeb ben-Nār"' [Electronic Campaigns with the Slogan 'al-Sisi President for Egypt', and the Brotherhood: 'Playing with Fire'], *al-Watan*, 21 February 2013. http://www.elwatannews.com/news/details/134765 (accessed 29 June 2021).

67 Reda, interview.

68 Wesam, interview.

69 Habermas, *The Theory of Communicative Action*, 375.

70 Brecht De Smet, 'Revolution and Counter-Revolution in Egypt', *Science & Society* 78, no. 1 (2014): 11–40.

71 Norris, Kern, and Just, *Framing Terrorism*, D'Angelo and Kuypers, *Doing News Framing*.

Chapter 6

1 Mosco, *The Political Economy of Communication*.

2 Timothy E. Cook, 'The News Media as a Political Institution: Looking Backward and Looking Forward', *Political Communication* 23, no. 2 (2006): 159–71.

3 Abdulla, *Egypt's Media in the Midst of Revolution*, 23–4.

4 Fatima El-Issawi, 'The Role of Egyptian Media in the Coup', in *IEMed Mediterranean Yearbook 2014* (Barcelona: European Institute of the Mediterranean, 2014).

5 Richter and Gräf, 'The Political Economy of Media', 32.

6 Habermas, *The Theory of Communicative Action*, 375.

7 Herman and Chomsky, *Manufacturing Consent*, 1.

8 Mosco (2009) *The Political Economy of Communication*, 209–10.

9 Diab, *Prime-Time Nationalism*.

10 Diab, *Prime-Time Nationalism*, 80.

11 Diab, *Prime-Time Nationalism*, 81.

12 This section is partially based on a previously published article by the author: Maher Hamoud, 'Egypt's Private Press and Inciting for Violence against Journalists during the 2013 Military Coup', *Rowaq Arabi* 25, no. 3 (2020): 79–94.

13 Herman and Chomsky, *Manufacturing Consent*.

14 El-Issawi and Cammaerts, 'Shifting Journalistic Roles'.

15 BBC, 'Misr: Iġlāq Maqar Saḥifat al-Horreya wal-Adāla at-Tābeʾah lel-Iḫwān al-Muslimīn' [Egypt: Office of al-Horreya wal-Adala Newspaper of the Muslim Brotherhood Shutdown], 25 September 2013, https://www.bbc.com/arabic/middleeast/2013/09/130925_egypt_mb_newspaper (accessed 29 June 2021).

16 Noha Mellor, *Voice of the Muslim Brotherhood: Daʿwa, Discourse, and Political Communication* (Oxford: Routledge, 2017), 207.

17 Alexander Dziadosz, 'Egypt Secures Liberals' Homes after Calls for their Death', *Reuters*, 7 February 2013, https://www.reuters.com/article/us-egypt-islamists-idUSBRE9160R020130207 (accessed 29 June 2021).

18 Alaa, Ihsan and Wesam, interview.

19 Nour, interview.

20 Ihsan, interview.

21 Fatima El-Issawi, *Egyptian Media Under Transition: In the Name of the Regime, in the Name of the People?* (London: LSE, 2014).

22 Dashiell Bennett, 'Photographer May Have Captured His Own Death During Egypt Protests', *The Atlantic*, 10 July 2013, https://www.theatlantic.com/international/archive/2013/07/egyptian-photographer-captured-his-own-death/313486 (accessed 29 June 2021). The story disappeared from *The Telegraph*'s website sometime around 2019, but the exact text can be found in several other sources including *The Atlantic* here.

23 This section is partially based on a previously published article by the author: Hamoud, 'Egypt's Private Press and Inciting for Violence'.

24 El-Issawi and Cammaerts, 'Shifting Journalistic Roles'.

25 Committee to Protect Journalists, 'China, Egypt are Worst Jailers of Journalists Worldwide', 14 December 2015, https://cpj.org/2015/12/china-egypt-are-worst-jailers-of-journalists-world.php (accessed 29 June 2021).

26 Committee to Protect Journalists, 'China, Egypt are Worst Jailers of Journalists Worldwide'.

27 Nour, interview.

28 Nour, interview.

29 Alaa, interview.

30 Committee to Protect Journalists, 'Press Threatened and Detained as Egypt Marks Uprising Anniversary', 26 January 2015, https://cpj.org/2015/01/press-threatened-and-detained-as-egypt-marks-upris/ (accessed 20 November 2022).

31 Reda, interview.

32 Ihsan, interview.

33 CBS, 'Maspero: A Massacre of Christians in Egypt', 22 June 2014, https://www.cbsnews.com/news/maspero-a-massacre-of-christians-in-egypt (accessed 29 June 2021).

34 Mamdouh Wafi, '"Al-Mowātenūm al-Šurafā'", 'Adāh "Sereyah" li-Tarwē' al-Mo'āradah bi-Misr. Man Hom wa Man Yuḥarikohom?" [The 'Honourable Citizens, a 'Secret' Tool for Terrifying the Opposition in Egypt. Who are they and Who's behind Them?], *an-Nahar*, 7 June 2018, https://bit.ly/3w45sVH (accessed 29 June 2021).

35 Reda, interview.

36 CPJ mistakenly labelled the pro-military al-Fagr as 'independent' newspaper in their report on 26 January 2015.

37 Committee to Protect Journalists, 'China, Egypt are Worst Jailers of Journalists'.

38 This section is partially based on a previously published article by the author: Hamoud, 'Egypt's Private Press and Inciting for Violence'.

39 Brian Whitaker, 'Battle Station', *The Guardian*, 7 February 2003, https://www.theguardian.com/media/2003/feb/07/iraqandthemedia.afghanistan (accessed 29 June 2021).

40 Philip Seib, 'Hegemonic No More: Western Media, the Rise of Al-Jazeera, and the Influence of Diverse Voices', *International Studies Review* 7, no. 4 (2005): 601–15.

41 Omar Chatriwala, 'What Wikileaks Tells Us About Al Jazeera', *Foreign Policy*, 19 September 2011, http://foreignpolicy.com/2011/09/19/what-wikileaks-tells-us-about-al-jazeera (accessed 29 June 2021).

42 Nour, interview.

43 Reporters without Borders, 'Heavy Toll on Journalists in Two Months since Army Takeover', 2 September 2013, https://rsf.org/en/news/heavy-toll-journalists-two-months-army-takeover (accessed 29 June 2021).

44 Reda, interview.

45 State Information Service, 'Statement by the State Information Service (SIS) on Current Events in Egypt', 17 August 2013.

46 Joshua Hersh, 'Egyptian Government Slams Foreign Press as Journalists Come Under Assault', *Huffington Post*, 18 August 2013, https://www.huffingtonpost.com/2013/08/18/egypt-foreign-press_n_3775634.html?guccounter=1 (accessed 29 June 2021).

47 Alaa, interview.

48 Yasmin El Banhawy, 'Why is the Egyptian State Monopolizing the Entertainment Industry?', *Open Democracy*, 24 June 2019, https://www.opendemocracy.net/en/

north-africa-west-asia/why-egyptian-state-monopolizing-entertainment-industry (accessed 29 June 2021).

49 *The Economist*, 'How Egyptian Entertainment Has Changed under Military Rule', 10 April 2021, https://www.economist.com/middle-east-and-africa/2021/04/10/ how-egyptian-entertainment-has-changed-under-military-rule (accessed 29 June 2021).

50 *The Economist*, 'How Egyptian Entertainment Has Changed under Military Rule'.

51 El Banhawy, 'Monopolizing the Entertainment Industry'.

52 *The Economist*, 'Egyptian Entertainment under Military Rule'.

53 Badr, interview.

54 Badr, interview.

55 Aseel, interview.

56 Ramadan, 'Who is to Conquer': 10.

57 Baraa, interview.

58 *The Economist*, 'Egyptian Entertainment under Military Rule'.

59 *The Economist*, 'Egyptian Entertainment under Military Rule'.

60 Mohamed al-Aswany, 'An Industry under Threat: Ramadan 2019, Brought to You by Egyptian Media Group', *Mada Masr*, 23 December 2018, https://www. madamasr.com/en/2018/12/23/feature/culture/an-industry-under-threat-ramadan-2019-brought-to-you-by-egyptian-media-group (accessed 29 June 2021).

61 The Economist, 'Egyptian Entertainment under Military Rule'.

62 Ramadan, 'Who is to Conquer': 12.

63 Youssef, 'Drama Production under State Control'.

64 Ramadan, 'Who is to Conquer': 13.

65 El Banhawy, 'Monopolizing the Entertainment Industry'.

66 Al-Aswany, 'An Industry under Threat'.

67 Baraa, interview.

68 *The Economist*, 'Egyptian Entertainment under Military Rule'.

69 Beshara, interview.

70 Badr, interview.

71 Tayseer, interview.

72 Tamam, interview.

73 El Banhawy, 'Monopolizing the Entertainment Industry'.

74 Gehad, interview.

75 Al-Aswany, 'An Industry under Threat'.

76 *The Economist*, 'Egyptian Entertainment under Military Rule'.

77 Human Rights Watch, 'Egypt: Campaign to Crush Artistic Freedom', 16 August 2018, https://www.hrw.org/news/2018/08/16/egypt-campaign-crush-artistic-freedom (accessed 29 June 2021).

78 Gehad, interview.

79 Beshara, interview.

80 *The Economist*, 'Egyptian Entertainment under Military Rule'.

81 Aseel, interview.

82 Ramadan, 'Who is to Conquer': 13.

83 Beshara, interview.

84 El Banhawy, 'Monopolizing the Entertainment Industry'.

85 *The Economist*, 'Egyptian Entertainment under Military Rule'.

86 Rasha Allam and Dinana Hesham, 'The Future of TV and Online Video Platforms: A Study on Predictors of Use and Interaction with Content in the Egyptian Evolving Telecomm', Media & Entertainment Industries', *SAGE Open* 3 (2021): 9.

87 El Banhawy, 'Monopolizing the Entertainment Industry'.

88 Al-Aswany, 'An Industry under Threat'.

89 Kassem, interview.

90 Badr, interview.

91 *The Economist*, 'Egyptian Entertainment under Military Rule'.

92 Human Rights Watch, 'Egypt: Rab'a Killings Likely Crimes against Humanity', 12 August 2014, https://www.hrw.org/news/2014/08/12/egypt-raba-killings-likely-crimes-against-humanity (accessed 29 June 2021).

93 *The Economist*, 'Egyptian Entertainment under Military Rule'.

Chapter 7

1 Mosco, *The Political Economy of Communication*, Hardy, *Critical Political Economy of the Media*.

2 Habermas, *The Theory of Communicative Action*, 375.

3 Sara Tonsy and Aly el-Raggal, 'How Did Sisi Reproduce Authoritarianism in Egypt?', *Rowaq Arabi* 26, no. 1 (2021): 47–63.

4 Daniel C. Hallin and Paolo Mancini, *Comparing Media Systems: Three Models of Media and Politics* (Cambridge: Cambridge University Press, 2004).

5 Daniel C. Hallin and Paolo Mancini, *Comparing Media Systems Beyond the Western World* (Cambridge: Cambridge University Press 2011).

6 Beshara, interview.

7 Beshara, interview.

8 El-Hamalawy, interview.

9   Beshara, interview.
10 Beshara, interview.
11 El-Hamalawy, interview.
12 Badr, interview.
13 Beshara, interview.
14 Badr, interview.
15 Badr, interview.
16 El-Hamalawy, interview.
17 Badr, interview.
18 Badr, interview.
19 Fadl, interview.
20 Fadl, interview.
21 Fadl, interview.
22 Fadl, interview.
23 Badr, interview.
24 El-Hamalawy, interview.
25 Badr, interview.
26 Badr, interview.
27 El-Hamalawy, interview.
28 Fadl, interview.

Bibliography

Abbas, Mohamed. 'Al-Sisi: Abdel Naser Kān Maḥzūz' [Al-Sisi: Abel Naser was Lucky]. *Al-Masry al-Youm*, 5 August 2014, https://www.almasryalyoum.com/news/details/495094 (accessed 28 June 2021).

Abdel Kader, Youssef. 'Man Howa Salah Diab?' [Who is Salah Diab?]. *DotMasr*, 9 November 2015, https://bit.ly/2Tgdoph (accessed 28 June 2021).

Abdel Rahman, Awatif. *Dirāsāt fil-Saḥafa al-Misrya wal-Arabya: Qadāyā Moʿāsira* [Studies in Egyptian and Arab Press: Current issues]. Cairo: al-Arabi, 1989.

Abdelrahman, Maha. *Egypt's Long Revolution: Protest Movements and Uprisings*. Abingdon: Routledge, 2015.

Abdulla, Rasha. *Egypt's Media in the Midst of Revolution*. Washington DC: Carnegie Endowment for International Peace, 2014.

Abercrombie, Nicholas and Brian Longhurst. *Dictionary of Media Studies*. London: Penguin, 2007.

Abu Awad, Mohamed. 'Tarek Nour wa-Tijārah bisomʿat al-Misriyīn' [Tarek Nour and Trading in the Reputation of Egyptians]. *Al-Youm al-Sabea*, 3 June 2019, https://bit.ly/3hxmhmP (accessed 29 June 2021).

Abu Bakr, Yahya, Saad Labib and Hamdy Kandil. *Development of Communication in the Arab States: Needs and Priorities*. Paris: UNESCO, 1985.

Abul-Saoud, Wael. 'Jamilāt fi Malafāt al-Qadāya (2): Ḥasnaʾ Misr al-Jadidah allai Ataḥat bel Mušīr' [Beauties in Court Files (2): Heliopolis Lady who Overthrew the Field Marshal]. *Al-Jarida*, 30 June 2014, https://www.aljarida.com/articles/1462359571481952800 (accessed 28 June 2021).

Adly, Amr. 'Mubarak (1990–2011): The State of Corruption'. *Arab Reform Initiative* (2011): 1–19.

Akhbar al-Youm. 'Al-Baz: Somʿat Tarek Nour "ʿala al-Maḥak" wa Otālebhu be-Iʿlān Themateh al-Māleyah' [Al-Baz: Tarek Nour's Reputation is 'at Stake' and I Demand him to Declare his Financial Liability]. 28 November 2018, https://bit.ly/3qyXToD (accessed 29 June 2021).

Al-Arabi al-Jadid. '70 Daqiqah Tasrībāt: Al-ʾImārāt Mawalat "Tamarod"' [70 Minute Leaks: The UAE Funded Tamarod]. 1 March 2015, https://bit.ly/3hg3dco (accessed 29 June 2021).

Al-Arabi al-Jadid. "Lejān Elektrōneya Tudāfeʿ ʿan al-Sisi, Taʿlimāt ʾam Tawāred Ḥawāṭer?" [Electronic Committees Defend al-Sisi, Orders or Telepathy?]. 2 November 2017, https://bit.ly/361hZi8 (accessed 29 June 2021).

Al-Aswany, Mohamed. 'An Industry under Threat: Ramadan 2019, Brought to You by Egyptian Media Group'. *Mada Masr*, 23 December 2018, https://www.madamasr. com/en/2018/12/23/feature/culture/an-industry-under-threat-ramadan-2019-brought-to-you-by-egyptian-media-group (accessed 29 June 2021).

Al-Gallad, Magdy. "Al-ḥyāh ʿAla Aktāf Gamāl Mubārak' [Life on the Shoulders of Gamal Mubark]. *Al-Masry al-Youm*, 8 July 2009, https://www.almasryalyoum. com/news/details/1902511 (accessed 28 June 2021).

Al-Gallad, Magdy. 'Ana Sursār, wa Anta Ayḍan' [I am a Cockroach, and You too]. *Al-Watan*, 2 July 2015, https://www.elwatannews.com/news/details/762787 (accessed 28 June 2021).

Al-Gallad, Magdy. 'Riḥlah fi ʿAql al-Sisi' [A Journey in al-Sisi's Mind]. *Masrawy*, 20 January 2018, https://bit.ly/3gZUPic (accessed 28 June 2021).

Al-Khafaji, Isam. *Tormented Births: Passages to Modernity in Europe and the Middle East*. London: I.B. Tauris, 2004.

Al-Khalij al-Jadid. 'Al-Lejān al-Elektrōneyah fi Misr, al-Tanzim wal-Tamwil, wal-Mahām' [The Electronic Committees in Egypt: Organization, Funding and Missions]. 10 March 2020, https://bit.ly/3dsRG8v (accessed 29 June 2021).

Al-Mal. 'Tarek Nour, Ḥayātuh, wa Qissat Najāhuh, wa Kifāhuh' [Tarek Nour, his Life, his Success Story, and his Perseverance]. 3 August 2020, https://www.almaal.org/ tariq-nour-s-life-and-success-story#i-6 (accessed 4 March 2021).

Al-Rawi, Ahmed and Adel Iskandar. 'News Coverage of the Arab Spring: State-Run News Agencies as Discursive Propagators of News'. *Digital Journalism*, (2021): 1–22.

Al-Wafd. 'Hiwār, Tamer Morsy: Iʿlām al-Misriyīn Tuʿid Bināʾ Sūq al-Dirāmā wal-Iʿlān' [Interview with Tamer Morsy: EMG is Rebuilding the Drama and Advertising Markets]. 14 May 2018, https://bit.ly/3gZx0Hs (accessed 29 June 2021).

Al-Waziry, Hany. 'Hamalāt Elektrōneyah Tarfaʿ Šeʿār "al-Sisi Raʾīsan li-Misr", wal-ʾIḥwān: "Laʿeb ben-Nār"' [Electronic Campaigns with the Slogan 'al-Sisi President for Egypt', and the Brotherhood: 'Playing with Fire']. *Al-Watan*, 21 February 2013. http://www.elwatannews.com/news/details/134765 (accessed 29 June 2021).

Allam, Rasha and Dinana Hesham. 'The Future of TV and Online Video Platforms: A Study on Predictors of Use and Interaction with Content in the Egyptian Evolving Telecomm'. Media & Entertainment Industries, *SAGE Open* 3 (2021).

Allam, Rasha. 'From Flabby to Fit: Restructuring the Public Broadcasting System in Egypt'. *Global Media and Communication* 17, no. 3 (2021): 297–320.

Amin, Samir Amin. *Theory is History*. New York: Springer, 2014.

Archive-It. 'Egypt Politics and Revolution'. https://archive-it.org/collections/2358?fc=meta_Creator%3AAl-Masry+Al-Youm (accessed 28 June 2021).

Atef, Noha. 'Pourquoi les radios locales disparaissent à Alexandrie?' [Why Do Local Radio Stations Disappear in Alexandria?]. *Open Edition Journals*, no. 17 (2018).

Badr, Hanan. 'Social Movements and Social Media in a Post-Revolutionary Political Culture: Constitutional Debates in Egypt'. In *Digital Media and the Politics of Transformation in the Arab World and Asia: Studies in International, Transnational and Global Communications*, edited by Carola Richter, Anna Antonakis, Cilja Harders. New York: Springer, 2018, 161–86.

Badr, Hanan. 'Before the "Arab Spring": How Challengers Pushed Counter-Issues in Egypt's Hybrid Media System'. *Media, War & Conflict* 14, no. 4 (2019) 522–41.

Badr, Hanan. 'Egypt's Media System: Historic Legacies and Blocked Potentials for Independent Media', *Publizistik* 65 (2020): 63–79.

Bahgat, Hossam. 'Looking into the Latest Acquisition of Egyptian Media Companies by General Intelligence'. *Mada Masr*, 21 December 2017, https://www.madamasr.com/en/2017/12/21/feature/politics/looking-into-the-latest-acquisition-of-egyptian-media-companies-by-general-intelligence (accessed 28 June 2021).

BBC. 'Misr: Iġlāq Maqar Saḥifat al-Horreya wal-Adāla at-Tābeʾah lel-Iḫwān al-Muslimīn' [Egypt: Office of al-Horreya wal-Adala Newspaper of the Muslim Brotherhood Shutdown]. 25 September 2013, https://www.bbc.com/arabic/middleeast/2013/09/130925_egypt_mb_newspaper (accessed 29 June 2021).

Beinin, Joel. 'Labor, Capital, and the State in Nasserist Egypt, 1952–1961'. *International Journal of Middle East Studies* 21, no. 1 (1989): 71–90.

Beiser, Elana. 'China, Turkey, Saudi Arabia, Egypt are World's Worst Jailers of Journalists'. *Committee to Protect Journalists*, 11 December 2019, https://cpj.org/reports/2019/12/journalists-jailed-china-turkey-saudi-arabia-egypt (accessed 28 June 2021).

Bennett, Dashiell. 'Photographer May Have Captured His Own Death During Egypt Protests'. *The Atlantic*, 10 July 2013, https://www.theatlantic.com/international/archive/2013/07/egyptian-photographer-captured-his-own-death/313486 (accessed 29 June 2021).

Benson, Rodney. 'Bringing the Sociology of Media Back in'. *Political Communication* 21, no. 3 (2004): 103–25.

Bush, Ray. 'Politics, Power and Poverty: Twenty Years of Agricultural Reform and Market Liberalisation in Egypt'. *Third World Quarterly* 28, no. 8 (2007): 1599–1615.

CBS. 'Maspero: A Massacre of Christians in Egypt'. 22 June 2014, https://www.
    cbsnews.com/news/maspero-a-massacre-of-christians-in-egypt (accessed
    29 June 2021).

Chammah, Maurice. 'The Scene of the Crime: October 9th, Maspero, and Egyptian
    Journalism after the Revolution'. *Arab Media and Society* 15, Spring (2012): 1–20.

Chatriwala, Omar. 'What Wikileaks Tells Us About Al Jazeera'. *Foreign Policy*, 19
    September 2011, http://foreignpolicy.com/2011/09/19/what-wikileaks-tells-us-
    about-al-jazeera (accessed 29 June 2021).

Committee to Protect Journalists, 'Press Threatened and Detained as Egypt Marks
    Uprising Anniversary', 26 January 2015, https://cpj.org/2015/01/press-threatened-
    and-detained-as-egypt-marks-upris (accessed 20 November 2022).

Committee to Protect Journalists. 'China, Egypt are Worst Jailers of Journalists
    Worldwide'. 14 December 2015, https://cpj.org/2015/12/china-egypt-are-worst-
    jailers-of-journalists-world.php (accessed 29 June 2021).

Cook, Timothy E. 'The News Media as a Political Institution: Looking Backward and
    Looking Forward'. *Political Communication* 23, no. 2 (2006): 159–71.

Curran, James and Michael Gurevitch. *Mass Media and Society.* 4th edn. London:
    Bloomsbury, 2005.

D'Angelo, Paul and Jim A. Kuypers. *Doing News Framing Analysis: Empirical and
    Theoretical Perspectives.* Abingdon: Routledge 2010.

De Smet, Brecht and Koenraad Bogaert. 'Resistance and Passive Revolution in Egypt
    and Morocco'. In Cemal Burak Tansel (ed.), *States of Discipline: Authoritarian
    Neoliberalism and the Contested Reproduction of Capitalist Order.* London:
    Rowman & Littlefield International, 2017.

De Smet, Brecht. 'Revolution and Counter-Revolution in Egypt'. *Science & Society* 78,
    no. 1 (2014): 11–40.

De Smet, Brecht. *A Dialectical Pedagogy of Revolt: Gramsci, Vygotsky, and the Egyptian
    Revolution.* Leiden: Brill, 2015.

Della Ratta, Donatella, Naomi Sakr and Jakob Skovgaard-Petersen. *Arab Media
    Moguls.* London: I.B. Tauris, 2015.

Diab, Osama. '*Prime-Time Nationalism: The Rational and Economic Underpinnings of
    the June 30 Nationalist "Hysteria"'*. PhD diss., Ghent University, Ghent, 2018.

Discogs. 'Americana A.A.V'. https://www.discogs.com/label/639716-Americana-AAV
    (accessed 29 June 2021).

Diwan, Ishac and Marc Schiffbauer. 'Private Banking and Crony Capitalism in Egypt'.
    Business and Politics 20, no 3 (2018): 390–409.

Diwan, Ishac. 'Understanding Revolution in the Middle East: The Central Role
    of the Middle Class'. *Middle East Development Journal* 5, no. 1 (2013): 1350004-1-
    1350004-30.

Doyle, Gillian. *Understanding Media Economics*, 2nd edn. London: SAGE, 2013.

Dziadosz, Alexander. 'Egypt Secures Liberals' Homes after Calls for their Death'. *Reuters*, 7 February 2013, https://www.reuters.com/article/us-egypt-islamists-idUSBRE9160R020130207 (accessed 29 June 2021).

Egypt Today. 'Tamer Morsi Appointed as new Egyptian Media Group CEO'. 22 February 2018, https://www.egypttoday.com/Article/1/43531/Tamer-Morsi-appointed-as-new-Egyptian-Media-Group-CEO (accessed 29 June 2021).

Egypt Today. 'UMS finishes "Egypt: A Piece of Heaven" documentary series'. 30 September 2019, https://bit.ly/2UG4mCo (accessed 29 June 2021).

El Banhawy, Yasmin. 'Why is the Egyptian State Monopolizing the Entertainment Industry?' *Open Democracy*, 24 June 2019, https://www.opendemocracy.net/en/north-africa-west-asia/why-egyptian-state-monopolizing-entertainment-industry (accessed 29 June 2021).

El-Hamalawy, Hossam. 'Al-Internet wal-Thawrah' [The Internet and the Revolution]. *Bawabat al-Ishteraky*, 24 January 2021, https://revsoc.me/politics/43522 (accessed 29 June 2021).

El-Issawi, Fatima and Bart Cammaerts. 'Shifting Journalistic Roles in Democratic Transitions: Lessons from Egypt'. *Journalism* 17, no. 5 (2016): 549–66.

El-Issawi, Fatima. 'The Role of Egyptian Media in the Coup'. In *IEMed Mediterranean Yearbook 2014*. Barcelona: European Institute of the Mediterranean, 2014.

El-Issawi, Fatima. *Egyptian Media Under Transition: In the Name of the Regime, in the Name of the People?* London: LSE, 2014.

El-Nawawy, Mohammed and Sahar Khamis. 'Blogging against Violations of Human Rights in Egypt: An Analysis of Five Political Blogs'. *International journal of communication*, (2014): 1–18.

Elbendary, Amina 'TV Meets the Madding Crowd'. *Al-Ahram Weekly*, 14 June 2001, 14–20.

Emara, Houssein. 'Harakat Tamarod al-Misreyah, Man Hom wa Mādhā Yorīdoūn?' [Egypt's Tamarod Movements: Who are They and What They Want?]. *France 24*, 26 June 2013, https://bit.ly/3xhOt3m (accessed 29 June 2021).

Entman, Robert. 'Framing: Toward Clarification of a Fractured Paradigm'. *Journal of Communication* 43, no. (1993): 51–8.

Fadel, Leila and Ernesto Londoño. 'Egypt's State-Run Media Starting to Shift from Pro-Mubarak Coverage'. *The Washington Post*, 9 February 2011, http://www.washingtonpost.com/wp-dyn/content/article/2011/02/09/AR2011020906234.html (accessed 29 June 2021).

Farah, Nadia Ramsis. *Religious Strife in Egypt: Crisis and Ideological Conflict in the Seventies*. New York: Gordon & Breach Science Publishers, 1986.

Faris, David M. 'New Media and Democracy in the Arab World'. In James D. Wright (ed.), *International Encyclopedia of the Social & Behavioral Sciences*. 2nd ed. Amsterdam: Elsevier Ltd., 2015.

Fathi, Mohamed. 'Intišār al-Hawātef al-Maḥmūlah Yafūq Muʿadal al-Mawālīd fi al-Šarq al-Awsat' [The Spread of Mobile Phones Exceeds Birth Rates in the Middle East]. *Al-Masry al-Youm*, 11 December 2012, https://www.almasryalyoum.com/news/details/261478 (accessed 29 June 2021).

Fuchs, Christian. 'Information and Communication Technologies and Society: A Contribution to the Critique of the Political Economy of the Internet'. *European Journal of Communication* 24, no. 1 (2009): 69–87.

Fuchs, Christian. *Critical Theory of Communication: New Readings of Lukács, Adorno, Marcuse, Honneth and Habermas in the Age of the Internet*. London: University of Westminster Press, 2016.

Fuchs, Christian. *Reading Marx in the Information Age: A Media and Communication Studies Perspective on Capital, Volume 1*. Abingdon: Routledge, 2015.

Gaddis, John Lewis. *We Now Know: Rethinking Cold War History*. New York: Oxford University Press, 1998.

Gamson, William and Andre Modigliani. *The Changing Culture of Affirmative Action*. Greenwich: JAI Press, 1987.

Gamson, William. 'Media Discourse as a Framing Resource'. In Ann N. Crigler (ed.), *The Psychology of Political Communication*. Ann Arbor: University of Michigan Press, 1998.

Ghareeb, Edmund. 'New Media and the Information Revolution in the Arab World: An Assessment'. *Middle East Journal* 54, no. 3 (2000): 395–418.

Gololy. 'Magdy al-Gallad: CV'. https://bit.ly/3dmuybV (accessed 28 June 2021).

Good News. 'Magdy al-Gallad: 700 Alf Junayh Mukafaʾat Nehāyat al-ḫidmah min al-Masry al-Youm wa 200 Alf Junayh Rāteb Šahri fi al-Watan' [Magdy al-Gallad: EGP 700,000 End of Contract from al-Masry al-Youm and 200,000 Monthly Salary from al-Watan]. 6 March 2012, http://www.masress.com/gn4me/4086359 (accessed 28 June 2021).

Grawert, Elke and Zeinab Abul-Magd. *Businessmen in Arms: How the Military and Other Armed Groups Profit in the MENA Region*. Lanham: Rowman & Littlefield, 2016.

Guaaybess, Tourya. 'Broadcasting and Businessmen in Egypt: Revolution Is Business'. In Donatella Della Ratta, Naomi Sakr and Jakob Skovgaard-Petersen (eds), *Arab Media Moguls*. London: I.B. Tauris, 2015.

Habermas, Juergen. *The Theory of Communicative Action: Volume 2: Lifeword and System: A Critique of Functionalist Reason*. Boston: Beacon Press, 1985.

Hafez, Kai and David L. Paletz. *Mass Media, Politics, and Society in the Middle East*. Cresskill: Hampton Press, 2001.

Hafez, Kai. 'Radically Polarized Publics and the Demise of Media Freedom in Egypt'. *Égypte/Monde Arabe* 12, no. 1 (2015): 37–49.

Hafez, Kai. *Radically Polarized Publics and the Demise of Media Freedom in Egypt*. Copenhagen: University of Copenhagen, 2013.

Hallin, Daniel C. and Paolo Mancini. *Comparing Media Systems Beyond the Western World*. Cambridge: Cambridge University Press 2011.

Hallin, Daniel C. and Paolo Mancini. *Comparing Media Systems: Three Models of Media and Politics*. Cambridge: Cambridge University Press, 2004.

Hamoud, Maher, 'Editor's Letter: Egyptians between the Two Gamals (5 of 5): Sisi in Nasser's Suit, Sadat's Tongue and Mubarak's Fist. *Daily News Egypt*, 5 December 2013, https://dailynewsegypt.com/2013/12/05/egyptians-between-the-two-gamals-5-of-5-sisi-in-nassers-suite-sadats-tongue-and-mubaraks-fist (accessed 28 June 2021).

Hamoud, Maher. 'Egypt's Military Coup of 2013: An Analysis of the Private Press in 112 Days'. *New Middle Eastern Studies* 9, no. 2 (2019): 133–48.

Hamoud, Maher. 'Hegemony and the Interest of Egypt's Business Elite in Post-Mubarak Press'. *New Middle Eastern Studies* 9, no. 1 (2019): 115–32.

Hamoud, Maher. 'Egypt's Private Press and Inciting for Violence against Journalists during the 2013 Military Coup'. *Rowaq Arabi* 25, no. 3 (2020): 79–94.

Hamzawy, Amr. 'Qānūn Jarāʾem Taqniyat al-Maʿlūmāt, ʾIstikmāl Ḥisār Ḥoreyat al-Taʿbīr ʿan al-Raʾy fi Miṣr' [Cyber Criminal Law: Continuing the Siege on Freedom of Expression in Egypt]. *Al-Quds al-Arabi*, 3 December 2018, https://bit.ly/35Y3MT5 (accessed 29 June 2021).

Hanieh, Adam. *Money, Markets, and Monarchies: The Gulf Cooperation Council and the Political Economy of the Contemporary Middle East*. Cambridge: Cambridge University Press, 2018.

Hardy, Jonathan. *Critical Political Economy of the Media: An Introduction*. Abingdon: Routledge, 2014.

Harvey, David. *The New Imperialism*. Oxford: Oxford University Press. 2003.

Herman, Edward S. and Noam Chomsky. *Manufacturing Consent: The Political Economy of Mass Media*. New York: Pantheon Books, 2002.

Hersh, Joshua. 'Egyptian Government Slams Foreign Press as Journalists Come Under Assault'. *Huffington Post*, 18 August 2013, https://www.huffingtonpost.com/2013/08/18/egypt-foreign-press_n_3775634.html?guccounter=1 (accessed 29 June 2021).

Human Rights Watch. 'Egypt: Rabʿa Killings Likely Crimes against Humanity'. 12 August 2014, https://www.hrw.org/news/2014/08/12/egypt-raba-killings-likely-crimes-against-humanity (accessed 29 June 2021).

Human Rights Watch. 'Egypt: Campaign to Crush Artistic Freedom'. 16 August 2018, https://www.hrw.org/news/2018/08/16/egypt-campaign-crush-artistic-freedom (accessed 29 June 2021).

Hussin, Mostafa el-Sayed. 'The Sisi Firewall: Cyber-Suppression Strategies and the Future of Cyberspace in Egypt'. *Arab Center for Research and Policy Studies*, (2020): 1–6.

Iskandar, Adel. 'Egyptian Youth's Digital Dissent'. *Journal of Democracy* 30, n. 3 (2019): 154–64.

Joffe, Lawrence. 'Abdel-Halim Abu Ghazala: Egyptian defence minister with strong anti-communist views'. *The Guardian*, 30 September 2008, https://www.theguardian.com/world/2008/sep/30/egypt (accessed 28 June 2021).

Joya, Angela. *The Roots of Revolt: A Political Economy of Egypt from Nasser to Mubarak*. Cambridge: Cambridge University Press, 2020.

Kamal Eddin, Sami. 'Mohammed Al-Amin: Milliārdīr 'Fulūl' al-I'lām' [Mohammed Al-Amin: Billionaire of the Media's 'Remnants']. *Al-Ahrām al-'Arabi*, 13 December 2012, http://arabi.ahram.org.eg/News/17973.aspx (accessed 17 November 2018).

Kamal Eddin, Sami. *Al-Ṣaḥāfa al-Ḥarām* [Forbidden Press]. Giza: Kayan, 2013).

Kandil, Hazem. *Soldiers, Spies, and Statesmen: Egypt's Road to Revolt*. New York: Verso, 2012.

Kemp, Simon. 'Digital 2021: Egypt'. *DataReportal*, 11 February 2021, https://datareportal.com/reports/digital-2021-egypt?rq=egypt (accessed 29 June 2021).

Khamis, Sahar. 'The Transformative Egyptian Media Landscape: Changes, Challenges and Comparative Perspectives'. *International Journal of Communication* 5 (2011): 1159–77.

Loveless, Matthew, Nael Jebril and Vaclav Stetka. *Media and Democratisation: What is Known about the Role of Mass Media in Transitions to Democracy*. Oxford: Reuters Institute for the Study of Journalism, 2013.

Matar, Dina. 'Contextualising the Media and the Uprisings: A Return to History'. *Middle East Journal of Culture and Communication* 5 (2012): 75–9.

Mattelart, Armand and Michèle Mattelart. *Theories of Mass Communication: A Short Introduction*. London: SAGE, 1998.

McFadden, Tom Johnston. *Daily Journalism in the Arab States*. Columbus: Ohio State University Press, 1953.

McQuail, Denis. *McQuail's Mass Communication Theory*. 6th edn. London: SAGE, 2010.

Mellor, Noha. *The Making of Arab News*. New York: Rowman & Littlefield Publishers, 2005.

Mellor, Noha. *Arab Journalists in Transitional Media*. New York: Hampton Press, 2011.

Mellor, Noha. *Voice of the Muslim Brotherhood: Da'wa, Discourse, and Political Communication*. Oxford: Routledge, 2017.

Mendel, Toby. *Political and Media Transitions in Egypt: A Snapshot of Media Policy and Regulatory Environment*. Washington DC: Internews, 2011.

Mitchell, Timothy. *Rule of Experts: Egypt, Techno-Politics, Modernity*. Berkeley: University of California Press, 2002.

Mohie, Mostafa. 'One, Two, Three, Four Media Laws: How Media Legislation in Egypt is Staging State Control'. *Mada Masr*, 6 December 2016, https://www.madamasr. com/en/2016/12/06/feature/politics/one-two-three-four-media-laws-how-media-legislation-in-egypt-is-staging-state-control (accessed 28 June 2021).

Morgan, Trish. 'Adorno and the Political Economy of Communication'. *The Political Economy of Communication* 1, no. 2 (2013): 44–64.

Mosco, Vincent. *The Political Economy of Communication*, 2nd edn. London: SAGE, 2009.

Nasser, Munir K. *Egyptian Mass Media under Nasser and Sadat*. Columbia: Association for Education in Journalism and Mass Communication, 1990.

Nasser, Munir K. *Press, Politics, and Power: Egypt's Heikal and Al-Ahram*. Ames: The Iowa State University Press, 1979.

Norris, Pippa, Montague Kern and Marion Just. *Framing Terrorism: The News Media, the Government and the Public*. Abingdon: Routledge, 2004.

Paul, Katie. 'Facebook Removes Two Middle East-Focused Fake Account Betworks'. *Reuters*, 2 March 2020, https://www.reuters.com/article/us-facebook-gulf-idUSKBN20P2XH (accessed 29 June 2021).

Poniwozik, James. 'What You See vs. What They See'. *Time*, 7 April 2003, http:// content.time.com/time/magazine/article/0,9171,1004593,00.html (accessed 28 June 2021).

Raafat, Samir. 'The Mass: From the 60's Music Scene'. *Egy.Com*, 4 October 1997, http:// www.egy.com/people/97-10-04.php (accessed 29 June 2021).

Radsch, Courtney C. *Cyberactivism and Citizen Journalism in Egypt: Digital Dissidence and Political Change*. London: Palgrave, 2016.

Ramadan, Sarah. 'Who is to Conquer: Drama Production between the Private Sector and Intelligence Services'. *Association for Freedom of Thought and Expression* (2020): 4–20.

Rayman, Noha. 'Is the Egyptian Press Ready for Democracy? Evaluating Newspaper Coverage as an Indicator of Democratization'. *Arab Media and Society* 17, Winter (2013): 1–28.

Reporters without Borders. 'Egyptian Media Group'. https://egypt.mom-rsf.org/en/ owners/companies/detail/company/company/show/egyptian-media-group (accessed 28 June 2021).

Reporters without Borders. 'Heavy Toll on Journalists in Two Months since Army
    Takeover'. 2 September 2013, https://rsf.org/en/news/heavy-toll-journalists-two-
    months-army-takeover (accessed 29 June 2021).

Reporters without Borders. 'Tamer Morsi'. https://egypt.mom-rsf.org/en/owners/
    individual-owners/detail/owner/owner/show/tamer-morsi (accessed 29 June
    2021).

Richter, Carola and Bettina Gräf. 'The Political Economy of Media: An Introduction'.
    In Nadja-Christina Schneider and Carola Richter (eds), *New Media Configurations
    and Socio-Cultural Dynamics in Asia and the Arab World*. London: Bloomsbury,
    2015.

Richter, Carola, Indira Dupuis and Hanan Badr. 'Media pushing for political
    transformation: A comparative analysis of issue contestation in Poland before
    1989 and Egypt before 2011'. *The International Communication Gazette* 83, no. 4
    (2021): 32–46.

Rizk, Yasser. 'Ayyām Lahā Tārīkh' [Days that have History]. *Al-Masry al-Youm*, 21 June
    2014, http://www.almasryalyoum.com/news/details/468406 (accessed 28 June
    2021).

Sayigh, Yezid. *Owners of the Republic: An Anatomy of Egypt's Military Economy*
    (Beirut: Carnegie Middle East Center, 2019.

Schapals, Aljosha Karim and Zahera Harb. '"Everything Has Changed, and Nothing
    Has Changed in Journalism": Revisiting Journalistic Sourcing Practices and
    Verification Techniques during the 2011 Egyptian Revolution and Beyond'. *Digital
    Journalism*, (2021): 1–19.

Seib, Philip. 'Hegemonic No More: Western Media, the Rise of Al-Jazeera, and the
    Influence of Diverse Voices'. *International Studies Review* 7, no. 4 (2005): 601–15.

Shea, Joey and Alexei Abrahams. 'Disinformation Wars in Egypt: The Inauthentic
    Battle on Twitter between Egyptian Government and Opposition'. *Just Security*,
    26 October 2020, https://www.justsecurity.org/72961/disinformation-wars-in-
    egypt-the-inauthentic-battle-on-twitter-between-egyptian-government-and-
    opposition (accessed 29 June 2021).

Shechter, Relli. 'Glocal Mediators: Marketing in Egypt during the Open-Door Era
    (Infitah)'. *Enterprise & Society* 9, no. 4 (2008): 76–87.

Shechter, Relli. 'Press Advertising in Egypt: Business Realities and Local Meaning'. *The
    Arab Studies Journal* 10, no. 11 (2002): 44–66.

Skovgaard-Petersen, Jakob. 'An Introduction'. In Donatella Della Ratta, Naomi
    Sakr and Jakob Skovgaard-Petersen (eds). *Arab Media Moguls*. London: I.B. Tauris,
    2015.

State Information Service. 'Statement by the State Information Service (SIS) on
    Current Events in Egypt'. 17 August 2013.

Taher, Mohamed and Marwa Fatafta. 'Misr: Tārīḫ Tawīl min Morāqabat al-Internet wal-ʾItisālāt' [Egypt: A Long History of Surveilling Internet and Communications]. *Access Now*, 6 October 2020, https://bit.ly/3y5L8EJ (accessed 29 June 2021).

Tarek Nour Communications. 'About Us'. http://www.tareknour.com/en/about-us (accessed 29 June 2021).

Tarek Nour Communications. 'Schweppes, Hassan Abdin 1983'. *YouTube*, 2001, https://www.youtube.com/watch?v=tWLa1nhHfDU (accessed 29 June 2021).

Tawfiq, Mohamed. 'Šarikāt al-Diʿāyah fi Misr Tantaqid Saytarat al-JayŠ ʿalā ʾIʿlānāt al-Turuqʾ [Egypt's Advertising Companies Criticize the Army's Control over Road Billboards]. *Al-Arabi al-Jadid*, 30 September 2015, https://bit.ly/36efrxj (accessed 29 June 2021).

The Economist. 'How Egyptian Entertainment Has Changed under Military Rule'. 10 April 2021, https://www.economist.com/middle-east-and-africa/2021/04/10/how-egyptian-entertainment-has-changed-under-military-rule (accessed 29 June 2021).

Tkacheva, Olesya et al. *Internet Freedom and Political Space*. Brussels: RAND Corporation, 2013.

Tonsy, Sara and Aly el-Raggal. 'How Did Sisi Reproduce Authoritarianism in Egypt?', *Rowaq Arabi* 26, no. 1 (2021): 47–63.

Tripp, Charles. *The Power and the People: Paths of Resistance in the Middle East*. Cambridge: Cambridge University Press, 2013.

Tuchman, Gaye. *Making News: A Study in the Construction of Reality*. New York: Free Press, 1978.

Wafi, Mamdouh. '"Al-Mowātenūm al-Šurafā'", ʾAdāh "Sereyah" li-Tarwēʿ al-Moʿāradah bi-Misr. Man Hom wa Man Yuḥarikohom?' [The 'Honourable Citizens, a 'Secret' Tool for Terrifying the Opposition in Egypt. Who are they and Who's Behind Them?]. *An-Nahar*, 7 June 2018, https://bit.ly/3w45sVH (accessed 29 June 2021).

Wahid, Maryam. 'Al-Khāriṭa al-Iʿlāmiyya al-Misriyya baʿda al-Thawra: Arqām wa-Tashrīʿāt wa-Qaḍāyā' [The Egyptian Media Map after the Revolution: Numbers, Legislations and Issues]. *Al-Arabiya Studies Institute*, 12 February 2013, https://web.archive.org/web/20170509221740/http://www.alarabiya.net/articles/2013/02/12/265930.html (accessed 28 June 2021).

Whitaker, Brian. 'Battle Station'. *The Guardian*, 7 February 2003, https://www.theguardian.com/media/2003/feb/07/iraqandthemedia.afghanistan (accessed 29 June 2021).

Winseck, Dwayne and Dal Yong Jin. *The Political Economies of Media: The Transformation of the Global Media Industries*. London: Bloomsbury Academic, 2011.

Youssef, Nevin. 'Hal Bāta al-Intāj al-Deramī fī Misr taḥta Saytarat al-Dawlah?' [Has Drama Production in Egypt Become under State Control?]. BBC, 6 May 2019, https://www.bbc.com/arabic/middleeast-48178108 (accessed 29 June 2021).

Zayani, Mohamed. 'Media, Popular Culture and Contestatory Politics in the Contemporary Middle East'. *International Journal of Media and Cultural Politics* 7, no. 1 (2011): 85–99.

Zemni, Sami and Koenraad Bogaert. 'Trade, Security and Neoliberal Politics: Whither Arab Reform? Evidence from the Moroccan Case'. *The Journal of North African Studies* 14, no. 1 (2009): 91–107.

Zemni, Sami, Brecht De Smet and Koenraad Bogaert. 'Luxemburg on Tahrir Square: Reading the Arab Revolutions with Rosa Luxemburg's The Mass Strike'. *Antipode* 45, no. 4 (2013): 888–907.

Zhuravskaya, Ekaterina, Maria Petrova and Ruben Enikolopov. 'Political Effects of the Internet and Social Media'. *Annual Review of Economics* 12, (2020): 415–38.

Index

www.ingramcontent.com/pod-product-compliance
Lightning Source LLC
Chambersburg PA
CBHW062021270326
41929CB00014B/2279